SUMMERLAND

Anne Stiles Quatrano

SUMMERLAND

Recipes for Celebrating with Southern Hospitality

Photographs by Brian Woodcock

RIZZOLI
NEW YORK

New York Paris London Milan

Contents

Our Journey to the South

As this book is printed, my husband and partner, Clifford Harrison, and I are celebrating our twentieth anniversary of the opening of our restaurant Bacchanalia. This is an amazing milestone for us. We moved to Georgia in 1992, started a farm, opened a small restaurant, fostered a local food movement, and have sustained our lofty goals through a few recessions and the ever-changing culinary climate in Atlanta. In those twenty years, we have moved Bacchanalia, opened three more restaurants and a retail store, and had the good fortune of working with an outstanding group of very talented chefs and service professionals.

Here is our story.

Clifford was born and raised in Hawaii, and I in Connecticut. We are both the product of the late Baby Boom era. Our mothers cooked from the freezer and from cans—in fact, both of us recall Spam making an occasional appearance at the dinner table. My paternal, Italian side of the family loved to cook and would always lay out a spread of delicacies for family and guests to enjoy. To this day, my favorite comfort foods involve tomato sauce, which we referred to as "red gravy." I cooked all through my childhood. I loved feeding people.

The restaurant industry offered me my first glimpse of independence when I waited tables during college to earn recreational funds. I thrived in the team environment, and I still have a close group of friends from those days. (Luckily, what happened in the '80s stayed in the '80s.)

By my mid-twenties, I decided it was time to round out my education with formal culinary training. So, I packed up my belongings in a decrepit Volkswagen and drove to San Francisco to attend the California Culinary Academy. While I was in school, I took a front-of-the-house job at the Zuni Cafe, where Judy Rodgers had recently taken over as chef. After a few months, I secured a rare apprenticeship with Judy in the kitchen, an experience I will always cherish.

During my time in culinary school I also met Clifford. We found that our style of cooking and our drive to succeed were perfectly in step. After graduation, we moved back to the East Coast to cook on Nantucket and then in Manhattan, often running kitchens together.

Our journey to the South began in the summer of 1992. Young and energetic, we had been let go of our jobs at a restaurant in Huntington, New York, for what the owners saw as insubordination. (I admit, I was more vocal than Clifford about our ability to run the entire business.)

Clifford's big idea was to relocate to the South. We were anxious to start our own restaurant. Atlanta had just been chosen to host the 1996 Summer Olympics, so the city instantly became a place of interest. Conveniently, my mother owned sixty acres of land in Cartersville—some forty miles northwest of Atlanta—that had been in her family since before the Civil War.

My family's history with this land began with my great, great, great grandfather, William Henry Stiles. He was born on January 1, 1809, in Savannah, Georgia, and studied law at Yale before returning to the South, opening his own law practice in Savannah in 1832. The following year, he married Eliza Ann Mackay. They had three children: Mary Cowper, William Henry Jr., and Robert Mackay. In addition to practicing law, W.H. usually farmed more than one plantation. In 1840, the federal government sent W.H., serving as a solicitor general for eastern Georgia, to pay the Cherokee Indians for the lands in north Georgia they had deeded to the United States. Impressed by the soil and climate there, my great, great, great grandfather purchased some of the newly acquired lands and settled on the banks of the Etowah River in Cass (now Bartow) County. After moving, he divided his time between his Cass County estate, known as Etowah Cliffs (which now lies in ruins and is the site for an ancestral cemetery) and his business and agricultural interests in the coastal region of Savannah.

The W.H. Stiles family used the north Georgia foothills as their summer retreat from the heat of the low country—thus the name of the property: Summerland. My mother, Gulielma Stiles, was born on this land and had called the farm home until she was seven, when the family moved into the town of Cartersville proper. After that, a family of tenant workers cared for the property until the mid 1980s. Then, the original house fell to vandals and fire in the late 1980s.

By the time Clifford and I arrived, the property was in an abysmal state—covered with nothing but soybeans and corn, the soil neglected and depleted. But we were not dismayed; we both felt as if we had come home. Clifford wanted to cultivate the land and have room to exercise his horse, Boyd Drifter. I saw great potential for a new house surrounded by an herb garden. We moved into a double-wide trailer that squatters had parked on the property and assumed their $69-dollar-a-month mortgage. For a few months, the trailer was home to not only Clifford and myself, but also our longtime friend and prep cook, Souleymane, and my mother. Boyd Drifter could not fit in the trailer, but he made his home within a crooked fence that Clifford and I had hastily and naively constructed. We threw ourselves into building, repairing, planting, and—most importantly—looking for a location in Atlanta to open our restaurant, Bacchanalia.

That fall, we signed a lease on a historic house in the Buckhead neighborhood. My mother was our sole investor, against the advice of her friends and some of our extended family. We converted the garage into our kitchen and made the house into our dining rooms, which could seat fifty diners at full capacity. By January 1993, we had a restaurant. In those early days, Bacchanalia had exactly four employees: Clifford, myself, Souleymane, and my sister, Frances, who moved down from Connecticut to manage the front of the house. (Miraculously, she still holds this job.)

For three months, very few guests came through the doors. Finally, we got our big break when Gerry Klaskala, then the chef of the Buckhead Diner, dined at Bacchanalia with his wife, Sally. Pleased with his meal, Gerry tipped off the local press. Nathalie Dupree and Elliot Mackle dined with us on a weeknight, and by the weekend, we had a glowing review and a steady flow of guests. We have not looked back. Thank you, Gerry.

Over the past two decades, our businesses have grown and changed. But we have stayed true to our mission of serving the best food to our diners in a warm, welcoming, and gracious atmosphere.

Meanwhile, Summerland Farm has flourished as our home and as the source for much of the produce we serve in our restaurants. Some people are surprised to learn that Clifford and

I make the eighty-mile round trip to Atlanta every single day—sometimes more than once!—and that we don't keep an apartment in the city. But after twenty years on the farm, we can't imagine living anywhere else.

To our delight in the hot summer months, Cartersville is consistently several degrees cooler than Atlanta, due to its foothills elevation. We grow intensely on a few acres, and our animals—including chickens, goats, and horses—roam and graze on another thirty acres. (Our ten dogs divide their time between the house, the porch, and the fields.) Closer to the river the fields give way to woods, with wild muscadine grapevines snaking among the trees.

The crops we raise include greens (mustard, chard, and kale), lettuces, tomatoes, beans, okra, potatoes, melons, squash, eggplant, peppers, corn, radish, fennel, and strawberries—just to name a few. We have peach trees that swell with ripe fruit in the summer; as well as pecan, walnut, and chestnut trees that were first planted by my ancestors. Closest to the house is the herb garden, which was our first foray into cultivation. We've now been tending those herbs for nearly twenty years.

During that time, we have had the privilege of being very patient farmers. The process has been one of trial and error, and we have been rewarded by more success than we could have imagined. When the hens aren't laying or we find ourselves in the middle of a historic drought, we have been able to rely on the restaurant business to support the growth of the farm. We know that not all farmers have the same luxury. Our own experiences with Summerland Farm make us all the more appreciative of the other hardworking, talented, and passionate farmers and ranchers we work with.

Speaking of hardworking and talented, we currently have two full-time employees, Maya and Sandee, who manage the property and oversee the farming operations. Clifford essentially works two full-time jobs: days in the fields, and nights at the restaurants (usually Floataway Café). When we have a task such as harvesting that demands extra hands, our restaurant workers take turns helping.

One long-term goal for Summerland Farm that we are close to fulfilling is a twelve-month growing cycle. In early 2013 we constructed a high tunnel, which allows us to grow crops in the winter and protect them from frost. Whether it is May's strawberries or January's turnips, there is something coming out of the ground at Summerland Farm—and making its way to our restaurant kitchens—virtually all year long. Thanks to composting, rotating, and other sustainable practices, our soil gets richer and healthier every year. Clifford and I may or may not have another restaurant or business in us, but we are determined to make our farm and food harvest what continually sets our restaurants apart.

Over the course of my career as a chef, I have discovered that, as much as I love preparing great food, I have an equal passion for the inedible gestures of hospitality. I enjoy the process of feeding people, from devising a menu and setting the table to attending to details such as flowers and seating arrangements.

Here, in *Summerland*, we bring you a compilation of our favorite menus and tables, from our home and our restaurants. It is a window into our world through the plate. We thank you all for your patronage.

From Pasture to Plate

A Celebration of the Pig

Serves 20

Sourwood Smash

Coppa | **Pork Pâté**

Head Cheese | **Hunter's Loop Sausage**

Madeira or Dry Sherry

Pork Sugo with Pasta | **Salad of Bitter Greens**

An American Zinfandel or Italian Nebbiolo

Leaf Lard Chocolate Chip Sandwich Cookies

Spanish conquistadors first brought hogs to the Caribbean and the North American mainland some five hundred years ago. So the pig's place in the Southern diet was established long before there was a "South" to speak of. The semi-feral hogs of Ossabaw Island, Georgia—near my maternal family's native Savannah—are now a prized heritage breed, raised in small herds throughout the country. It is one of a handful of heritage breeds being preserved and celebrated these days thanks to responsible farmers, passionate chefs, and curious eaters. As they say, you have to eat it to save it. And that's what we like to do with the pig.

Today at Summerland Farm, our pig, Hamlet, is a pet, with no chance of becoming prosciutto. But my mother remembers a time when the hog slaughter was an autumn tradition. The cooler nights in the north Georgia foothills afforded the perfect time to butcher the pigs without giving the meat a chance to spoil. In the weeks leading up to the hog killing, my ancestors would feed the pigs chestnuts and apples to develop a flavorful balance of meat and fat. The ritual demanded the work of everyone on the farm—men and women alike—to raise the scaffolding, assemble the scalding pots, prepare the smokehouse, and carry out the butchering and preserving. They made use of every part of the animal; nothing was wasted.

Today, we practice the same nose-to-tail butchering that my ancestors did. We consider it the fiscally, environmentally, and ethically responsible thing to do. Hogs arrive for the restaurants nearly every week, all year long, so the butchering ritual is no longer relegated to the cold fall nights. Nonetheless, the sweet meat of a pasture-raised pig slaughtered in the autumn is still our favorite.

And so, we dedicate this month to the process of butchering, curing, and serving the whole animal. Don't be intimidated if you are a newcomer to home butchering and curing. Any one of these dishes would be a great place to start. Though I like to think that my team of butchers are uniquely talented, there's really no magic involved in curing. Use high-quality meat from a local farmer or trusted butcher, measure precisely, keep your tools and ingredients very cold as you work, and you will impress yourself with the results. Unless you have a great deal of time and refrigerator space, I suggest you divide the menu items among a group of intrepid friends. When the curing process is complete, you can all come together for a pork-centric, potluck-style supper. You can start out with a charcuterie plate featuring the coppa, head cheese, hunter's loop and pâté—this will let your curing handiwork really shine! For a clever menu, re-create a pig butchering diagram using white marker or chalk on black paper, and label the appropriate parts with each guest's dish. There's no need to get formal—rustic, earthy tableware complements the visual and gustatory appeal of the dishes. We used a variety of surfaces and vessels for plating, including mango wood cutting boards, copper pots, carved soapstone bowls, and miniature ceramic Staub cocottes.

Sourwood Smash

A beer-based cocktail seems a perfect match for celebrating what is great about the hog. Here we like to use a traditional Belgian wheat beer, which is on the lighter side. This makes for a refreshing aperitif with a warm kick from a little old-fashioned corn whiskey.

Corn moonshine whiskey (preferably Ole Smokey Moonshine)

Freshly squeezed lemon juice

Sourwood honey water (recipe follows)

Orange bitters (preferably Peychaud's)

Lemon bitters (preferably Fee brothers)

Wheat beer (preferably Allagash White)

For each cocktail, fill a cocktail shaker with ice, 1 ounce whiskey, 1 ounce lemon juice, ¾ ounce honey water, 2 dashes orange bitters, and 1 dash lemon bitters. Mix together with a cocktail spoon and strain into a highball glass filled with ice. Top off with 3 ounces of the beer. ★

Sourwood Honey Water
Makes 2 cups

Many believe sourwood honey to be the best-tasting honey on Earth. Bees collect nectar from the increasingly rare sourwood trees, which bloom throughout the upper South from June to August. The result of their work has a gingery twang that pairs well with whiskey. This will keep for several weeks in the refrigerator and will make a great sweetener for other cocktails or iced tea.

1 cup sourwood honey

Pour the honey into a pint jar and add 1 cup of water. Close the lid and shake until dissolved. ★

Coppa

Serves 20 as an appetizer

Coppa is a delicious whole-muscle cure, more similar to a ham than a salami. Thinly sliced, it is delicious as an antipasto. If you enjoy capicola on an Italian sandwich, you will love this homemade version. We like to serve it with little rye toasts, grainy mustard, and small leaves of watercress.

5 pounds pork shoulder

70 grams granulated sugar

92 grams kosher salt

5 grams black peppercorns

8 grams garlic powder

6 grams Insta Cure #2 (see "Curing Salt," below)

5 grams coriander seed

3 grams fresh thyme leaves

6 grams fennel seeds

2 grams crushed red pepper flakes

Ask your butcher to trim the pork shoulder to isolate the large muscles and remove the excess fat and sinew. Keep the meat cold.

Combine the sugar, kosher salt, peppercorns, garlic powder, Insta Cure, coriander, thyme, fennel, and red pepper flakes in a spice grinder or mortar and pestle and grind to a coarse powder.

Rub the meat with half of the spice mixture (refrigerate the remaining mixture in a sealed container). Place the rubbed pork in a 2-gallon sealable plastic bag and force as much air as you can out of the bag. Refrigerate for 9 days.

Remove the pork from the bag and rinse under cold water. Dry thoroughly with paper towels and let sit to air dry for 30 minutes. Repeat the process, rubbing on the remaining spice mixture, and refrigerate for 9 more days.

Rinse the meat under cool running water and pat dry. Allow the meat to air-dry for at least 2 hours on a stainless-steel rack in the refrigerator.

Fit the muscles back together to form a tight package, as if you are reassembling the shoulder before it was trimmed. Wrap tightly in cheesecloth (you will need several feet of cheesecloth) by rolling the cheesecloth completely around the meat and torqueing, or turning, both ends in opposite directions until the cloth is very tight. Tie both ends with

butcher's twine and tie twine around the bundle a few times to keep the cloth tight. As with anything in life, this is easier with the help of a friend. Place in the warmest part of the refrigerator—usually the top shelf—either hung between the racks or set on a stainless-steel cooling rack with a pan underneath. Let the meat cure in the refrigerator for 30 to 45 days, after which point it should have lost 35 percent of its weight. To serve, slice thinly. This will keep for several months if sealed well and refrigerated. ★

Curing Salt

Insta Cure #1, which is also called "Prague Powder #1" and "pink salt," is a curing salt, a mixture of salt and sodium nitrite. In sausages and other meat preparations such as pâtés, it plays two roles: It preserves the bright pink color of the meat and it prevents the growth of certain harmful microbes during the curing or smoking process.

Insta Cure #2 is a similar curing salt but also contains sodium nitrate; it is used for dry-cured sausages that require no cooking.

For food safety, it is essential that you use the exact amount of Insta Cure specified in each recipe. You can ask your local butcher to provide you with some Insta Cure, or you may order online through such sources as sausagemaker.com.

Pork Pâté

Makes 2 terrines, serves 20 as an appetizer

A pâté is another way to utilize the trim after butchering an entire animal. It can also be prepared with the shoulder or butt, the leg, or even parts of the belly. This terrine combines pork with the delicate flavors of leeks and slightly sweet, herbaceous marjoram. Serve simply with toast.

4 pounds lean pork shoulder, cut into 1-inch cubes

1 ¼ pounds unsalted pork fatback, cut into 1-inch cubes

33 grams kosher salt

6 grams Insta Cure #1 (see "Curing Salt," page 16)

80 grams foie gras scraps
(you may substitute chicken liver or duck liver)

½ pound baby leeks, cleaned and cut into thin rounds

½ cup lightly toasted pine nuts

½ cup fresh marjoram leaves

Place the meat and fat cubes in a resealable plastic storage bag and chill in the freezer for 30 minutes.

Preheat the oven to 275° F. Line two 9 by 2 by 2 ½-inch terrine molds with plastic wrap, leaving enough overhang to cover the tops of the pâtés.

Use a meat grinder fitted with the fine die to grind the meat and fat into a large bowl. Add the kosher salt, Insta Cure, and foie gras and mix well.

Pack each mold with a layer of the ground meat about ¾ inch thick. Then layer one-fourth of the leeks on the meat in each terrine. Sprinkle one-fourth of the pine nuts and marjoram on top of each. Pressing down as you go, spread another layer of meat in each terrine, then top with the remaining leeks, pine nuts, and marjoram as before. Top with a third layer of meat and tightly wrap the plastic around the finished terrines.

Place the terrines in a baking dish with sides at least 2 inches high. Add enough warm water to reach at least halfway up the sides of the terrines. Carefully transfer the baking dish to the oven and bake the pâtés until the internal temperature registers 140° F when a meat thermometer is inserted into the center of one, about 1 hour. This time is an estimate; the most reliable and accurate test is an instant-read thermometer. We suggest checking the temperature after 60 minutes as this terrine is best if not overcooked.

Let cool slightly at room temperature. Place a 2-pound weight (a box of kosher salt works well as a weight) on top of each terrine and refrigerate until completely cool, about 3 hours. Unmold and slice. (The pâté will keep for a couple of weeks in the refrigerator.) ⋆

Simmering the pork for Head Cheese

Head Cheese

Head Cheese

Serves 20 as an appetizer

Head cheese is not a cheese at all, but a rich terrine. It is a lovely use of the head of the animal and requires very little special equipment or ingredients. The natural gelatins in the head set this terrine perfectly. Serve with grainy mustard and cornichons.

1 pig's head (about 18 pounds)

2 cups plus 1 tablespoon kosher salt

2 quarts Chicken Stock (page 244)

1 carrot, roughly chopped

1 onion, roughly chopped

1 stalk celery, roughly chopped

2 bay leaves

3 tablespoons Champagne vinegar

2 tablespoons yellow mustard seeds

2 tablespoons chopped fresh parsley leaves

1 tablespoon chopped fresh cilantro leaves

Freshly ground pepper

Remove the outer skin (mask) of the head by peeling it off the bone. You can have your butcher do this, but the only equipment needed is a small sharp knife: Start above the ears on either side and run your knife between the bones of the skull and the skin, working slowly around the entire head. The ears come off with the mask. Remove the tongue as well, and set aside. Discard (or reserve for another use) the bones and the rest of the head.

Prepare the brine by dissolving the 2 cups salt in 2 gallons cold water; a 5-gallon bucket is a great vessel for this. Place the mask and tongue in the brine, cover, and refrigerate for 24 hours. You may need to place a plate or a weight on the top of the bucket or container you are brining in to keep the pork completely immersed.

Remove the mask and tongue from the brine and rinse under cold running water. Discard the brine. Place the mask and tongue in a large stockpot with the stock, carrot, onion, celery, bay leaves, and 2 quarts water. Bring to a simmer, then cook over low heat, uncovered, for 3 to 4 hours, until tender. Remove the mask and tongue from the cooking liquid and set aside to cool. Strain the cooking liquid through a fine-mesh strainer into a container and let cool to room temperature.

Line two 9 by 2 by 2 1/2-inch terrine molds with plastic wrap, leaving plenty of overlap for wrapping.

When the mask is cool enough to handle, remove any firm cartilage from the ears, discard it, and chop the rest of the mask coarsely. Peel the tongue, discarding the peel, and chop the meat coarsely. Place the chopped meat in a large bowl and set aside to cool to room temperature. Once cooled, add the vinegar, mustard seeds, parsley, cilantro, the remaining 1 tablespoon salt, and pepper to taste and mix by hand. Add the room-temperature cooking liquid, a little at a time, until the mixture becomes pastelike (you will need 2 to 3 cups). Adjust the seasoning, if necessary, and press into the terrine molds. Wrap the overhanging plastic around each terrine and place a weight on top (a 2-pound box of salt should work). Alternatively, you can roll the head cheese into a roulade by wrapping plastic wrap around the mixture and forming it into a log shape, torqueing the wrap tightly. Refrigerate the head cheese for at least 24 hours before slicing and serving. It will keep for up to 2 weeks, covered tightly in the refrigerator. ∗

Hunter's Loop Sausage

Serves 20

This is the simplest of our fermented salamis. The idea behind the name is that the sausage could be looped over the hunter's shoulder and carried into the woods. The texture is such that you will be able to see and feel the larger and smaller chunks of meat as well as glistening bits of fat—a charcuterie lover's dream, and a great way to showcase a high-quality pig. Since this is a dry, uncooked sausage, you will need a meat starter culture, also called Bactoferm, which is a live culture that starts the fermentation process. You can order Bactoferm from sausagemaker.com. This preparation does have a significant cure time, but it will be worth your wait. Serve with mustard, olives, or sharp aged sheep's milk cheese.

1 package hog casings, for 5 pounds sausage (about 6 feet in length)

5 pounds lean pork, cut into 2-inch cubes

1 ½ pounds pork fatback, cut into 1- to 2-inch cubes

7.3 grams Insta Cure #2 (see "Curing Salt," page 16)

6.5 grams kosher salt

.9 grams (¼ teaspoon) Bactoferm, CHR Hansen F-RM 52 (see note above)

2 to 3 tablespoons distilled water

15 grams dextrose

3 ½ teaspoons fennel pollen

5 teaspoons whole black peppercorns, cracked

2 garlic cloves, grated finely on a Microplane

Soak the casings in cool water in the refrigerator for 12 to 24 hours; we like to change the water at least twice during the soaking period. Rinse the casings thoroughly, holding each open and running cool water through the casings to rinse completely.

Place the cubed meat and fatback in the resealable storage bag and freeze for 30 minutes. Using a meat grinder fitted with the medium grinding plate, grind two-thirds of the meat and fat into a medium stainless-steel bowl; replace the medium plate with the fine plate, and grind the remaining one-third meat and fat into the same bowl. Add the Insta Cure and kosher salt to the meat and loosely incorporate. Cover the mixture and refrigerate until it becomes sticky, about 20 minutes.

In a small bowl combine the Bactoferm with the distilled water and a pinch of the dextrose. Allow to sit for a minimum of 20 minutes to allow the beneficial bacteria to become active but no more than 2 hours.

In a small bowl, combine the remaining dextrose, the fennel pollen, and peppercorns and mix by hand thoroughly. Add the garlic and the Bactoferm mixture and mix again. Add this to the bowl with the meat and fat and loosely incorporate until it becomes pastelike.

For this step a sausage stuffing tube would help; this is a tube that fits onto the end of a meat grinder and keeps the casing open as the grinder presses the mixture in. Also, there is an attachment for grinders available for stand mixers that has a tube that will hold the casings open while the grinder pushes the sausage into the casing. Use the sausage grinder or grinder attachment without the blade and die to push the sausage into the casings. Load a length of casing on the stuffing tube and tie off the open end with butcher's twine. Start your mixer or grinder and allow the casing to fill slowly and evenly. Once a length of the casing is full, tie off the end that was on the tube and create a link approximately every 24 inches by twisting links in one direction and then the other or by tying around the diameter of the sausage with butcher's twine and tightening the knot. For each link you create, fold it so that it makes a loop and tie the ends together. Repeat this process until all of the sausage is stuffed into the casing. Prick the air pockets in the sausage with a needle.

Hang the hunter's loop for 24 hours in a warm part of your home, shed, or garage in order to activate the cultures and start the fermentation process. You are looking for an environment with a temperature of around 80° F.

Move the hunter's loop to your refrigerator and hang for 6 or more weeks. It should be firm all the way through when you slice into a piece. To serve, slice thinly. ⋆

Pork Sugo with Pasta

Serves 20

A sugo (meaning "gravy" or "sauce" in Italian) is a hearty braise that can utilize many different scraps and trim from the breakdown of an animal. We use pork shoulder, which is often referred to as pork butt. This cut is relatively easy to obtain, braises well, and is very cost effective. The sugo can easily be stored in small containers and frozen for later meals. Hand-cut fresh pasta or store-bought egg noodles coated with a small portion of this unctuous stew makes a simple, delicious meal. A few shavings of truffle would add a delicious pop of flavor for a special occasion. We usually serve this dish in soapstone bowls, which do an excellent job of retaining heat and highlight the pleasing earthiness of the dish.

For the Brine and Pork

2 cups kosher salt

1 cup packed light brown sugar

2 tablespoons black peppercorns

4 garlic cloves, smashed

1 tablespoon juniper berries

2 dried chiles

4 bay leaves

4 fresh thyme sprigs

2 fresh rosemary sprigs

4 fresh parsley stems

4- to 5-pound pork shoulder or butt

For the Sugo

Kosher salt

Freshly ground pepper

1 tablespoon vegetable oil

4 white onions, diced small

2 carrots, diced small

2 celery stalks, diced small

6 garlic cloves, smashed

½ cup tomato paste

1 (750 ml) bottle cabernet sauvignon

2 bay leaves

6 fresh thyme sprigs

2 fresh rosemary sprigs

2 quarts Chicken Stock (page 244)

For Serving

8 discs (2 full recipes) Fresh Pasta Dough (page 244), rolled out and hand-cut into ½ inch-wide noodles

Kosher salt

Sprigs of fresh herbs (thyme, parsley, or rosemary)

1 black truffle (optional)

To brine the pork: Heat 1 gallon water in a 12-quart stockpot over high heat. Add the salt, brown sugar, peppercorns, garlic, juniper berries, chiles, bay leaves, thyme, rosemary, and parsley stems and bring to a boil. Once the sugar and salt have dissolved, remove from the heat, cover, and let steep for 15 minutes. Add 1 gallon iced water. Once the mixture is cool, add the pork, cover, and refrigerate for 24 hours.

Remove the pork from the brine, rinse under running cold water, and place on a stainless-steel cooling rack set over a baking sheet. Let the pork dry in the refrigerator for 24 hours. Discard the brine.

To make the sugo: Allow the pork to come to room temperature, about 30 minutes, then thoroughly season with salt and pepper.

Preheat the oven to 350° F. In a large Dutch oven, heat the oil and sear the pork shoulder, turning, until all its surfaces are dark brown. Remove the meat from the pot and allow it to rest while you cook the vegetables.

Add to the pot the onions, carrots, celery, and garlic. Cook over low heat, stirring occasionally, until deeply browned, about 30 minutes. Add the tomato paste and cook, stirring, until browned. Add the wine, bring to a simmer over medium heat, and reduce until almost dry, about 15 minutes. Add the bay leaves, thyme, and rosemary, place the pork shoulder on top, and add enough of the stock to almost cover the meat and vegetables. Cover the pot with a tight-fitting lid, place in the oven, and braise for 3 to 3½ hours, until the pork is tender.

Allow the pork to cool in the braising liquid. (You may prepare the pork in advance up to this point; it will keep, immersed in its braising liquid and covered in the refrigerator, for up to 3 days.) Remove the pork and strain the braising liquid through a fine-mesh sieve lined with cheesecloth into a 4-quart sauté pan. Place over medium heat and simmer, skimming frequently, until slightly reduced.

Pull the meat from the pork, tearing the lean meat into strands and disposing of all fat and undesirable trim. Add the meat back to the reduced braising liquid and cook uncovered over medium heat until most of the liquid is gone, about 30 minutes. Adjust the seasoning.

To serve, cook the pasta in a large pot of salted boiling water until al dente, 2 to 3 minutes. Serve the sugo over the pasta topped with herb and thin truffle shavings, if you like. ⋆

Clockwise from top left: Hunter's Loop Sausage | Ham and dried sausages from our larder
Salad of Bitter Greens | The makings of Pork Pâté

Salad of Bitter Greens

Serves 20

Bitter chicory greens, such as escarole, endive, and radicchio, are among my favorite autumn vegetables. Although they usually require little more than lemon, salt, pepper, and a dash of fruity extra virgin olive oil to set off their flavor, the sweet-tart crunch of the apple added here is a nice foil for the bitterness of the greens. Don't worry if you can't find the exact varieties of greens listed. Feel free to use any kind of radicchio, endive, or escarole, particularly if there are locally grown varieties at your farmers' market. This salad is a fresh, healthy counterpoint to the pork recipes on this menu, and the presentation is even lovelier if you mix red and green varieties of leaves.

2 heads Treviso radicchio

2 heads chioggia radicchio

2 heads frisée

2 heads young escarole

1 cup toasted pecan pieces

2 tablespoons Clarified Butter (see page 246)

1 teaspoon sugar

Kosher salt

4 apples, cored and thinly sliced

Juice of 2 lemons

¼ cup extra virgin olive oil

Freshly cracked pepper

Preheat the oven to 350 ° F. Line a baking sheet with parchment paper.

In batches, peel apart the heads of greens and immerse in a bath of plenty of cool clean water. Use your hands to swish around, then lift out the greens, letting the water drip off. Use a salad spinner to dry the greens.

Toss the pecans with the clarified butter in a nonstick pan and toast over medium heat, stirring, until the nuts are fragrant, 2 to 3 minutes. Season the nuts with the sugar and salt to taste. Spread the nuts out on the parchment-lined baking sheet and bake for 5 minutes.

In a large salad bowl, toss the apples and greens together with the lemon juice and olive oil, adding salt and pepper to taste. Garnish with the pecans and serve. ★

Leaf Lard Chocolate Chip Sandwich Cookies

Makes 24 cookie sandwiches

To finish our celebration of pork, what could be more appropriate than baking with lard? Leaf lard is rendered from the fat that surrounds the pig's kidneys. If you're worrying that your dessert will taste like a pork chop, relax: Leaf lard has virtually no "piggy" taste. Its clean flavor and smooth texture makes delicious pastries and doughs—many home cooks and pastry chefs alike swear by it for a perfectly flaky pie crust. Look for lard at your farmers' market or local butcher (lard from Mangalitsa pigs is the best); do not use the hydrogenated kind that comes in a box. We use leaf lard here to make delicious chocolate chip cookies. You can stop there, or take it one step further by preparing a lard-based buttercream to sandwich between two cookies. With a cold, frothy glass of local milk, we cannot think of a finer way to end this homage to the pig.

For the Lardo Buttercream

⅔ cup leaf lard, at room temperature

5 tablespoons confectioners' sugar

1 teaspoon pure vanilla extract

1 ½ teaspoons fleur de sel

1 ounce Lardo (page 213), frozen and finely diced (optional)

For the Cookies

1 cup packed dark brown sugar

2 ¼ cups granulated sugar

10 tablespoons (1 ¼ sticks) butter, at room temperature

1 cup leaf lard, at room temperature (may substitute butter)

1 tablespoon baking soda

1 tablespoon fleur de sel

3 large eggs, at room temperature

1 tablespoon pure vanilla extract

1 tablespoon white balsamic vinegar

4 ½ cups (24 ounces) all-purpose flour

4 cups (24 ounces) coarsely chopped chocolate, 58 percent cacao

To make the lardo buttercream: Whip the lard until light and fluffy in a bowl of a stand mixer fitted with the whisk attachment on medium to high speed. Reduce the speed to medium and add the confectioners' sugar and vanilla and whisk until thoroughly incorporated. Add the fleur de sel and diced lardo (if using) and mix until just bound together. (The buttercream can be made up to several days in advance; before icing, bring it to room temperature and whip until smooth.)

To make the cookies: In a stand mixer fitted with the paddle attachment, cream together the brown sugar, granulated sugar, butter, lard, baking soda, and half of the salt on medium speed. Once the mixture is uniform and light in color, add the eggs, one by one, thoroughly incorporating after each addition. Add the vanilla and vinegar and mix for 1 minute. Add half the flour and mix on low speed until almost completely incorporated. Add the remaining flour and partially incorporate. Add the chocolate and mix by hand until just barely incorporated. Wrap the dough in plastic and refrigerate until firm, at least 1 hour or up to several days.

Preheat a convection oven to 325° F or a conventional oven to 350° F. Line 2 baking sheets with parchment paper.

Scoop 24 balls of dough, each about 1 tablespoon, on each of the parchment-lined baking sheets, leaving 1 ½ inches between each ball for them to spread as they bake. Bake the cookies, rotating the baking sheet halfway through, for 7 minutes. The edges should be uniformly browned and the top of the cookies should look slightly undercooked. Let cool for a few minutes on the baking sheets to set, then transfer to a cooling rack to cool completely. The cookies will be best if baked the day they are served.

To assemble the cookies: Spread 1 tablespoon buttercream on the bottom of one cookie, sprinkle with a little of the remaining fleur de sel, then place a second cookie on top, bottom side down, to make a sandwich. Repeat to make 24 sandwich cookies. Once assembled, the cookies will keep for a few hours before serving. Store in an airtight container at room temperature. ✶

★

October

The Old Red Barn

An Autumn Repast

Serves 6

Mint Julep

Potted Quail Livers

Wilted Autumn Greens with Honey Mustard Vinaigrette

Roasted Quail with Wild Mushrooms | **Roasted and Fresh Baby Carrot Salad**

A Complex Pinot Noir with Rich Fruit

Meadow Creek Dairy Grayson with Toasted Hazelnuts and Honey

Madeleines | **Meyer Lemon Gelato**

In some pockets of the South, quail are just as beloved as pork and fried chicken. Georgia is one such place: The bobwhite quail was declared the official state gamebird in 1970. Though much of the state's former quail habitat has been given over to development in recent decades, Georgia is still home to several tracts of prime quail-hunting acreage. Our own Summerland Farm backs up to the Etowah River, and quail like to make their nests in the tall grass by the riverbanks. Clifford and I don't hunt, but we occasionally host guests who do. They've had good luck at Malbone Plantation, another Stiles family property adjacent to Summerland Farm. Whether freshly bagged or purchased from a farm, quail make an excellent autumn supper.

Though Clifford isn't a hunter, he is an avid equestrian. Growing up in Hawaii, he was a caretaker at a stable, and over the years he picked up the sport of polo. Now we raise horses on Summerland Farm, and Clifford plays polo throughout the South when his schedule permits. Our land is great for a trail ride, and I envision this meal as the perfect repast to follow a hunt or a long ride. October in our part of Georgia is cool but usually not cold—it's one of my favorite times of the year to be outside. Plenty of vegetables and herbs are still coming out of the ground, and the hills on the horizon are bursting into autumn color.

I love the way this menu comes together. The ingredients are simple, seasonal, and pleasing to the eye and the palate. Quail are a great main course for entertaining because each guest gets his or her own bird, which makes for an elegant presentation. The mint julep is often thought of as a spring cocktail, but it is really delicious any time of year, and the presentation of a mint julep cup packed with a dome of crushed ice, a sprig of mint, and a striped drinking straw is so much fun. The sweetness of the cocktail plays well against the rich potted quail liver crostini, accompanied by grapes and Marcona almonds for pre-dinner nibbling. Fall vegetables and a rich cheese set off the main dish of roasted, stuffed whole quail, and dessert is a sweet-tart gelato accompanied by a perfectly delicate madeleine.

We staged this supper at my cousin Frederick's barn on Malbone Plantation. The old red barn is into its second century now, and makes a picturesque, rustic setting for a meal. Guests coming up from Atlanta are always stunned that, after driving for less than an hour, they feel so far removed from the city. We set a wooden table with mismatched chairs and dined alfresco on a stunning mix of old transferware, new Vietri china, and crystal and linens from William Yeoward. For centerpieces, we interspersed antique trophy cups and ceramic horses with tuberose garlands around their necks. With a few seasonal adjustments, this menu would also work well for a Derby or steeplechase party in the spring, or even at room temperature for a polo tailgating picnic.

Mint Julep

We grow julep mint, a variety developed just for this iconic Southern cocktail, in the herb garden at Summerland farm; it is fragrant, delicious, easy to grow, and thrives in the Georgia climate. If you grow julep mint or any other variety of mint, snip it just before using to achieve the freshest taste. You can certainly use fresh mint from the farmers' market or grocery store, but mint is a great plant to grow at home, even for the beginning gardener. It's almost impossible to kill!

Many people think of the mint julep as a spring or summer drink, associated in particular with the Kentucky Derby. But the brightness of the mint with the warmth of the bourbon is just as appropriate in the fall. The preferred serving vessel is the traditional pewter or silver mint julep cup, but a double old fashioned glass is a good substitute.

Fresh mint leaves

Granulated or turbinado sugar

Bourbon (preferably Blanton's)

For each mint julep, use a muddler to crush 6 mint leaves and 1 tablespoon sugar together in the bottom of a silver julep cup or tall glass. Add 1 ounce water and stir. Mound the cup with ice—crushed ice is preferable. Pour 2 1/2 ounces bourbon over the ice (do not stir). Serve with a silver mint julep spoon or straw or other fancy straw. ⋆

Potted Quail Livers

Makes four 8-ounce jars, serves 6 with ample leftovers

This savory recipe is excellent for entertaining, as it will keep for up to 2 weeks. Its almost mousselike consistency is fantastic on a fresh homemade baguette (page 242), especially when accompanied by grapes, Marcona almonds, and plumped raisins (soak golden raisins in warm water for about 10 minutes). Take a jar of these potted livers along on a picnic, or to a dinner party as a crowd-pleasing appetizer or hostess gift. If you cannot find quail livers, chicken livers provide an equally delicious result. We include a pinch of Insta Cure here, but since its only role is to preserve the pleasing pink color of the spread, you may omit it if you like. But if you do so, it is important to seal the top with fat if you plan on making the spread more than a few days in advance.

1 tablespoon plus 1 cup (2 sticks) cold butter, cubed

2 shallots, diced (about 2 tablespoons)

2 garlic cloves, thinly sliced

1 pound fresh quail livers, deveined

½ cup tawny port

Kosher salt

Freshly ground pepper

Pinch of sugar

Pinch of Insta Cure #1 (see "Curing Salt," page 16)

1 tablespoon duck fat (optional) or
Clarified Butter (see page 246)

In a large sauté pan, heat the 1 tablespoon butter over medium heat. Add the shallots and garlic and cook until translucent, stirring occasionally. Add the livers and cook, tossing the pan once to ensure even cooking, until medium rare, about 5 minutes (or 10 minutes for chicken livers). Transfer the livers to the bowl of a food processor fitted with the metal blade. Add the port to the pan and cook, stirring to loosen the brown bits from the bottom, until reduced by half. Season with kosher salt, pepper, and sugar.

Pulse the livers a few times to puree, then add the port-shallot mixture from the pan and pulse a few more times. Slowly add the cubes of cold butter, about 4 at a time, and pulse until the butter is completely incorporated. Add the Insta Cure, which will keep the color bright. Adjust the seasoning with kosher salt, pepper, and sugar if needed.

Push the mixture through a fine-mesh strainer into a bowl. Spoon the mixture into four half-pint jars leaving ½ inch of space at the top. Place lids on the jars, or cover tightly with plastic wrap. Refrigerate until chilled completely, about 1 hour. Top with duck fat or clarified butter that has been heated in a small saucepan just until warm or melted, if you like. This layer of fat seals the top and prevents oxidation and discoloration. Store in the refrigerator for up to 2 weeks. ★

Wilted Autumn Greens
with Honey Mustard Vinaigrette

Serves 6

This is a perfect autumn salad: not so much cooked as wilted greens in a warm, savory-sweet vinaigrette. Here in the South, we are lucky to have so many different greens that grow remarkably well virtually all year round. From the traditional collards, spinach, mustard, and turnip greens to the international varieties that have recently made their way here, including bok choy, tatsoi, and komatsuna, there are a variety of tastes and textures to choose from. No matter where you live, experiment with seasonal greens until you find your favorites. If you're shopping at the farmers' market, most of the vendors will be happy to let you have a few nibbles for taste-testing. The same goes for the squash—you can use butternut, acorn, pumpkin, African, or any similar variety. At Summerland Farm, we are lucky to have American chestnut trees planted by my ancestors, and even luckier that those trees survived the chestnut blight that killed most American chestnuts in the first half of the twentieth century. Fresh chestnuts—often grown in California—are available in many natural foods stores in the cooler months. If you can't find chestnuts, hazelnuts or cashews would make a good substitute.

1 medium African or small butternut squash

2 Moonglow or Asian pears, cored, peeled, and diced (about 1 cup)

1 tablespoon olive oil

½ cup (about 12) chestnuts

10 shallots, peeled

⅓ pound (about 2 bunches) tender komatsuna leaves or fresh spinach, torn

⅓ pound (about 2 heads) tatsoi, torn

⅓ pound (about 2 bunches) mustard greens, torn

For the Vinaigrette

8 ounces bacon, diced

2 tablespoons Dijon mustard

2 tablespoons local honey

¼ cup Champagne vinegar

1 teaspoon chopped fresh thyme

1 teaspoon freshly ground pepper

⅓ cup canola oil

Preheat the oven to 400° F.

Peel the squash: First cut into two cross sections, scrape out the seeds, and place the squash, flat side down, on a cutting board. Work around the squash with a sharp knife or peeler, making sure to remove the layer of lighter colored flesh under the skin as well as the skin. Dice into ½-inch cubes to make about 1 cup (reserve any leftovers for another use).

Arrange the diced squash and pears on a baking sheet and toss with the oil. Roast until browned, about 20 minutes; set aside at room temperature.

Make a cross slit on the rounded end of each chestnut with a sharp paring knife. Place on a baking sheet and roast for 15 minutes, or until the cut sections on the bottoms of the nuts just start to curl. Peel the chestnuts as soon as they are cool enough to handle, as they will peel the easiest while hot. Cut into quarters and set aside.

Reduce the oven temperature to 350° F. Wrap the shallots in parchment paper and then in aluminum foil. Bake until tender and slightly caramelized, about 1 hour. Once the shallots are cool enough to handle, chop coarsely and set aside.

To make the vinaigrette: In a large sauté pan, cook the bacon over medium heat until crispy; transfer the bacon to a paper towel–lined plate and reserve the fat in the pan. Once the fat has cooled slightly, strain through a fine-mesh strainer into a measuring cup that has a spout. In a blender or food processor, combine the mustard, honey, vinegar, thyme, and pepper and blend for 30 seconds. Slowly add the strained warm bacon fat and the oil through the cap of the blender or the feed tube of the food processor, blending until thoroughly combined. Pour the vinaigrette into a large mixing bowl.

Add the squash and pears, chestnuts, shallots, bacon, komatsuna, tatsoi, and mustard greens to the mixing bowl and toss with the warm vinaigrette. Serve immediately. ⋆

Roasted Quail with Wild Mushrooms

Serves 6

This recipe is a wonderful way to celebrate the spoils of the Southern hunt, though it is just as delicious when made with farm-raised quail. If quail livers aren't included with the quail, chicken livers would be a good substitute. The size of a quail makes each bird a perfect individual portion for a dinner party. To make the stuffing, we've used another reward of the "hunt": wild mushrooms. When we forage in the woods near Summerland Farm, the mushrooms we most often find are chanterelles and hen-of-the-woods, especially prolific during a moist season. If you are foraging, be absolutely sure you know what you are looking for, as poisonous varieties can sometimes look dangerously similar to edible ones. To be on the safe side, visit a gourmet market or natural foods grocery store for a nice choice of mushrooms. We serve the quail on a bed of Wilted Autumn Greens (page 38).

1 pound wild mushrooms, such as chanterelle, hen-of-the-woods, black trumpet, or a mixture

1 teaspoon plus 1 tablespoon olive oil

1 cup white port

10 ounces boneless, skinless chicken breasts, cubed

6 quail livers

2 large egg whites

¼ cup heavy cream

6 (14-ounce) whole semi-boneless quail

Kosher salt

To clean the mushrooms, wash in a bowl of cold water, gently tossing so as not to bruise them. Repeat 2 times. Using a paring knife, trim the ends and scrape the stems, removing the outer layer. Let dry thoroughly on paper towels at room temperature or uncovered in your refrigerator—this could take up to a couple of hours and can be done the day before.

In large sauté pan over high heat, heat the 1 teaspoon oil. Add the mushrooms and cook until browned. Reduce the heat to medium and add the port, scraping up any brown bits on the bottom. Reduce until the liquid is a syrupy consistency, about 10 minutes.

In a food processor fitted with a steel blade, puree the chicken cubes and livers; slowly add the egg whites, then the cream. Mix until thoroughly combined. Pass the poultry puree through a fine-mesh strainer into a bowl. Roughly chop the cooled mushrooms and add (with any residual juice) to the bowl with the poultry puree.

Preheat the oven to 325° F. Season the quail inside and out with salt.

Scoop the poultry puree into a pastry piping bag fitted with a ½-inch round tip or a large plastic storage bag with one ½-inch corner snipped. Pipe puree into each quail body and tie the legs together with butcher's twine.

Heat a large cast-iron or heavy-bottomed ovenproof sauté pan over medium heat. Add the remaining 1 tablespoon oil and brown the quail on all sides. You may need to work in batches. Transfer the pan to the oven (use two pans or transfer to a large roasting pan if necessary) and roast the quail for 30 minutes, or until a meat thermometer inserted in the center of the quail registers 155° F. Let rest in the pan for 5 minutes before serving. ∗

Roasted and Fresh Baby Carrot Salad

Serves 6

Though we recommend using young, small carrots for this recipe, we are definitely not referring to the peeled and bagged nubs sold as "baby carrots" in the supermarket. Traditional orange carrots make for a bright, beautiful salad, but you can also add visual interest by using heirloom varieties in shades of purple, yellow, and white. We roast some of the carrots and leave some of them raw, creating a wonderful contrast in flavor and texture between the sweet, slightly soft, roasted carrots and the fresh, crunchy raw curls. Pistachios and pumpkin seeds add a pleasing crunch; you could just use one or the other, but the two flavors together are even more interesting. Pecans or sesame seeds would also work well. For me, the coriander seeds bring the whole dish together—something about their flavor both highlights and rounds out the earthiness of the carrots. To assemble the salad, begin with the humble-looking roasted carrots on the bottom and build from there. If you are unable to find carrots with their tops still attached, watercress would also make a nice garnish.

3 pounds baby carrots (about 24), cleaned and peeled

4 tablespoons olive oil

Kosher salt

1 cup golden raisins

1 cup dry white wine, such as a pinot grigio or sauvignon blanc

¼ teaspoon granulated sugar

½ teaspoon coriander seeds

½ cup hulled pumpkin seeds

½ cup pistachios

1 tablespoon freshly squeezed lemon juice

1 teaspoon honey

Pea shoots, for garnish

Carrot greens or watercress, stemmed, for garnish

Preheat the oven to 400° F.

Toss 14 of the carrots with 1 tablespoon of the oil and salt to taste. Spread out in a single layer on a baking sheet and roast for 10 to 15 minutes, until tender. While the carrots roast, combine the raisins, wine, and sugar in a medium saucepan. Cook over low until the raisins are plump, about 10 minutes. Drain off any remaining liquid and discard.

In a large bowl, combine 2 cups ice and 2 cups cold water to make an ice bath. Use a mandolin with the safety guard or a sharp knife to shave the remaining carrots lengthwise as thin as possible. Place the shaved raw carrots in the ice bath to help the carrots curl and stay crisp.

Lightly toast the coriander seeds over medium heat in a dry nonstick pan just until they become fragrant, about 3 minutes. Crush them slightly in a mortar and pestle or with the flat side of a chef's knife and set aside. Toast the pumpkin seeds in the same way until just fragrant, about 3 minutes. Roughly chop and set aside. Toast the pistachios in the same way until just fragrant, about 5 minutes. Roughly chop and set aside.

Whisk together the coriander, lemon juice, honey, and remaining 3 tablespoons oil in a large bowl. Add the roasted carrots, raisins, and pistachios and toss. Transfer to the center of a serving platter. Drain the carrot curls and scatter on top, along with the pumpkin seeds. Garnish with pea shoots and carrot tops and serve. ★

Madeleines

Makes 12 little cakes

We serve these delicate, shell-shaped sponge cakes warm at the end of every meal at Bacchanalia. They are best served immediately out of the oven but, luckily, you can prepare the batter up to a few days in advance. The madeleines bake quickly, producing a crisp exterior that yields to a pleasantly spongy interior. The flavor is sweet, but not too sweet, with a zing of fresh lemon and orange zest. Madeleine pans, with their elongated, seashell-shaped molds, are available at most kitchenware stores.

½ cup (1 stick) butter

2 large eggs

¾ cup granulated sugar

1 teaspoon finely grated orange zest

1 teaspoon finely grated lemon zest

¼ teaspoon pure vanilla extract

¼ teaspoon kosher salt

1 cup all-purpose flour

1 teaspoon baking powder

Confectioners' sugar, for dusting

Melt the butter in a medium saucepan and hold it warm over very low heat. In a large bowl, whisk together the eggs, granulated sugar, orange and lemon zests, vanilla, and salt. Add the flour and baking powder and whisk together. Gradually stir in the melted butter until incorporated. Scoop the batter into a pastry piping bag fitted with a ½-inch round tip or a large plastic storage bag with one corner snipped. (The batter can be refrigerated in the piping bag or plastic bag for up to 2 days.)

Preheat the oven to 325° F. Coat 12 molds of a madeleine pan with nonstick cooking spray—we use it even with nonstick pans as the madeleines tend to stick.

Pipe the batter into the prepared molds, filling each about halfway. Bake for 6 to 8 minutes; they should be golden brown and a toothpick inserted will come out clean. They should release from the pans easily. In a perfect world, these would come out of the oven and be served directly to your guests. (We make them all night to ensure they are hot and crisp.) But you may bake them in advance and store the cooled cakes in an airtight container at room temperature for up to 2 days. Then reheat in a 325° F oven for a couple of minutes. Just before serving, dust with confectioners' sugar. ★

Meyer Lemon Gelato

Makes 1 quart, serves 6 with leftovers

Meyer lemons, once available only in northern California, are now cultivated in Florida and widely available in the fall. The sweet, floral, slightly acidic fruit can be used to make an excellent gelato. Paired with a warm Madeleine (page 44), it is the perfect ending to this autumn meal. The gelato can be made up to several weeks ahead of time and stored in the freezer. Let it soften for 15 to 20 minutes before serving. For the best results, use high-quality, fresh, and ideally local milk, cream, and eggs.

2 cups whole milk

1 cup heavy cream

4 large egg yolks

2/3 cup granulated sugar

2 teaspoons grated Meyer lemon zest

3 tablespoons freshly squeezed Meyer lemon juice (from about 3 lemons)

Candied Lemon or Orange Zest (page 52), for garnish

In a heavy-bottomed medium saucepan, combine the milk and cream over medium to low heat. Cook, stirring occasionally so a skin doesn't form, until tiny bubbles form on the surface. Remove from the heat.

In a medium heat-resistant bowl such as Pyrex or stainless steel, whisk the egg yolks until smooth. Gradually whisk in the sugar until it is well incorporated and the mixture is thick and pale yellow. You can do this by hand or using a hand mixer. Very slowly pour in the hot milk-cream mixture while whisking continuously; it's important to pour slowly so the eggs don't curdle.

Return the mixture to the saucepan and place over low heat. Cook, stirring frequently with a wooden spoon, until the custard is thick enough to coat the back of the spoon, 5 to 7 minutes. Do not bring to a boil. Gently whisk in the lemon zest and juice.

Strain the custard through a fine-mesh strainer into a clean heatproof bowl and place plastic wrap directly on the surface to prevent a skin from forming; let cool for 5 minutes. Meanwhile, make an ice bath by filling a large bowl with 2 cups ice and 2 cups cold water. Place the bowl with the custard in the bath; uncover and stir the custard with a spoon until cooled. Once completely cool, cover and refrigerate until very cold, at least 4 hours and up to 24 hours.

Pour the custard into the container of an ice cream machine and churn per the manufacturer's instructions. Transfer to a clean plastic container and freeze for at least 2 hours before serving. Scoop out and garnish with candied zest. ⋆

★

Give Thanks
All the Fixings for a Crowd

Serves 12

Cranberry Cocktail

Roasted Turkey with Gravy Two Ways

Apple-Cranberry Dressing | Nanny's Cranberry Mold

Roasted Brussels Sprouts with Bacon

Mrs. Carver's Buttered Rutabagas

Sweet Potato Puree with Toasted Meringue

Yukon Gold Potato Puree | Yeast Rolls

A Full-Bodied Chardonnay

Warm Pumpkin Pudding with Hard Sauce

Liz Lorber's Famous Hummingbird Cake | Pecan Pie

My paternal grandmother, Nanny, always laid out a tremendous bounty at Thanksgiving, and her recipes are the ones I re-create year after year. They are too delicious—and too comforting—to give up. Every Thanksgiving, we prepare the same menu for customers to take home to their family tables that I serve my guests at the farm. At Star Provisions, this means several hundred pounds of dressing, dozens of gallons of gravy, and a hundred roasted turkeys—it's all hands on deck.

Our restaurants are closed on Thanksgiving Day, but we are so busy before and after the holiday that some of our staff can't make it home. I invite anyone who wants to come to Summerland Farm for this meal of traditional Thanksgiving favorites. Some years, this has meant that Clifford and I play host to more than thirty guests, but there is always plenty to eat. We give thanks for each other, for the food, and for the day of rest before we return to the holiday hustle.

For years, we have been roasting two birds—and not just because we have so many mouths to feed. We love the heritage turkeys from Frank Reese's Good Shepherd Ranch in Kansas for their rich, flavorful dark meat. But we can't give up the succulence of a good organic turkey, which has a much larger breast than the heritage breeds. Rather than make the difficult choice, we compromise with at least one of each.

Years ago, we added some turkeys to the menagerie at Summerland Farm, with the intention of bringing them to the Thanksgiving table. But when their time came, we couldn't bring ourselves to kill them. We had grown attached to their inquisitive personalities and their striking red wattles, and their funny way of tottering around the chicken yard. Now, they all share a name—"Lucky"—and at seven years old, they've had quite a run.

In addition to the turkeys, we prepare plenty of traditional sides—from yeast rolls to meringue-capped sweet potatoes—most of which are borrowed from my grandmother's Thanksgiving table. The apple-cranberry dressing is a favorite of my sister Frances, who runs the front of the house at Bacchanalia and always joins us at Summerland Farm for Thanksgiving. To start things off, we serve a festive cranberry cocktail. And the meal ends with an embarrassment of desserts. I can never seem to narrow down which one I want the most, so I make them all! (No guest has ever complained about this.)

With so many people coming and going, I keep the meal fairly casual. I do like to bring out my Thanksgiving china (Johnson Brothers transferware), but I pair it with chocolate-brown ceramic chargers and neutral table linens. Instead of creating flower arrangements, I fill glass bottles and apothecary jars with unshelled walnuts and pecans and arrange them down the middle of the dining table. When the holiday is over, I leave the nuts in the pantry at one of the restaurants, so nothing is wasted. After all, making good use of what you have is a demonstration of gratitude in itself.

Cranberry Cocktail

In a fitting homage to cranberry sauce, why not add some cranberry to your sauce? We make this simple, tart cocktail with the liquid from poached cranberries. You can use any vodka, but our favorite for this particular cocktail is Prairie, an organic, corn-based vodka from Minnesota. This is a festive and refreshing way to get in the Thanksgiving spirit.

Vodka (preferably Prairie)

Cranberry poaching liquid (see below)

Orange bitters (preferably Peychaud's)

Poached Cranberries (recipe follows), for garnish

Candied Orange Zest (recipe follows), for garnish

For each cocktail, combine 1 ½ ounces vodka, 1 ounce cranberry poaching liquid, and 4 dashes bitters in a cocktail shaker with ice. Shake and strain into a chilled glass. Skewer poached cranberries and candied orange zest to garnish. ★

Poached Cranberries
Makes 2 cups cranberries and
2 cups poaching liquid

4 oranges

2 cups granulated sugar

Pinch of kosher salt

1 pound fresh cranberries

Peel the oranges with a vegetable peeler and then juice them. Combine 1 cup water with the orange zest and juice, sugar, and salt in a 2-quart saucepan over medium heat. Bring to a boil, reduce the heat to low, and simmer for 2 minutes. Add the cranberries and simmer for 10 minutes, until tender but not bursting. Cool slightly and then strain the poaching liquid into a container; reserve the cranberries in another container and refrigerate both. This can be made up to 2 days in advance. ★

Candied Citrus Zest
Makes 1 pint

4 oranges or 6 lemons

3 cups granulated sugar

¾ cup superfine sugar

Peel just the zest from the fruit using a channel knife working in a circular fashion to create long strips of zest. You do not want any of the bitter white pith from the underside of the colored zest, so scrape off any that remains with the knife.

Stir the granulated sugar into 5 cups water in a 4-quart saucepan and bring to a boil over medium to high heat. Lower the heat to a simmer, add the zest, and simmer uncovered for 1 ½ hours.

Preheat the oven to 200° F. Line a baking sheet with parchment paper. Transfer the zest to a small bowl with a strainer or slotted spoon. (Reserve the syrup for another use; it is great for sweetening iced tea or in cocktails.) Add the superfine sugar and toss. Transfer the zest to the prepared baking sheet. (Reserve the leftover sugar for another use as above.)

Place the baking sheet in the oven for up to 1 hour to dry out the zest. Check every 20 minutes to be sure it is not browning. If it starts to brown, turn off the oven and leave the zest in the oven with the door slightly ajar until dry to the touch. The candied zest can be made ahead of time and will keep well for several weeks in an airtight container at room temperature. ★

Roasted Turkey with Gravy Two Ways

Serves 12 to 16; for a 16 to 20 pound turkey

To brine or not to brine—that is the Thanksgiving question. Though some people believe that it negatively affects the texture of the bird, I am a faithful briner. I feel that the application of salt enhances the flavor of the meat and helps keep it moist during cooking. A simple overnight brine of 1 cup salt to 1 gallon cold water is all you need. For a heritage bird, I might take it a step further and flavor the brine with aromatics as in the recipe below. A dry rub would work as well: Just salt the bird liberally and let it sit in the refrigerator for 12 to 24 hours; rinse under cold water and dry thoroughly before roasting. This also helps seal in moisture and impart flavor.

For the Aromatic Brine

7 quarts water

2 cups kosher salt

1 cup brown sugar

2 medium onions, quartered

½ cup celery scraps (leaves and small stems)

6 garlic cloves, crushed

4 sprigs fresh thyme

6 fresh bay leaves

2 tablespoons whole coriander seeds

2 tablespoons whole black peppercorns

1 tablespoon fennel seeds

1 gallon ice

Fill a 10-quart stockpot with the water and add the salt, brown sugar, onions, celery scraps, garlic, thyme, bay leaves, coriander, peppercorns, and fennel seeds. Heat over medium heat until the sugar and salt have dissolved—it does not have to come to a boil. Remove from the heat and cool slightly. Transfer to a 5-gallon bucket and add the ice. This should bring down the temperature to a cool 40° F or below. Remove the giblets from the turkey and reserve for the gravy (opposite). Add the turkey to the brine, making sure it is completely submerged. If needed, place a plate on the top of the turkey to keep it submerged. Cover and refrigerate for 24 hours. ★

For the Turkey

1 (18-pound) turkey, brined (see opposite)

1 cup (2 sticks) butter

Leaves from 4 sprigs fresh sage

2 teaspoons kosher salt

1 teaspoon freshly ground black pepper

Preheat the oven to 425° F.

Melt the butter slowly over very low heat. Rinse the turkey inside and out. Pat it dry with paper towels. If you've brined the turkey, drain it and discard the brine. Gently run your fingers between the skin and meat on either side of the breast bone and arrange the sage leaves between the skin and breast. Pour one-fourth of the melted butter over the bird and rub it into the skin with your hands. (Reserve the remaining melted butter for basting.) Tuck the drumsticks under the folds of skin or tie together with butcher's twine. Season with salt and pepper.

Place the bird on a rack in a roasting pan and insert an ovenproof meat thermometer into the thickest part of a thigh. The thermometer should point toward the body and should not touch the bone. Place the turkey in the oven. After 30 minutes, baste the turkey with melted butter and reduce the oven temperature to 350° F. Continue to roast, basting with the melted butter every 30 minutes (this promotes even browning). If you feel the turkey is browning too quickly, cover with a tent of aluminum foil. Roasting times will vary depending on the size of your bird. It typically takes about 3 hours total for an 18-pound bird, but the best and safest way to know when your turkey is cooked is to check the meat thermometer. Once it registers 160° F, remove the turkey from the oven.

Transfer the turkey to a cutting board and allow it to rest, uncovered, for 30 minutes. Reserve the drippings in the roasting pan for the gravy (see opposite). ★

Gravy Two Ways

Makes 8 cups

Here are two techniques for making gravy (with a roux or with a slurry), and each has its staunch defenders. If the gravy is cooked long enough without being allowed to burn, both methods create a rich and delicious gravy without any residual taste of uncooked flour. The roux, made of equal parts fat and flour, takes a little more time and requires several minutes of constant stirring and monitoring. This technique is beloved in Louisiana and elsewhere—including in classical French cooking—for the depth of flavor it imparts. The slurry method is how most of our grandmothers made gravy, and I find it a bit easier. With the slurry method, be sure to cook the gravy until you can no longer taste the flour. Keep it on the stove for a few minutes more than you think you should, resisting the inclination to stop as soon as the flour is incorporated into the stock.

To make the gravy with a roux: Place 1 cup of the reserved fat in a 4-quart saucepan and add the flour. Discard the remaining fat. Stirring constantly with a wooden spoon, cook the roux over low heat until the mixture looks like wet sand. Continue to cook slowly for 5 minutes. A little color is okay and will add a toasted quality to the gravy. Slowly add the warm stock from the roasting pan, 1 cup at a time, stirring to incorporate after each addition. Continue to cook over low heat until the gravy is thickened.

Strain through a fine sieve just in case there are any lumps. Season with salt and pepper to taste. Add the diced giblets if desired. Reserve in saucepan until ready to serve; reheat if needed. (The gravy will keep, well covered, in the refrigerator for several days for leftovers.) *

Giblets from 1 turkey (gizzard, neck, heart, and liver)

6 cups Chicken Stock (page 244) or cold water

1 stalk celery, roughly chopped

1 onion, roughly chopped

Turkey pan drippings

1 cup all-purpose flour

Kosher salt

Freshly ground pepper

Rinse the giblets and place them in an 8-quart stockpot with the stock, celery, and onion. Simmer over low heat, uncovered, for 1 hour. Strain the stock through a fine strainer into a saucepan and set aside. Reserve the giblets; discard all other solids. Finely dice the gizzard, heart, and liver and set aside for the gravy; discard the neck.

Skim the fat off the top of the pan drippings in the roasting pan using a large spoon and reserve. Place the roasting pan over low heat, add the 6 cups chicken or turkey giblet stock, and stir to scrape up and incorporate the flavorful browned bits from the bottom of the pan.

To make the gravy with a slurry: Discard the reserved fat. Mix the flour into 1 1/2 cups cold water in a jar with a lid and shake vigorously for about 2 minutes, until the flour is incorporated without any lumps, creating a slurry. Over medium heat, slowly add the slurry to the roasting pan, stirring constantly with a wooden spoon. Bring to a simmer and reduce the heat to low, continuing to cook for 10 to 15 minutes.

Roasted Turkey with Gravy Two Ways

An adequately full plate

Apple-Cranberry Dressing

Serves 12

When I was growing up in Connecticut, we called this "stuffing." In the South, it is "dressing." Regardless of semantics, this is a comforting, classic Thanksgiving favorite. It is very close to my grandmother's recipe, although she (like so many of our mothers and grandmothers!) used Pepperidge Farm stuffing and doctored it up some. For the most reliable results, I prefer to cook the dressing on its own in a casserole dish instead of stuffing it into the uncooked turkey. I love the flavors of the sage and celery with the sweetness of the apple. I often add browned and crumbled sweet Italian sausage, but it is quite good without the pork.

1 (2-pound) loaf of sourdough bread

1 pound (4 sticks) butter

2 stalks celery, medium diced

2 sweet onions, medium diced

2 apples (preferably Gala or Yates),
peeled, cored, and medium diced

10 leaves fresh sage, thinly sliced

Freshly ground pepper

Kosher salt

2 cups Chicken Stock or Turkey Stock (page 244)

½ cup dried cranberries

Preheat the oven to 350° F. Dice the bread into 1-inch cubes and place on a baking sheet. Toast in the oven until golden brown, about 15 minutes; set aside. If baking the dressing right away, leave the oven at 350° F. (You can toast the bread several days in advance and store in an airtight container or bag.)

Melt the butter in large sauté pan over medium heat. Add the celery and onions and sauté until softened, 5 minutes.

Add the apples and sauté for another 5 minutes. Add the sage and season with salt and pepper. Add the stock and cook for 10 minutes, until it just comes to a simmer. Add the cranberries and stir.

Place the toasted bread cubes in a large bowl and pour the hot vegetables and stock over them; toss until well coated. Transfer to a 9 x 14-inch casserole dish and bake, uncovered, for 30 minutes, until the top is crispy. ★

Nanny's Cranberry Mold

Serves 12 to 16

For years after my grandmother's death, I tried to re-create her lovely cranberry mold, but to no avail—mine always fell into a puddle as soon as I removed the mold. A few years ago, my great-aunt Frances instructed me to use a little gelatin, as Nanny had always done. Now it is perfect. Though I grew up eating this dish in Connecticut, it is right at home on the Southern Thanksgiving table, where congealed salads are a holiday staple. And it tastes much fresher than cranberry sauce from a can! I like to make it in smaller 1-cup ramekins in order to set a small mold at each corner of the table.

1 pound fresh cranberries

2 cups granulated sugar

1 tablespoon grated orange zest

1 cup freshly squeezed orange juice (from 3 medium oranges), strained

1½ tablespoons freshly squeezed lemon juice

1 sheet gelatin, or ¾ teaspoon powdered gelatin

Combine the cranberries, sugar, orange zest and juice, lemon juice, and 1 cup water in a 2-quart saucepan over medium heat. Bring to a simmer, reduce to low heat, and cook until the cranberries are soft and tender, about 10 minutes. Strain through a fine-mesh sieve into a medium bowl, being careful not to press too hard on the cranberries (which would make the mixture cloudy). Discard the solids or reserve to use as a cocktail garnish (see page 52) or as a special treat for your chickens.

In a small bowl, soften the gelatin sheet in 1 cup cold water for about 3 minutes. Remove the sheet from the water and squeeze out the water. Add the gelatin sheet to the strained warm cranberry liquid (or sprinkle on the powdered gelatin) and stir well until dissolved.

Immediately pour the liquid into a decorative 4-cup mold or four 8-ounce molds or ramekins. Refrigerate, uncovered, for at least 1 hour, or until set. Once set you can cover with plastic wrap. (This can be prepared up to 3 days in advance.)

When ready to unmold, fill a bowl large enough to hold a mold with warm water. Place a mold in the bowl so the water comes partway up the sides (you don't want water to slosh over the top of the mold, though). Let the mold sit in the warm water for a minute or two. Take the mold out of the water, wipe off excess water, and invert a serving plate on top of the mold. Flip it over, lift up the mold, and the gelatin will slip out onto the plate. ★

Roasted Brussels Sprouts with Bacon

Serves 12

This delicious vegetable is the most popular side dish we serve at Abattoir and Floataway Café. I don't bother with blanching the Brussels sprouts—I prefer to cook them from a raw state so that they maintain that fantastic crunch. The outside leaves are especially delicious when they begin to caramelize in the hot pan. And bacon is the perfect salty, savory accompaniment to the pleasant, earthy bitterness of the Brussels sprouts. Using high-quality bacon—we like Benton's, from Madisonville, Tennessee (it's available by mail order)—makes a big difference in a dish like this one with just a few ingredients.

½ pound bacon, diced

2 teaspoons olive oil

3 pounds Brussels sprouts, outer leaves trimmed, halved

Kosher salt

Freshly ground pepper

Preheat the oven to 400° F.

In a 12-inch cast-iron or heavy-bottomed skillet, cook the bacon until crispy. Remove the bacon with a slotted spoon and transfer to a bowl lined with paper towels to drain; set aside. Reserve the bacon fat for another use.

In a clean 12-inch skillet, heat the olive oil over high heat. Add the Brussels sprouts and cook, tossing or shaking the pan, until browned, about 5 minutes. Add the bacon, season with salt and pepper, and transfer to a 9 x 14-inch baking dish. Roast for 15 minutes, until the Brussels sprouts are caramelized and brown. Serve hot. ★

Mrs. Carver's Buttered Rutabagas

Serves 12

There is a small "meat and three"—a type of Southern lunch establishment where you choose a protein and three vegetables, often from a steam table—around the corner from Bacchanalia and Star Provisions called Carver's Country Kitchen. It used to be a general store, but now the small kitchen serves up home-cooked meats and vegetables from 11 a.m. until they run out. You can eat in the restaurant at an assortment of mismatched tables, or take a Styrofoam container to go. The rutabagas are my favorite—rich, buttery soul food with just a slight kick of nutmeg. They make a delicious and comforting addition to the Thanksgiving table, where they fit right in with my family's classics.

Kosher salt

4 medium rutabagas

1 cup (2 sticks) cold butter, diced

¼ teaspoon freshly grated nutmeg

Freshly ground pepper

Bring an 8-quart pot of water to a boil and add 1 tablespoon salt.

Meanwhile, peel the rutabagas: They are very dense and the skin can be ¼ inch thick, so best to cut off the bottom of the root first to stabilize, then work around the root, slicing away the skin from the top to the bottom in sections. There is often a lighter colored underskin that should also be removed as it can be bitter.

Cut the peeled rutabagas into 1 ½-inch cubes and add to the boiling water. Reduce the heat to medium and cook until tender, 10 to 15 minutes. They should be tender to the touch while retaining their shape. Drain in a colander, then return to the pot. Add the butter, nutmeg, salt, and pepper and gently fold together; avoid breaking apart the rutabaga cubes. Serve immediately. ★

Sweet Potato Puree with Toasted Meringue

Serves 12

I still find this old favorite irresistible on my Thanksgiving table, even after we've pureed hundreds of pounds of sweet potatoes to sell at Star Provisions. This dish is a take on the classic candied yams, made slightly more sophisticated with warm spices and a toasted meringue topping. Of course, marshmallows can easily sub in for the meringue if you do not have time to whip up the meringue—or if you prefer the marshmallows for sentimental reasons. In that case, simply cover the top of the baked sweet potatoes with a layer of mini marshmallows and return to the oven for 10 minutes to toast.

For the Sweet Potatoes

3 pounds sweet potatoes, skin on

1 cup (2 sticks) cold butter, cut into cubes, plus extra for greasing the pan

½ cup maple syrup

1 teaspoon ground ginger

½ teaspoon ground cinnamon

¼ teaspoon freshly grated nutmeg

1 teaspoon kosher salt

1 teaspoon white pepper

For the Meringue

1 ¼ cups egg whites (from about 10 large eggs), at room temperature

⅛ teaspoon cream of tartar

⅛ teaspoon pure vanilla extract (preferably Nielsen-Massey)

3 cups granulated sugar

To make the sweet potatoes: Preheat the oven to 350° F. Butter a 9-inch round casserole dish. Place the sweet potatoes on a baking sheet and bake until they are soft and give to the touch when squeezed in the center. This should take 1 to 2 hours, depending on the size of the potatoes.

Peel the sweet potatoes while still warm. Place in the bowl of a food processor and puree until smooth. Add the butter, maple syrup, ginger, cinnamon, nutmeg, salt, and white pepper. Transfer to the prepared casserole. (You can prepare the casserole in advance up to this point; it will keep, covered in the refrigerator, for up to 2 days.) When you are ready to serve, bake the casserole for 30 minutes, until heated through.

To make the meringue: In the clean bowl of a stand mixer fitted with the whisk attachment, beat the egg whites, cream of tartar, and vanilla. Bring to soft peaks and slowly add the sugar; the meringue should be shiny and silky—do not overwhip.

Preheat the broiler. Top the sweet potatoes with dollops of meringue. Toast about 4 inches from the broiler for about 5 minutes, until golden brown. (Alternatively, you may toast the meringue using a propane torch: Hold the torch 5 to 6 inches from the meringue and move it in sweeping motions across the meringue until it is golden brown, being careful not to hold the flame over one place too long.) Serve immediately. ★

Clockwise from top left: Roasted Brussels Sprouts with Bacon | Mrs. Carver's Buttered Rutabagas
Yukon Gold Potato Puree, Nanny's Cranberry Mold, and Apple-Cranberry Dressing | Sweet Potato Puree with Toasted Meringue

Yukon Gold Potato Puree

Serves 12

For many people, myself included, it wouldn't be Thanksgiving without mashed potatoes. We like to cook our potatoes in their jackets to keep the excess moisture out, then we can add our own moisture in the form of butter and milk. The potatoes may be mashed by hand, but for the smoothest texture we suggest pushing them through a ricer or food mill for a nice smooth puree. They are sublime with a splash of gravy (page 55) on top.

5 pounds Yukon gold potatoes, skin on

Kosher salt

2 cups half-and-half or whole milk

1 pound (4 sticks) cold butter, cut into small cubes

Freshly ground pepper

In a large pot, cover the potatoes with cold water and a pinch of salt. Bring to a boil over high heat. Reduce to a simmer and cook for 20 to 30 minutes. To test if the potatoes are done, insert a paring knife in the middle of one: If it slips out easily, they are done. Drain.

Meanwhile, in a 2-quart saucepan, warm the half-and-half over low heat.

While still hot, peel the potatoes. (They will absorb the butter and milk better when hot.) To avoid burning your hands, hold the hot potato in a kitchen towel to peel. Push the potato flesh through a food mill or ricer into a 4-quart saucepan, or mash by hand.

Place the potatoes over low heat and, stirring constantly with a wooden spoon, slowly add some of the warm half-and-half and then several cubes of the butter; continue stirring and alternating adding the half-and-half and butter until smooth. Remove from the heat and season with salt and pepper to taste. (The potatoes can stay at room temperature for a couple of hours; reheat in the saucepan over low heat while stirring constantly.) ★

Yeast Rolls

Makes 24 rolls

After gravy, these rolls are the second most popular item in the Star Provisions Turkey Day repertoire. But what our customers might not know is that they are easy to make at home. The sugar helps activate the yeast, making the rolls virtually foolproof. Brushing the tops with butter when they are hot out of the oven is optional, but why not pull out all the stops for the holidays?

1 cup milk

1 ½ teaspoons dry yeast

2 large eggs

4 ounces granulated sugar

1 pound 2 ounces all-purpose flour

2 ¼ teaspoons kosher salt

3 tablespoons butter, softened

1 teaspoon olive oil

1 tablespoon Clarified Butter (see page 246)

Heat the milk in a 1-quart saucepan over low heat until 140° F. Transfer to the bowl of a stand mixer fitted with a dough hook attachment and add the yeast. Let the milk-yeast mixture sit for 5 minutes, until it is foamy. Add the eggs and sugar and mix to combine on low speed. Add the flour and salt and mix until the dough just starts to form; this should take a couple of minutes. This is a wet dough. Add the soft butter and mix on low speed for 3 to 5 minutes to form a soft, not tacky, dough.

Rub the inside of a 6-quart bowl with the oil. Turn the dough into the bowl, cover with plastic wrap, and let rise until doubled in size, about 1 hour.

Spray two 9-inch round baking pans with nonstick cooking spray. Divide the dough into 24 equal pieces and shape each into a round ball by rolling it between the flat of your palm and a dry surface. The dough will be smooth, not sticky.

Arrange 12 balls per pie pan: 8 around the outer edge and 4 in the middle. The balls will be touching and this is fine. Cover with dry kitchen towels and allow to rise for 45 minutes at cool room temperature (68° F), until doubled in size. Preheat the oven to 350° F.

Bake the rolls for 15 to 20 minutes, until golden brown. Immediately after removing the rolls from the oven, brush the tops with the butter. (The rolls will reheat well but are best served the day they are baked.) ★

Warm Pumpkin Pudding with Hard Sauce

Serves 12

Sticky toffee pudding, a favorite British dessert, is not really a pudding at all. Rather, it is a moist sponge cake, usually made with chopped dates, that is doused with a toffee sauce. Sticky toffee pudding has become quite popular here in the States in the last few years. This is our Thanksgiving rendition of that dessert, made with pumpkin instead of dates. Whether you use canned or fresh pumpkin puree, be sure to drain it first using cheesecloth, paper towels, or a fine-mesh sieve. If the pumpkin is too wet, the finished cake will be difficult to unmold from the pan.

Instead of a toffee sauce, we top our pumpkin "pudding" with a hard sauce. It's just a mixture of sugar, butter, and liquor (here we use bourbon)—hence the "hard" part of the name—that is frequently used to glaze fruitcakes. The combination of sweet, moist pumpkin cake and boozy, buttery sauce is hard to resist!

2 cups all-purpose flour

1 teaspoon baking powder

½ teaspoon kosher salt

1 pound (4 sticks) butter, plus extra for greasing the pan, softened

½ cup granulated sugar, plus extra for the pan

4 cups packed brown sugar

3 large eggs

1 cup buttermilk

1 teaspoon pure vanilla extract

2 cups pumpkin puree

1 cup sorghum syrup (see page 228)

2 cups heavy cream

Hard Sauce (recipe below)

Preheat the oven to 300° F. Butter a 9-inch Bundt pan, preferably nonstick, and sprinkle with granulated sugar.

Into a medium bowl, sift together the flour, baking powder, and salt. In the bowl of a stand mixer fitted with the paddle attachment, combine 2 sticks of the softened butter, the granulated sugar, and 1 cup of the brown sugar. Mix on medium speed until creamy and light. Add the eggs one at a time, mixing well after each addition. Add the buttermilk and vanilla. If the mixture looks broken or separated do not worry, it will come together. Fold in the dry ingredients by hand using a spatula. Fold in the pumpkin puree.

Scrape into the prepared pan and bake for 35 to 40 minutes, until a toothpick inserted in the center comes out clean.

Meanwhile, make the glaze: Combine the remaining 2 sticks butter and 3 cups brown sugar, the sorghum syrup,

and cream in a stainless-steel saucepan over low heat until the butter melts and the mixture is combined.

As soon as the cake comes out of the oven, prick it all over with a skewer and drizzle half of the glaze over the cake; cool the cake in the pan. You can cover and let rest at room temperature for a few hours before reheating to unmold.

When you are ready to unmold, warm the cake in a 350° F oven for 15 minutes. Immediately unmold into a shallow serving bowl or a deep plate with a rim; there will be a considerable amount of glaze running over. Warm the remaining glaze over low heat and pour over the slightly warmed, unmolded cake. Serve immediately with the hard sauce on the side. ★

Hard Sauce
Makes 2 cups

½ cup (1 stick) butter, softened

1 cup confectioners' sugar

3 tablespoons bourbon

In the bowl of a stand mixer fitted with the whisk attachment, whip the butter until soft and creamy. Add the confectioners' sugar and bourbon and mix until combined. The sauce can be made up to 2 days in advance; keep it covered at room temperature and whip it again before serving. Serve at room temperature. ★

Liz Lorber's Famous Hummingbird Cake

Makes one 3-layer cake, serving 12

Liz and Henry Lorber are very good friends who spend most Thanksgivings with us on the farm. Liz, an accomplished baker, has worked in our kitchens and other restaurant kitchens, but most notably makes and ships cakes overseas to our troops. All of her cakes are excellent, but her Hummingbird Cake is my favorite. Hummingbird Cake—a moist spice cake with pecans, pineapple, and banana, iced with cream cheese frosting—has been a Southern favorite since the seventies when it first appeared in *Southern Living* magazine. For years, it held the record as the most-requested recipe from the magazine's archives. Liz's version is always part of our Thanksgiving dessert buffet—and the leftover cake is eagerly anticipated by our staff at Bacchanalia and Star Provisions.

3 cups all-purpose flour

2 cups granulated sugar

1 tablespoon baking soda

1 teaspoon ground cinnamon

1 teaspoon kosher salt

3 extra-large eggs

1 cup canola or vegetable oil

2 cups diced ripe bananas (3 to 4 bananas)

1 (8-ounce) can crushed pineapple with juice

1 cup chopped pecans, plus extra for assembly (optional)

2 teaspoons pure vanilla extract

Cream Cheese Frosting (recipe follows)

Preheat the oven to 350° F. Coat three 9-inch round cake pans with nonstick cooking spray and line the bottoms and sides with parchment paper. To make the parchment paper liners: Trace the bottom of the cake pan onto a piece of parchment. Cut out 3 circles and line the bottoms of the pans. Cut strips of parchment 2 to 3 inches wide and line the sides of the pans as well. Spray the parchment with nonstick spray to ensure easy unmolding.

Combine the flour, sugar, baking soda, cinnamon, and salt in a large mixing bowl. Use a wire whisk to blend well and break up any lumps. Add the eggs and oil and mix with a wooden spoon just until the ingredients are combined; do not overbeat. Stir in the bananas, pineapple and juice, pecans, and vanilla.

Divide the batter evenly among the prepared pans. Rap each pan sharply on the counter to remove any air bubbles, then place in the oven. Bake for 30 to 40 minutes, until a toothpick inserted in the center of each cake comes out clean. Place the pans on a rack and cool for 20 minutes, then turn out on the rack to cool completely before frosting. (The cake can be made up to 2 days in advance: Wrap each layer tightly after completely cooled and store at room temperature.)

To assemble the cake, trim the tops of the cakes so they are level. Place one cake on a 10-inch cake plate or stand, trimmed side down. Frost the top with ¼ cup frosting, spreading evenly. Place the second cake, trimmed side down, on the frosted layer, and frost the top with ¼ cup of frosting. Top with the third cake, trimmed side down. Place 1 cup frosting on the top of the cake and work it onto the sides and top roughly, continuing to add frosting as needed. Press pecan pieces on the sides of the cake if desired. The cake will keep for up to 2 days, covered, at room temperature. ⋆

Cream Cheese Frosting

Makes enough to ice one 3-layer cake

8 ounces cream cheese, at room temperature

1 cup (2 sticks) butter, at room temperature

5 cups confectioners' sugar, sifted

Pinch of kosher salt

1 teaspoon pure vanilla extract

Combine the cream cheese and butter in the bowl of a stand mixer fitted with a whisk attachment. Beat well on high for at least 5 minutes, stopping the mixer to scrape the bowl down often, until no lumps remain. Add the confectioners' sugar 1 cup at a time, beating well and stopping the mixer to scrape down the bowl as needed. Add the salt and vanilla extract. ⋆

Pecan Pie

Makes one 9-inch pie, serving 12

Georgia is one of the nation's top producers of pecans, and these sweet, rich nuts make a fantastic pie. If pressed to name their favorite dessert, many Southerners would choose pecan pie. Warm, rich, and filled with the flavor of brown sugar, it's a Thanksgiving staple. Elliott pecans, which are grown in Georgia and northern Florida, are small, sweet, and especially delicious. It's worth seeking them out if you can. If you live in a state that produces pecans, any fresh, local variety is a great alternative. That said, this pie will be delicious no matter what kind of pecans you use.

For the Pie Dough

1 cup all-purpose flour

½ teaspoon sugar

½ teaspoon kosher salt

½ cup (1 stick) cold butter, diced

3 tablespoons ice water

For the Filling

1 ½ cups packed dark brown sugar

1 cup maple syrup

½ cup (1 stick) butter, melted

3 tablespoons all-purpose flour

1 cup whole milk

3 large eggs

1 teaspoon pure vanilla extract

1 teaspoon kosher salt

1 ½ cups pecans, lightly toasted

To make the dough: In a large bowl, combine the flour, sugar, and salt. Add the butter and rub between the palms of your hands until it becomes the texture of coarse meal. Sprinkle with the ice water and work the dough with your hands just until incorporated. Roll the dough into a ball and flatten into a disc. Wrap in plastic wrap and refrigerate for at least 2 hours or up to 2 days before rolling out.

Preheat the oven to 350° F.

Roll out the pie dough on a lightly floured surface into a 12-inch round that is about ⅛ inch thick. Line a 9-inch pie pan with the dough and crimp the edges. Freeze until ready to fill and bake. (You may prepare the pie shell up to this point up to a week in advance; keep it well covered in the freezer.)

To make the filling: In a 2-quart saucepan over medium heat, combine the brown sugar, maple syrup, butter, and flour. Stir constantly to avoid burning and cook just until the sugar has melted and all has come together.

In a medium bowl, mix together the milk, eggs, vanilla, and salt. Pour the warm sugar-flour mixture into the milk and eggs, a quarter at a time, while continually stirring to keep the eggs from curdling. Arrange the toasted pecans in the pie shell and slowly pour in the filling. Bake for 40 to 50 minutes, until the center of the pie is set but still quivers when shaken. Let cool on a wire rack for at least 1 hour before serving. (The pie may be made up to 1 day in advance; store, covered, at room temperature.) ★

The Holiday Retreat

Our Traditional Menu

Serves 4

Champagne

Broccoli Soup with Sabayon and Shaved Périgord Truffle

Bay Scallops with Bacon Vinaigrette | Standing Rib Roast of Beef

Glazed and Pickled Hakurei Turnips with Their Greens

Yorkshire Pudding | Slow-Roasted Sweet Onions

Bordeaux or Cabernet Sauvignon

Selection of Southern Cheeses with Preserved Cherries

Stump de Noel | Dessert Eggnog

The holiday season starts early in our world. I begin ordering the Christmas merchandise and decorations for Star Provisions during the summer, so I find myself dreaming of snowflakes, icicles, and fir trees on some of the hottest days of the year. To see my Christmas fantasy come to life in November is truly spectacular and will put even the worst Grinch or Scrooge into the spirit of the season. The month between Thanksgiving and Christmas is one of our busiest times of the year. No matter the season, our goal is to serve the best food to our diners in the most hospitable atmosphere. But we always try to make the holidays in our restaurants that much more special, as we find ourselves hosting a variety of holiday dinners and private parties. Needless to say, I love to feed people, and it delights me that they choose us for their special-occasion meals.

As much as we enjoy hosting a rotating cast of guests on Thanksgiving, Clifford and I look forward to spending a quiet, cozy Christmas Day at Summerland Farm with each other and with our four-legged children—all ten of them. We fill a tub with toys and bones for the dogs and let them have at it in the yard.

For ourselves, we prepare a meal of classic, comforting holiday dishes with a few special touches that nod to the festive occasion. We're usually lucky enough to have broccoli coming out of the garden in December, and it makes a colorful, satisfying soup course. Since it's Christmas, we shave a few truffles on top! For me, a standing rib roast is the perfect main dish for Christmas dinner, especially when accompanied by traditional Yorkshire puddings. We finish the meal with our "stump de Noel," a slightly less daunting, but still impressive, take on the traditional European buche de Noel.

We set the table with colors and textures that are elegant and wintry but subtle—deep grayish-purple linens are a soothing substitute for red or green, and juniper berries stand in for the more expected holly. While the table setting would be appropriate for any winter meal, the rest of the house leaves no doubt as to which holiday we're celebrating. We usually put up two or even three Christmas trees, and we decorate the house inside and out with garlands and lights. And of course, we hang our stockings by the fireplace with care, hoping that Santa Claus will bring us a few extra truffles.

Broccoli Soup with Sabayon and Shaved Périgord Truffle

Serves 4

Clifford and I plant broccoli in early September, and it thrives through the end of the year. The plant grows tall and strong, with sturdy, vibrant green leaves. When we harvest the plants in late November and December, the leaves and stems are just as delicious as the tight flowers. We make a soup at Christmas that uses the whole plant, accented by the richness of our farm eggs and the decadence of the Périgord truffle. If you grow your own broccoli or buy it at a farmers' market, you should have enough leaves for this recipe. Otherwise, spinach makes a fine substitute. You can use either broccoli stock or chicken stock: The soup will please vegetarian palates if made with broccoli stock, but of course it is only vegan if you leave off the sabayon.

For the Broccoli Soup

1 large russet potato, peeled and cubed

½ yellow onion, roughly chopped

1 sprig fresh thyme

Kosher salt

2 cups broccoli florets
(about 1 head of broccoli)

2 cups broccoli leaves or spinach leaves

About 4 cups Chicken Stock (page 244)
or Broccoli Stock (page 245),
or to taste

Freshly squeezed lemon juice to taste

For the Sabayon

4 large egg yolks, preferably farm fresh

¼ teaspoon freshly squeezed lemon juice

¼ teaspoon kosher salt

½ cup heavy cream

Périgord truffle

Extra virgin olive oil

To make the broccoli soup: In a 2-quart saucepan, combine the potato, onion, and thyme and cover with plenty of water. Cook over medium heat, uncovered, until the potato and onion are soft, about 20 minutes. Drain and discard the thyme. Transfer the remaining contents to a blender and puree on medium speed until smooth. Season with salt and let cool.

Bring a large pot of lightly salted water to a boil. Make an ice bath by filling a large bowl with 2 cups ice and 2 cups cold water. Drop the broccoli florets and leaves into the boiling water and cook for 2 to 4 minutes, until brilliant green. Remove and quickly plunge into the ice water bath, then drain and set aside.

In a blender, combine 1 cup of the potato puree, the broccoli florets and leaves, and the stock. Blend on medium speed until smooth. If you prefer a thicker soup, add a bit less than the 4 cups stock called for; if you prefer a thinner soup, add more. Strain the soup through a fine-mesh strainer. (At this point, you can cool, cover, and refrigerate the soup for up to 1 week. Add the lemon juice and salt just before serving, as adding lemon too long before will cause the soup to lose its vibrant green color.)

To make the sabayon: Set up a double boiler. (Alternatively, you can bring a saucepan half-filled with water to a gentle simmer over low to medium heat and rest a heatproof bowl on top of the pan, making sure the bottom of the bowl does not touch the water.) Whisk together the egg yolks, lemon juice, and salt in the top of the double boiler (or the bowl) until the whisk leaves a ribbon through the egg mixture or the mixture reaches approximately 140° F. Test the temperature with a deep-fry thermometer, or just use your finger: It should be quite warm to the touch, too warm to keep your finger in for very long.

Transfer the sabayon to the bowl of a stand mixer fitted with the whisk attachment and whisk on high speed until it has cooled and thickened. You are looking for the consistency of homemade mayonnaise. Taste for seasoning and transfer to another bowl.

Clean the bowl and whisk of the stand mixer. Whisk the cream until soft peaks form. Fold into the egg mixture. You should have 1 cup of sabayon, which will be more than you need. (You can make the sabayon up to 3 days in advance; it will keep, covered, in the refrigerator. Leftover sabayon is delicious reheated and spooned over eggs benedict the next day.)

To serve: Bring the soup to a simmer in a 4-quart saucepan over medium to low heat. Stir in the lemon juice and season with salt. Divide the soup among 4 warm bowls. To each add a spoonful of the sabayon and a few thin slices of Périgord truffle. Drizzle with the oil. *

Bay Scallops with Bacon Vinaigrette

Serves 4

During college, I spent my summers waitressing on Nantucket. After graduating, slightly misdirected, I found myself living on the island for a couple of winters. Although Nantucket is lovely and quiet in the off-season, most of the businesses shut down, and I found myself scrambling for employment. At the time, a job opening scallops seemed like as good an idea as any. But we were paid by the bucket, and after hours of standing on wooden pallets with my feet covered in cold shells, my daily earnings were only a few dollars. (Of course, I popped more than a few of the fresh, raw scallops into my mouth while I worked!) This was by no means my most profitable or successful job. But the scallops were exceptional—we still purchase ours from that same fishing company. This appetizer is a great way to show them off, and it is made even more special if you can find a white Alba truffle to shave on top.

For the Bacon Vinaigrette

¼ pound bacon, finely chopped

1 cup sherry vinegar

½ cup Chicken Stock (page 244)

½ cup maple syrup

3 tablespoons extra virgin olive oil

For the Scallops

1 teaspoon canola oil

40 Nantucket bay scallops (about ½ pound)

Kosher salt

¼ ounce Alba white truffle (optional)

To make the vinaigrette: In a 12-inch nonstick sauté pan over medium heat, cook the bacon until light golden. Use a slotted spoon to transfer the bacon to a plate lined with paper towels; set aside. Add the vinegar to the bacon fat in the pan and cook over medium heat for just a minute or two. Add the stock and maple syrup and cook until the mixture has reduced by about half. Whisk in the oil. Hold this mixture warm in a heat-proof bowl until ready to serve.

To make the scallops: In a 14-inch nonstick pan over high heat, heat the oil. While heating the pan, lay the scallops out on paper towels and pat dry to remove any moisture and season with salt. When the oil is hot, carefully add the scallops to the pan. Do not crowd the pan or the scallops will not brown, but rather steam, and they will not have the appealing texture and residual sweetness they get when caramelized. If you have a 14-inch nonstick skillet you should be able to cook all the scallops at one time without crowding the pan. If not you may need to cook in two batches. In order to allow the sugars in the scallops to caramelize and form a golden crust, do not touch the scallops for about 2 minutes. Then give the pan a slight shake back and forth to flip the scallops (or turn each scallop over using a spatula). Cook for another 2 minutes, until browned on the second side.

Immediately remove the scallops from the pan to avoid overcooking and arrange on 4 plates. Top with the crisped bacon and drizzle with the vinaigrette. If you have any Alba white truffles around, please shave a few on top—it is Christmas, after all. ★

Standing Rib Roast of Beef

Serves 4, with leftovers

My paternal grandmother always served a rib roast for Christmas. What I remember most was the decadent, savory Yorkshire Pudding (page 82) she made with the pan drippings. Even now, I serve standing rib roast as a special, Christmas-only dish. We source delicious beef and dry-age it for 28 days in our cold storage at Star Provisions. The result is a full-flavored, firm-textured roast. Find one that weighs at least 12 pounds, which will make for an impressive presence at the holiday table. (You and your family will be happy to have plenty of leftovers!) Ask your butcher to french the bones—he or she will cut the meat away from the end of each rib for an attractive, festive presentation. You can also do this at home, using a sharp knife to carefully scrape the meat and fat from the tip of each bone. We like to pull the roast out of the oven early (see the temperature guide below), as it will continue to cook as it rests.

1 pound baby carrots, peeled

1 pound fingerling potatoes, scrubbed

1 large onion, peeled and cut into 8 wedges

1 pound baby turnips

4 sprigs fresh flat-leaf parsley, plus more for garnish

4 sprigs fresh thyme, plus more for garnish

4 sprigs fresh rosemary, plus more for garnish

1 bay leaf

2 tablespoons olive oil

Kosher salt

Freshly ground pepper

1 (12-pound) rib roast of beef (7 bones), frenched

Preheat the oven to 450° F.

Toss all the root vegetables with the herbs, oil, and salt and pepper to taste. Spread the vegetables out in an even layer in the bottom of a roasting pan.

Pat the rib roast dry and liberally season with 1 tablespoon of salt and 1 tablespoon pepper. Place the roast fat side up on top of the bed of vegetables in the roasting pan. Roast for 30 minutes.

Reduce the oven temperature to 350° F and continue roasting for approximately 2 hours. Insert an instant-read thermometer into the thickest part of the roast; the thermometer should register 120° F for rare. (The internal temperature will continue to rise 10° F after removing the roast from the oven, resulting in a final temperature of 130° F.) For medium rare, continue cooking until the thermometer registers 130° F (yielding a temperature after resting of 140° F). For medium, continue cooking until the thermometer registers 140° F (yielding a temperature after resting of 150° F).

Remove the roast to a platter and loosely cover with aluminum foil; let rest for at least 30 minutes before carving. Reserve the pan drippings and increase the oven temperature to 450° F to cook the Yorkshire Pudding (page 82).

To carve, I like to run the knife between the bone and the meat to separate the ribs from the roast for serving. Then you can serve a rib and a slice or two of the roast on each plate. Serve with the roasted vegetables and garnish with more of the herbs. ⋆

Glazed and Pickled Hakurei Turnips with Their Greens

Serves 4

Turnips are a versatile, year-round crop for us in north Georgia. We are very fond of a Japanese variety called hakurei—a small, white, sweet turnip with delicate flesh that is just as tasty raw as it is cooked. This combination of pickled, glazed, and raw greens is an excellent foil for the Standing Rib Roast of Beef (page 78). If you cannot find hakurei turnips or a similar small, white variety, you can use the more common purple-topped turnips. Because those turnips are larger, you will need to peel and cut them into wedges for this recipe. This recipe also would make a terrific side dish for any wintry meal—if you are serving that way, then toss together all of the three preparations at the table.

For the Pickled Turnips

1 cup white wine vinegar

1 cup granulated sugar

1 tablespoon kosher salt

1 pound small hakurei turnips (about 12), washed and quartered, greens reserved

For the Glazed Turnips

2 cups Chicken Stock (page 244)

1 tablespoon kosher salt

1 fresh bay leaf

½ cup (1 stick) cold butter, cubed

1 pound small hakurei turnips (about 12), washed and quartered, greens reserved

For the Turnip Greens Salad

1 tablespoon extra virgin olive oil

1 teaspoon freshly squeezed lemon juice

Kosher salt

Freshly ground pepper

To make the pickled turnips: In a 2-quart saucepan, combine the vinegar, sugar, salt, and 1 cup water and bring to a boil over medium to high heat. Immediately remove from the heat. Put the turnips in a stainless-steel or ceramic bowl and add the vinegar mixture. Allow the turnips to cool in the liquid; set aside until ready to serve. (The pickled turnips can be made up to 1 week in advance; store them, covered, in the refrigerator.)

To make the glazed turnips: In a 2-quart saucepan, combine the stock, salt, and bay leaf and bring to a simmer over low heat. Reduce the liquid by half. Turn off the heat and whisk in the butter a few cubes at a time. When all the butter is thoroughly incorporated, add the turnips. Return to medium heat and simmer for 3 to 5 minutes, until the turnips are just fork-tender. Remove from the heat, discard the bay leaf, and adjust the seasoning.

To make the turnip greens salad: Wash and dry the greens reserved from the pickled and glazed turnips in a salad spinner. Thinly slice and place in a 2-quart bowl. Sprinkle with the oil, lemon juice, and salt and pepper to taste and toss.

Serve a scattering of the room-temperature pickled turnips, warm glazed turnips, and dressed turnip greens as a garnish for the roast. ★

Yorkshire Pudding

Serves 12

If the cooking gods are with you, as they always were with my grandmother, these individual Yorkshire puddings should puff in the oven, resulting in a light, airy top and a dense bottom. Nanny had an old *Gourmet* magazine cookbook that I still refer to from time to time, and she religiously followed its recipe for Yorkshire pudding every Christmas. This recipe is a slight variation on the classic, the result of years of tinkering in our kitchens. Now, I go back to it each year to accompany the annual Christmas rib roast (page 78). Although a deep popover pan yields the most dramatic results, there's nothing wrong with using a cupcake or muffin pan. Leftovers are delicious toasted.

4 large eggs

1 ½ cups whole milk

1 ½ cups all-purpose flour, sifted

2 ¾ teaspoons kosher salt

5 tablespoons hot pan drippings from the rib roast (page 78)

Whisk the eggs in a large bowl of a stand mixer fitted with a whisk attachment for 3 minutes. Add the milk and continue beating for 1 minute. Add the sifted flour in three intervals while continuing to whisk until smooth. Add the salt and 1 tablespoon of the pan drippings and mix until combined. Let the batter rest at room temperature for at least 30 minutes. (The batter can be made a few hours ahead and stored in the refrigerator, but you will need to take it out 1 hour before cooking so that it returns to room temperature.)

Preheat the oven to 450° F.

Fill each of the 12 cups of a popover pan with approximately 1 teaspoon of the pan drippings and put the pan in the oven for 5 minutes to heat. It is very important that the pan be very hot when the batter is added so that the puddings will "pop" or puff up. Remove the hot pan from the oven and immediately fill each popover cup halfway full with batter. Bake for approximately 20 minutes, until the puddings are puffed and golden brown; the centers should look hollow. Serve immediately. ★

Slow-Roasted Sweet Onions

Serves 4

Daniel Porubiansky was our executive chef at Bacchanalia for many years. He has a superlative resume and is long on talent. Daniel prides himself on recipes that he calls "DP Extra Classics," and this sweet onion preparation is one of them. It is unexpected and delicious in its simplicity, making it a perfect accompaniment to the rich, savory beef roast (page 78) and Yorkshire Pudding (opposite). I do not like aluminum foil to touch food, so I always use a lining of parchment paper when wrapping or sealing in foil.

2 sweet onions, peeled with root ends intact

6 tablespoons butter

2 teaspoons kosher salt

2 sprigs fresh rosemary

2 sprigs fresh thyme

Freshly ground pepper

2 tablespoons turbinado sugar or sugar in the raw

Preheat the oven to 375° F.

Top each onion with 2 tablespoons butter, 1 teaspoon salt, a sprig of rosemary and thyme, and pepper. Wrap each onion in two layers of parchment and then wrap in aluminum foil; seal the foil pouches tightly. Bake for about 2 ½ hours, until the onions are tender all the way through but not mushy. Allow the wrapped onions to cool slightly, then refrigerate until completely cooled, at least 2 hours or for as long as 3 days.

Unwrap the onions and cut into 1 ½- to 2-inch-thick slices, keeping the rings intact. Melt the remaining 2 tablespoons butter with the sugar in a 14-inch nonstick pan over medium heat. Add the onions, reduce the heat to low, and begin to very lightly caramelize the sugar, 4 to 5 minutes. You want to caramelize one side of each slice, swirling the pan as needed to get even color.

Remove the pan from the heat and immediately flip the onions with a spatula, being very careful to keep them intact; they are very delicate. You want to serve them this way, so that the beautiful caramelized side is up. Serve immediately or set aside in a warm place while you finish and slice the rib roast. ★

Stump de Noel

Serves 10

The Stump de Noel is an easier but no less impressive version of the traditional buche de Noel. Named after the European tradition of burning a yule log in December, the buche de Noel is a French holiday dessert that consists of a rolled sponge cake, intricately decorated to look like a piece of firewood. Our version is made with a chocolate layer cake and chocolate buttercream. Let your creativity run wild with the garnishes—or, if you'd rather keep it simple, just enjoy the frosted cake and tell your guests to use their imagination.

For the Chocolate Cake

4 ounces bittersweet chocolate

1 ½ cups cocoa powder

1 ½ cups all-purpose flour

½ teaspoon baking soda

1 teaspoon baking powder

½ teaspoon kosher salt

1 ½ cups (3 sticks) butter, at room temperature

½ cup packed light brown sugar

2 cups granulated sugar

6 large eggs

2 teaspoons pure vanilla extract

1 cup sour cream

To make the chocolate cake: Preheat the oven to 375° F. Coat three 8-inch round baking pans with nonstick spray and line the bottoms with parchment paper. To make the liners, trace one pan on parchment and cut out 3 rounds, then tuck them inside the pans, spraying both sides with nonstick cooking spray. Dust with flour.

Melt the chocolate in a stainless-steel bowl over slowly simmering water. Keep the chocolate warm until ready to use.

Sift the cocoa powder, flour, baking soda, baking powder, and salt into a large bowl. In the bowl of a stand mixer fitted with the paddle, cream the butter and brown and granulated sugars on medium speed for 10 minutes. Add the eggs one at a time, beating well after each addition. Add the vanilla and mix well. Reduce the speed of the mixer to low and alternately add the sour cream and flour mixture in three intervals until completely incorporated.

Remove the bowl from the mixer and fold in the melted chocolate with a rubber spatula. Divide the batter among the three prepared pans. Bake on the middle rack of the oven if possible for 30 minutes, or until a toothpick inserted in a center comes out clean. Cool in the pan. ⋆

For the Chocolate Buttercream

2 cups granulated sugar

1 cup egg whites (from 6 to 8 large eggs)

8 ounces bittersweet chocolate

1 ¼ pounds (5 sticks) unsalted butter, at room temperature, cut into small pieces

1 teaspoon pure vanilla extract

1 teaspoon kosher salt

To make the chocolate buttercream: Place the sugar and egg whites in a heatproof bowl. Place the bowl over a saucepan of lightly simmering water and whisk by hand or with a hand mixer for about 10 minutes, until the mixture is hot to the touch, about 140° F.

Transfer the egg white mixture to the bowl of a stand mixer fitted with the whisk attachment and whip on high until doubled in volume, about 5 minutes.

Melt the chocolate in a stainless-steel bowl over slowly simmering water. (Or melt in a microwaveable bowl in the microwave set on medium for 10 seconds; stir and then microwave for 10 more seconds if needed.) Keep the chocolate warm until ready to use.

With the mixer on medium speed, slowly add the butter pieces to the egg whites, 2 pieces at a time, fully incorporating them before adding more. Reduce the speed to low and add the vanilla and salt, then the melted chocolate. Scrape the bowl to ensure that all the butter and chocolate are completely incorporated. Transfer to a bowl until needed. Makes about 6 cups. (Cover and refrigerate for up to 5 days. Let come to room temperature and whip again before using.) ⋆

continued from page 83

For the Garnishes and Cake Assembly

**1 cup egg whites (from 6 to 8 large eggs),
plus 1 egg white for the rosemary branches**

1 ¾ cups granulated sugar

1 cup superfine sugar

4 sprigs fresh rosemary

1 teaspoon cocoa powder

To make the garnishes: Preheat the oven to 200° F.

Whip the 1 cup egg whites and the granulated sugar in the bowl of a stand mixer fitted with a whisk attachment until they form stiff peaks, about 15 minutes.

Place the meringue into a piping bag with a ⅜-inch round tip. Pipe the following onto a baking sheet lined with parchment: twelve 1-inch rounds that are ¾ inch tall (press the tip down with a wet finger to make a smooth top); twelve ½-inch rounds that are 1 inch tall (leave the pointed tip); four 1½-inch-wide triangles that are ¼ inch tall (pipe as close to a triangle as possible, but with one slightly rounded side; soften any peaks with a wet finger).

Bake the meringues for 15 to 20 minutes, until firm to the touch; do not let them brown. Let cool completely. Store in an airtight container for up to 5 days until ready to use.

Put the superfine sugar in a bowl. Whisk the 1 remaining egg white in a medium bowl until frothy, about 5 minutes. Dip each rosemary sprig in the whisked egg white, tap it to remove some moisture, then dip into the sugar. Let dry on a cooling rack.

To assemble the Stump de Noel: Trim the tops of the cakes so they are level. Place one cake on a 10-inch cake plate or stand, trimmed side down, and frost with ¼ cup buttercream; spread evenly. Place the second cake, trimmed side down, on the frosted layer, and frost with ¼ cup of buttercream. Add the third cake, trimmed side down, on the frosted layer. Place 1 cup of buttercream on the top of cake and work it onto the sides and top roughly. Reserve a few tablespoons buttercream to assemble the mushrooms and transfer the remainder to a piping bag fitted with a ⅜-inch round tip.

At three points around the cake, pipe buttercream up the side of the cake vertically to change the round shape of the cake to a more uneven tree stump shape. Take a small offset metal spatula and pull icing up the cake with the tip to create the effect of bark. On the top use the tip of the offset spatula to create rings that mimic the grain of the wood on the end of a stump.

To assemble the mushrooms, use a small amount of buttercream to attach the 12 tall, ½-inch meringues to the bottoms of the 12 short 1-inch meringues. Dust the tops with cocoa using a fine sifter. Arrange around and on top of the stump in a random fashion.

Insert the triangles into the sides of the cake with the rounded portion facing out to resemble lichen; dust with cocoa or powdered sugar using a fine sifter. Garnish with sugared rosemary sprigs; place them as if they are growing up the sides of the stump. ⋆

Dessert Eggnog

Serves 12

My college roommate, Lisa Mauro, turned me on to eggnog. I am sure that, at the time, the alcohol was 90 percent of the drink's appeal, but Lisa's eggnog is still the best I've ever had. I like to offer the bourbon-laced drink at the end of the meal so that guests can sip it by the fire. In fact, it could be served in lieu of dessert with just a few holiday cookies. This recipe is intended to serve 12 people, creating a nice opportunity for you to invite some additional guests to stop by after dinner. If you are entertaining a smaller crowd, you can scale down the recipe accordingly. You can add the alcohol prior to serving, or let guests pour their own, according to their tastes. I prefer incorporating into the base three different liquors—bourbon, rum, and cognac—as this mix is most pleasing on the palate. Clifford collects bourbon, so our guests always enjoy serving themselves from his impressive assortment. (And some of them seem to have bourbon tunnel vision, skipping the eggnog all together!)

6 large eggs, separated

¾ cup superfine sugar, or 1 cup confectioners' sugar

¼ cup cognac (optional)

¼ cup rum (optional)

½ cup bourbon (optional)

2 cups whole milk

3 cups heavy cream

Freshly grated nutmeg

In the bowl of a stand mixer fitted with the whisk attachment, whisk the egg yolks while gradually adding the sugar until the mixture is thick and glossy; this should take 10 minutes. If using alcohol, add it now, then add the milk and 2 cups of the cream, while mixing constantly on low speed. (This mixture can be refrigerated for up to 4 days. A covered glass container is best for storage. Refrigerate the egg whites, covered, separately.)

Just before serving, transfer the yolk mixture to a large bowl. Whisk the egg whites on high speed in the bowl of a stand mixer fitted with a whisk attachment until they form soft peaks. Gently fold the whipped whites into the yolk mixture. In the bowl of the stand mixer (you do not need to clean it), whisk the remaining 1 cup heavy cream on high speed until it forms soft peaks. Gently fold the whipped cream into the egg base mixture.

To serve, pour the eggnog into 6-ounce glasses and grate a bit of nutmeg on top of each. ⋆

Luck and Fortune in the New Year

A Fireside Brunch

Serves 6

Red-Eyed Cocktail

Citrus Salad with Dried Olives and Candied Zest

Hoppin' John | **Braised Winter Greens**

Browned Pork Chops with Tomato Gravy

Shirred Farm Eggs | **Breakfast Sausage**

A Spicy and Earthy Pinot Noir

Buttermilk Biscuits (page 244) | **Monkey Bread**

From Thanksgiving to New Year's Eve, my team works nonstop. On New Year's Day, I host a drop-in brunch for all of my employees. We catch our breath and thank each other for another year of hard work and wonderful food in the restaurants. Since opening in 2009, Abattoir has been the venue for this annual celebration. We build a fire in the dining room's fireplace, and the guests spill out onto the patio overlooking the railroad tracks. Georgia is one of the few places in the country where you could hold a New Year's party outdoors, and I think it makes the brunch all the more festive.

We put out plenty of tartan blankets, which come in handy if the temperature drops. We use more of the same throws as tablecloths, topping them with pinecones and birch boughs to create a natural, wintry atmosphere. Bowls of bright citrus fruits add a complementary pop of color. We set the table with casual green ceramic plates and chambray napkins, which pick up the colors of the tartan blankets-cum-tablecloths. The glassware is simple and inexpensive: stemless flutes for Champagne and stemless wineglasses for water or orange juice.

The menu is inspired and anchored by the traditional Southern New Year's Day meal of pork, greens, and black-eyed peas. Most culinary historians think that the tradition originated in the African-American community, among the descendants of enslaved peoples. Black-eyed peas were originally brought to the South from West Africa, where they migrated from slave quarters to white kitchens and quickly became the region's staple legume. Southerners have long eaten black-eyed peas on New Year's Day for good luck. They often appear in the form of Hoppin' John, the traditional Lowcountry dish of rice and black-eyed peas. Greens—whether collard, cabbage, turnip, or any other winter green—are eaten in hopes that they will bring money ("greenbacks," that is) in the year to come. Many recipes for Hoppin' John and greens call for a small amount of seasoning pork, such as a few slices of bacon or a smoked ham hock, to add flavor. For this menu, we gave the pork a starring role, serving succulent bone-in chops with a juicy tomato gravy.

We augment the classic New Year's Day meal with a handful of rich, comforting brunch favorites that sit easy on the post-party stomach, such as buttermilk biscuits and shirred farm eggs. This is a long menu for a brunch, but it hits all the right notes of sweet, savory, acidic, bitter, rich, starchy, and meaty. If I can round up my whole staff only once a year, I'm not going to hold back on saying "thank you." If you approach your own celebration for family and friends with the same mindset, you will all agree that it's a perfect way to kick off the New Year.

Red-Eyed Cocktail

A coffee-based cocktail is a perfect wake-up call on New Year's Day. The combination of bourbon and sweet, acidic orange shrub stimulates the appetite. A "shrub" is a preparation of vinegar and fruit that is aged and used to flavor drinks—similar to the way bitters are used. Prior to the modern era, shrubs were a means of preserving fruits to enjoy them long past their seasons. You will need to start the orange shrub at least a couple of weeks in advance to allow the flavors to meld and then mellow slightly. Because you never heat it up, a shrub maintains more of the bright fruit flavor than a cooked fruit syrup does. We like to keep different kinds of shrubs in our bar pantry to add a fresh-tasting fruit kick to our cocktails throughout the year. Orange shrub would enhance a variety of cocktails, from screwdrivers to Manhattans.

Hot brewed coffee

Heavy cream

Bourbon, preferably Black Maple Hill

Orange Shrub (recipe follows)

While brewing the coffee, whip the cream in a medium bowl using a whisk.

For each cocktail, stir 1 ½ ounces bourbon and 1 ounce orange shrub into 6 ounces coffee in a large mug. Float a dollop of the whipped cream on top and serve. ★

Orange Shrub
Makes 1 cup

2 oranges

½ cup Grade A maple syrup

½ cup aged sherry vinegar

2 whole star anise

Peel the oranges, discarding the peel. Place the whole oranges and maple syrup in a medium bowl and muddle to release the juices. Add the vinegar and star anise and stir. Transfer to a glass jar and seal. Store in a cool (68° F) dark place for 2 weeks, shaking or agitating the jar daily. Strain out the oranges and star anise, pour the liquid into a clean jar or bottle, and cap. The orange shrub will keep, refrigerated, for months. ★

Citrus Salad with Dried Olives and Candied Zest

Serves 6

Salty olives and tangy fruit are a wonderful combination in this bright salad. Citrus is the unsung hero of winter—its variety and quality make it your best bet for fruit during the colder months. Every January, I get a box of HoneyBell tangelos from Florida for my birthday, and it is always my favorite gift. Each individual fruit is a ball of sunshine waiting to be peeled. Though you could make this dish with only a few of the fruits mentioned, I suggest you go for maximum variety, as the array of sunny fruits will be as stunningly beautiful as it is delicious. The dried olives and candied lemon zest keep well at room temperature, making them versatile additions to your pantry. The olives are especially nice grated over pizzas and pastas, and the zest is a bright garnish for cocktails or desserts.

2 oranges

2 blood oranges

2 ruby red grapefruit

3 tangerines or HoneyBell tangelos

3 clementine oranges

1 Meyer lemon

1 lime

2 teaspoons fruity extra virgin olive oil, preferably French

1 tablespoon honey

Kosher salt

½ cup whole Dried Olives (recipe follows), for garnish

¼ cup Candied Citrus Zest, made with lemons (page 52), for garnish

2 sprigs fresh rosemary, leaves pulled from the stems, for garnish

Use a sharp paring knife to peel the oranges, grapefruit, tangerines, clementines, lemon, and lime: Cut the ends off each fruit so you have a flat surface on each end, then place one end down and slice sections of peel from end to end, working your way around the fruit and being sure to remove all the white pith.

Slice all the citrus into ½-inch-thick rounds and place in a large serving bowl. Drizzle the fruit with the oil and honey and sprinkle with salt to taste, being mindful that the olives are quite salty. Garnish with the dried olives, candied lemon zest, and rosemary leaves. ✶

Dried Olives
makes 2 pints
2 pounds pitted Kalamata olives, rinsed and drained

Preheat the oven to 120 to 140 ° F. (Alternatively, use a food dehydrator set between 120 and 140 ° F.) Use paper towels to blot excess oil from the olives. Line a baking sheet with a cooling rack and place the pitted olives on the rack. (The olives should not touch the bottom of the pan; air needs to circulate around the olives in order to properly dry them.)

Place the pan in the oven and dry the olives for 8 to 12 hours. The oven should be warm enough to remove all the moisture, but you want to be careful to avoid cooking the olives. (If your oven does not have a setting below 200 ° F, then preheat it to 200 ° F and turn it off after 1 hour of drying the olives, leaving the door closed for the remaining time.) The olives should be shriveled and dry to the touch when done. The olives can be dried ahead of time and will keep well for months in an airtight container at room temperature. ✶

Hoppin' John

Serves 6

Hoppin' John, a Southern bean and rice combination traditionally served on New Year's Day, is thought to bring whoever eats it a prosperous year. I like to make it with Sea Island red peas because of their nutty flavor and creamy texture. An heirloom from the Lowcountry region of South Carolina and Georgia, this field pea fell out of cultivation in the twentieth century but has recently been brought back by Anson Mills, the South Carolina–based purveyors of specialty grains and legumes. You can order Sea Island red peas from the Anson Mills website, or you can use dried black-eyed peas. You may soak the peas in advance to reduce the cooking time, but we find that they hold their shape better if they are cooked directly. The Hoppin' John will be delicious either way. I hope the dish brings you good luck!

½ pound bacon, diced

1 pound Sea Island red peas

1 onion, halved

2 garlic cloves, peeled

1 bay leaf

1 tablespoon olive oil

2 shallots, finely chopped

1 red bell pepper, cored and roughly chopped

1 cup Carolina Gold or other long-grain white rice

3 cups Chicken Stock (page 244)

1 tablespoon fresh thyme leaves

1 tablespoon chopped fresh flat-leaf parsley

Kosher salt

Freshly ground pepper

In a large stockpot over low to medium heat, slowly cook the bacon until translucent. Add the peas, onion, garlic, bay leaf, and 7 cups water. Bring to a boil, then reduce the heat to a simmer and cook, uncovered, until the peas are tender but not mushy, about 1 hour.

Drain the mixture in a colander. Discard the onion halves, garlic, and bay leaf and set aside the peas and bacon.

In the same pot, heat the oil over medium heat. Add the shallots, bell pepper, and rice and sauté until fragrant, 3 to 5 minutes. Add the stock, bring to a boil, and reduce the heat to low. Simmer, covered, for 15 minutes, or until the rice is tender. The rice should still be moist and there should be some stock left in the pot. Add the peas and bacon and stir in the fresh herbs. Season with salt and pepper and serve warm. ★

Braised Winter Greens

Serves 6

It is traditional to eat collard greens on New Year's Day to ensure wealth—green, of course, is the color of money—in the coming year. But greens are a constant staple on our restaurant menus and grow in our garden at least nine months out of the year. Typically, we harvest them young, when they are tender, so they cook much faster than more mature greens. In this braise, we mix the meaty texture of collard greens with the delicate flavor and texture of chard and the tangy bite of mustard greens. Any combination of greens will work—you could also use beet, turnip, and rutabaga greens, as well as kale or spinach. If the greens have large stems, we like to remove them and pickle them to be added as a garnish (this pickle is best made at least a day before serving). For the stock, you may substitute broth made from country ham or bacon; or, even better, add a hambone to the stock when you begin cooking. In the South we like to finish our greens with pepper vinegar, a condiment found in most grocery stores. If you can't find it, you can make your own by steeping a few hot chile peppers in a jar of apple cider vinegar for a week or two.

½ pound slab bacon, cut into ¼-inch pieces

2 tablespoons olive oil

5 tablespoons cold butter

1 sweet onion, diced

½ cup maple syrup or sorghum syrup (see page 228)

¼ cup sherry vinegar

½ teaspoon crushed red pepper flakes

1 bunch (about 1 pound) young mustard greens, stems reserved

1 bunch (about 1 pound) young Swiss chard, stems reserved

1 bunch (about 1 pound) young collard greens, stems reserved

6 cups Chicken Stock (page 244) or vegetable stock

Kosher salt

Pepper vinegar, for serving

Quick pickles (recipe follows), optional

Quick Pickles
Makes 1 pint

1 cup white wine vinegar

1 cup granulated sugar

1 tablespoon kosher salt

1 teaspoon fennel seeds

1 teaspoon coriander seeds

1 bay leaf

3 sprigs fresh thyme

2 cups mustard, chard, and/or collard stems, cut into 2-inch pieces

In a large stockpot over medium to low heat, add the bacon and cook, stirring, until it begins to brown, about 5 minutes. Add the oil and 2 tablespoons of the butter. Add the onion and sauté until transparent. Add the maple syrup, vinegar, and red pepper flakes. Stir to combine, then cook for 5 minutes.

Meanwhile, roughly chop or slice the greens. Add the greens to the pot and cook over medium to low heat until wilted, about 5 minutes. Add the stock and bring to simmer. Cook over medium heat until the greens are very tender, 15 minutes.

Season with salt, then stir in the remaining 3 tablespoons cold butter until melted and combined. Serve immediately (so the greens keep their vibrant color) with pepper vinegar and top with pickled stems, if you like. ⋆

Place the vinegar, sugar, salt, seeds, and herbs in a large saucepan with 1 cup water. Bring to a boil over medium heat, stirring, until the sugar dissolves.

Pack the stems into a pint jar. Pour the hot pickling liquid through a strainer into the jar.

Let cool, place a lid on the jar, and store in the refrigerator, where it will keep for several weeks. ⋆

Browned Pork Chops with Tomato Gravy

Serves 6

The recipe for this dish came to me thanks to a gentleman farmer and true Southern gourmand, Dub Taft. Dub's description of his family favorite begins, "Take some meat—in the South this means pork. . . ." He also supplied me with enough canned tomatoes from his farm to keep me in tomato gravy all winter. (If you don't have home-canned tomatoes, store-bought will work nicely.) Dub suggests making biscuits or cornbread to sop up the gravy. The Shirred Farm Eggs (page 100) are lovely served alongside the chops too.

6 (8-ounce) pork chops, with or without the bone

Kosher salt

Freshly ground pepper

6 (½-inch-thick) bacon slices

1 sweet onion, coarsely chopped

4 cups homemade canned tomatoes or 1 (28-ounce) can store-bought whole tomatoes

1 teaspoon sugar

Preheat the oven to 350° F. Season the pork chops with salt and pepper and set aside.

In a large cast-iron or heavy-bottomed skillet over medium heat, cook the bacon slices until crispy. Remove with a slotted spoon and drain on paper towels; set aside.

Brown the pork chops in the bacon grease over medium heat. (They should all fit in the large skillet in a single layer; if not, brown them in batches.) Cook until browned on both sides, 5 to 7 minutes per side, then transfer to a baking sheet. Bake for about 10 minutes, until the internal temperature of the chops reaches 140° F. Keep warm; the pork chops will continue to cook as they rest.

Meanwhile, discard all but 2 tablespoons of the bacon grease from the pan and place over low heat. Add the onion and sauté until translucent, about 5 minutes. Roughly chop the tomatoes, discarding any fibrous stem portions. Add the tomatoes with their juice to the pan. Cook for another 5 to 7 minutes over medium heat. The gravy should be very liquid, so add water if necessary. Season with the sugar, salt, and pepper.

To serve, place a pork chop and a slice of crispy bacon on each plate, then top with 3 to 4 tablespoons of the tomato gravy. ⋆

Shirred Farm Eggs

Serves 6

To eliminate some of the hassle from serving eggs at brunch, try baking the eggs in the oven, as we do with these easy shirred eggs. This will allow you to bake all of the eggs at one time to the perfect consistency without having to stand at the stove while your guests are drinking their Red-Eyed Cocktails (page 92) without you. We like to use small cast-iron skillets here, but ceramic ramekins will work just as well. Fresh eggs from pastured chickens make an enormous difference in the quality of any egg dish, plus they support your local farmer.

1 tablespoon butter, at room temperature

2 ½ cups heavy cream

1 sprig fresh rosemary, plus additional leaves for garnish

2 garlic cloves, peeled and crushed

12 large eggs

Kosher salt

Freshly ground pepper

Preheat the oven to 375° F. Use the butter to grease the insides of six shallow 4-inch ramekins or 4-inch cast-iron skillets and place them on a baking sheet.

Combine the cream, rosemary sprig, and garlic in a medium saucepan and bring to a simmer. Cook over medium heat for 10 minutes. Set aside to cool slightly. Fish out the garlic and rosemary and discard.

Once the cream has cooled, distribute it evenly among the ramekins (about ¼ cup in each). Crack two eggs into each ramekin, being careful to not break the yolks. Season the eggs with salt and pepper.

Bake in the oven for about 10 minutes, until the whites are just firm but the yolks are still soft. Serve immediately with a garnish of fresh rosemary leaves. ★

Breakfast Sausage

Makes 5 pounds, about 30 links or patties

This is my favorite breakfast sausage, and it works equally well in patty or link form. It has a residual sweetness from the maple syrup and a nice kick from the peppers and ginger. It makes a great gift in a basket with some grits and farm-fresh eggs. Be sure to use the best pork you can find—ideally a heritage breed from a local farmer—and measure your ingredients carefully. You'll be surprised how easy it is to make your own sausage at home, and your brunch guests will be impressed.

4 pounds boneless lean pork shoulder

1 ¼ pounds pork fatback

6 tablespoons maple syrup

¼ cup kosher salt

3 tablespoons finely chopped fresh sage

2 tablespoons finely chopped garlic

2 ½ teaspoons crushed red pepper flakes

1 teaspoon freshly ground black pepper

1 teaspoon Insta Cure #1 (see "Curing Salt," page 16)

½ teaspoon powdered ginger or 1 teaspoon finely grated fresh ginger

5 feet sheep casings (optional)

Vegetable oil, for cooking

Trim the pork shoulder of sinew and connective tissue. Cut the pork shoulder and fatback into 1- to 2-inch cubes, then place in the freezer for 10 to 15 minutes. Using a meat grinder fitted with the fine grinding plate, grind both the meat and the fat into a medium stainless-steel bowl. In a large stainless-steel bowl, combine ¼ cup of ice water with the maple syrup, salt, sage, garlic, red pepper flakes, black pepper, Insta Cure, and ginger. Mix to form a paste. Mix the paste into the ground meat and incorporate until sticky; it is best to use your hands.

Put the sausage mixture into a 2-gallon resealable plastic storage bag; make sure to get out as much of the air as possible to prevent oxidation. A trick to remove the air: Submerge the bag in a vessel of water, keeping the open end above the water line; this will push all the air out before you seal the bag. You can also use a vacuum-seal bag, if you have one. Refrigerate for at least 12 hours or up to 24 hours.

At this point you can make sausage patties or stuff the mixture into the sheep's casings to make links.

For patties, form the sausage mixture into 4-ounce rounds, about 4 inches in diameter. Stack the patties, separating them with wax paper, wrap well, and refrigerate for up to a week, or freeze for up to 3 months in an airtight bag.

For links, you will need to soak the casings in cool water in the refrigerator for 12 to 24 hours before making the links; we like to change the water at least twice during the soaking period. Rinse the casings thoroughly after soaking, holding each casing open and running cool water through it to rinse completely.

For this step a sausage stuffing tube would help: This is a tube that fits onto the end of your meat grinder and keeps the casing open as the grinder presses the mixture in. Also, there is an attachment for grinders available for stand mixers that has a tube that will hold the casings while the grinder pushes the sausage into the casing. (You should not stuff the sausage directly into casings as you are grinding, though; the sausage needs to cure overnight before going into the casings.) Use the sausage grinder or grinder attachment without the blade and die and with the stuffing tube attachment. Fit the casings onto the stuffing tube and then push the sausage into the casings. Once a length of casing is full, create links every 3 to 4 inches by twisting the sausage a few times in one direction and/or using butcher's twine to tie it off, remembering to tie off each end first. Repeat the process with the other casings until all the mixture is used. Prick the air pockets in the sausage with a needle. (The uncooked sausage links can be stored, tightly wrapped, in the refrigerator for up to a week or in the freezer for up to several months.)

To cook the sausage, place a large skillet over medium heat and add just enough oil to coat thinly. Add the patties or links and cook, turning, until browned on all sides and cooked through. This should take 10 to 15 minutes in total. ∗

Monkey Bread

Serves 6 to 8

A batch of monkey bread will not sit for long on your counter. The delicious, sweet pull-apart bread—an American favorite since at least the 1950s—has become a staple dessert at Abattoir. Pulling off pieces of the sticky caramelized bread and eating them with your fingers is appealing to young and old alike. We use bread flour because the gluten level is higher and results in a chewier and slightly denser monkey bread. All-purpose flour will work as well, but will yield a slightly lighter texture.

2 ½ cups milk

2 ½ tablespoons dry yeast

6 large eggs

9 ¼ cups bread flour or high-gluten flour

¾ cup granulated sugar

2 tablespoons kosher salt

2 ¼ cups (4 ½ sticks) unsalted butter,
at room temperature, cut into 1-inch cubes

For the Coating

2 cups granulated sugar

¼ cup ground cinnamon

1 ¾ cups (3 ½ sticks) unsalted butter

In a small saucepan, warm ½ cup of the milk over low heat until just warm to the touch. Remove from the heat, stir in the yeast, and let sit for about 5 minutes to activate the yeast.

In the bowl of a stand mixer fitted with a dough hook, combine the milk-yeast mixture, the remaining 2 cups milk, and the eggs until just incorporated.

In a separate medium bowl, combine the flour, sugar, and salt, then add to the ingredients in the mixer. Mix on low speed for 3 to 5 minutes, until everything comes together.

Add the butter, one piece at a time, continuing to mix on low speed and occasionally stopping to scrape the bowl to ensure that everything is incorporated. Mix until the dough will pull a "window"—when you can stretch a little piece of dough with your hands and see through a thin layer instead of the dough breaking or tearing.

Cover the bowl with plastic wrap and let the dough rest at room temperature for about 45 minutes to allow the yeast to develop. Then refrigerate for 1 hour if you can spare the time. (Refrigerating the dough makes it easier to shape the bread as the dough is quite sticky, but it is not imperative.)

To help remove the bread easily once it has baked, line the bottom and sides of an 8- to 9-inch angel food cake pan with parchment paper, generously coating both sides of the paper with nonstick baking spray. (To line the bottom of the pan, trace the bottom on a sheet of parchment paper and cut a ring to fit in the bottom of the tube pan.)

To make the coating: in a small bowl, mix the sugar and cinnamon. Melt the butter in a small saucepan. Let cool slightly.

Shape the dough into 1-ounce balls—about the size of golf balls—and dip each in the melted butter. Then roll in the cinnamon-sugar mixture and place in the prepared pan. Continue layering the balls randomly into the pan until all the dough has been used; the pan should be about halfway full. Cover the pan loosely with plastic wrap and let the dough sit in a warm place for about 1 ½ hours, or until it has doubled in size.

Preheat the oven to 375° F. Bake the monkey bread for 25 to 30 minutes, until a skewer or toothpick inserted in a piece of bread comes out clean and the top is caramelized and deep brown.

Let the pan cool for 10 minutes and then turn it upside down onto a plate and remove the bread from the pan. Serve immediately. ✶

A Labor of Love
Dinner for Your Valentine

Serves 2

My Bloody Valentine

Summerland Farm Egg Custard

Kumamoto Oysters with Caviar and Champagne Gelee

Crab Salad with Grapefruit, Fennel, and Apples

Root Vegetable Consommé with Celery Root Agnolotti

Squab with Beets and Beet Green Pesto

Champagne

Chocolate Soufflés | **Rose Macarons**

I am not a romantic, but I do throw myself into the things that I love. Bacchanalia was a labor of love that began more than twenty years ago. Clifford and I moved to Summerland Farm in June of 1992, and we opened Bacchanalia in early 1993. We took over the lease on a small house in the Buckhead neighborhood of Atlanta, and we did all of the renovations ourselves.

I won't pretend that we set out to make Bacchanalia a romantic destination. In fact, Clifford and I were perhaps more surprised than anyone that it has become known as one of Atlanta's most romantic restaurants over the last two decades. Maybe it was the cozy tables for two, which fit better in the small rooms than four-tops. Or the mismatched antique china I inherited from my grandmother, which served as our dishware when Bacchanalia was young. Somewhere along the way, our labor of love became a favorite restaurant of Atlanta's lovebirds, and we found ourselves adapting to what our customers wanted us to be. When they asked for "romantic" fare, we obliged with oysters and caviar. Our menus evolved as the diners' expectations heightened. As with any relationship, a willingness to be flexible has been key to our longevity.

Twenty years in, Valentine's Day is still one of Bacchanalia's biggest nights. And it's a point of pride for my sister Frances, who runs the front of the house, that she helps mastermind an engagement nearly every week. (At her insistence, we've even invested in miniature cloches, perfect for serving dessert with a ring on the side.) For customers who want to keep the romance at home, we offer a Valentine's Day mise en place at Star Provisions: a romantic meal for two that feels homemade but requires little more than heating and plating.

And so, inspired by my own labor of love, I offer you one to try at home. If you're really head over heels, and you're up for a little challenge, impress your honey with this dinner for two. You will have him or her literally eating succulent squab out of your hands . . . or licking it off, if—as in my case—your true love is a canine. Once you've made the effort of preparing this meal, especially if it's for a human sweetheart, be sure to serve it in a fittingly romantic atmosphere. Clusters of peonies in short, clear glass tumblers make a lush centerpiece. The pink candles and the pink glasses, which are handmade at Nouvel Studio in Mexico City, pick up the color of the peonies. Though the shades of pink and magenta nod to Valentine's Day, these accents are sophisticated, not cloying. This is the perfect occasion to get out your fine china and good silver—after all, you only need two place settings! Here, we used Villeroy and Boch plates. Finally, despite my aversion to romance, I couldn't resist baking and serving the chocolate soufflé in sweet tin charlotte molds with heart-shaped handles.

My Bloody Valentine

This cocktail is the perfect way to begin a romantic dinner for two: a simple combination of blood orange nectar, St. Germain elderflower liqueur, and prosecco. Elderflower liqueur has become quite popular in recent years, but I personally find it too sweet when used in large quantities. The acidity of the blood orange nectar is a perfect foil for the St. Germain—the drink has a slight floral taste, but no cloying sweetness. Prosecco is the Italian equivalent of Champagne, and I like its slightly yeasty flavor in this cocktail. Champagne would be delicious in this recipe as well. But there's no reason to spend a fortune on a bottle for a mixed drink. I like to serve this in an old-fashioned Champagne coupe, also known as a Marie Antoinette glass. (Legend has it that the glass was designed after the shape of the ill-fated French queen's breast.) The coupe is a more elegant, unexpected alternative to a Champagne flute, but a flute would work just as well.

Blood Orange Nectar (recipe follows)

St. Germain elderflower liqueur

Prosecco

For each cocktail, combine 1 ounce nectar, 1 ounce liqueur, and 2 ounces prosecco in a cocktail shaker filled with ice. Shake and strain into a chilled Marie Antoinette or Champagne coupe glass. ✶

Blood Orange Nectar
Makes 4 cups

2 cups freshly squeezed blood orange juice
(from 8 blood oranges)

Juice of 1 lemon

½ cup granulated sugar

Stir together the orange juice, lemon juice, and sugar with 2 cups water in a 2-quart saucepan over medium heat. Bring to a boil, then lower the heat and simmer for 5 minutes. Let cool slightly, then strain through a fine-mesh strainer into a 1-quart glass jar or similar container with a lid. Let cool. Store in the refrigerator in a glass jar with lid for up to 2 weeks. ✶

Summerland Farm Egg Custard

Serves 2

I absolutely love eggs; I could easily put an egg dish on every menu I create. With menus at our restaurants, we often try to start and end with something similar to give the meal symmetry. Here, we begin with this egg custard, and end with an egg-rich chocolate soufflé. This is a delicate, aromatic dish with lots of fresh herbs. I like to serve it in eggshells for a special presentation (see the deviled egg recipe in April, page 151, for instructions on topping eggs and reserving the shells for serving). But ramekins or demitasse cups would work well too. Since eggs are the star of custard, it's important that they be high-quality. Pasture-raised chickens tend to produce eggs with the most colorful and richest-tasting yolks.

1 tablespoon butter

½ small onion, finely chopped

1 garlic clove, thinly sliced

Kosher salt

¼ cup dry white wine, such as pinot grigio or sauvignon blanc

1 cup heavy cream

1 sprig fresh thyme

1 sprig fresh parsley

1 sprig fresh tarragon

2 fresh chives

1 bay leaf

2 large egg yolks, preferably from a local farm

Pink Peppercorn Granola (recipe follows)

Preheat the oven to 300° F. Place two 2-inch ramekins in an ovenproof saucepan or baking dish and set aside.

Slowly cook the butter, onion, and garlic in a 1-quart saucepan over low heat until the onion is translucent, about 5 minutes. Season with salt and add the wine. Continue to cook until there is almost no liquid remaining in the pan and it is very aromatic, 5 to 7 minutes. Add the cream, bring to a simmer, then remove the pan from the heat and add the thyme, parsley, tarragon, chives, and bay leaf. Allow to steep for 20 minutes. Return the pan to the stove, bring the mixture to a slow simmer, then strain through a fine-mesh strainer into a bowl; discard the solids.

Place the egg yolks in a small mixing bowl and, while the cream is still warm, slowly add a small amount of the cream to the yolks, whisking constantly. Continue to add the cream to the eggs, until all is incorporated. Strain through a fine-mesh strainer into a bowl and then divide between the two ramekins. Pour enough hot water into the pan with the ramekins to come halfway up the sides of the ramekins. Carefully place the pan in the oven. Bake for 15 to 20 minutes, or until the custards are just set: When you jiggle the ramekins, the custard should seem loose but with no liquid in the center. Do not overcook. Serve warm with Pink Peppercorn Granola sprinkled on top. ∗

Pink Peppercorn Granola
Makes 2 cups

Granola is a delicious, unexpected topping for the custards. Pink peppercorn is actually a dried fruit, with a slightly floral flavor and a bit of spice. Its lovely pink color is an appropriate nod to Valentine's Day. If you have leftover granola, its lightly spicy crunch would be delicious sprinkled on a salad, or even as a topping for scrambled eggs at breakfast the next morning.

1 tablespoon butter

2 cups rolled oats

¼ cup Marcona almonds, roughly chopped

2 teaspoons granulated sugar

Kosher salt

Freshly ground black pepper

¼ cup pink peppercorns

Preheat the oven to 300° F.

Melt the butter in 1-quart saucepan over low heat, then toss in the oats and stir to evenly coat with the butter. Add the almonds, sugar, salt, a few cracks of black pepper, and the peppercorns. Mix all the ingredients to combine.

Spread the granola out on a baking sheet and toast in the oven for 10 minutes, or until crispy, golden brown, and aromatic. Transfer to a food processor and pulse until coarsely chopped. Cool completely, then transfer to an airtight container. The granola will keep for several days at room temperature. ∗

Kumamoto Oysters
with Caviar and Champagne Gelée

Serves 2

Oysters, caviar, and Champagne would top almost anyone's list of aphrodisiacs. Here, we showcase them all in one luxurious bite. Though oysters from the Gulf of Mexico are readily available in Georgia, I actually prefer to use kumamotos from Washington State for this recipe. They have an elegant, deep, fluted cup with a sweet, creamy flavor that works wonderfully with the delicate flavors of the Champagne and caviar. If you don't have access to caviar, or don't want to spend the money, you could leave it out. But the saltiness of the caviar really adds to the balanced flavors of the dish, and it's a wonderful touch for a special occasion. If you want to continue with the Valentine's Day color scheme, try using pink Champagne for the gelée. For the gelée mold, I would suggest a 4- or 5-inch square or round flat-bottomed container.

1 cup dry Champagne

¼ ounce powdered gelatin or 1 sheet of gelatin

12 kumamoto oysters

Crushed ice or coarse sea salt

1 (30-gram) jar Petrossian osetra caviar

Micro sorrel

Heat ½ cup of the Champagne in a small saucepan over low heat. Sprinkle the powdered gelatin into the warm Champagne and stir to dissolve. (If using a gelatin sheet, cover the sheet with about 2 cups of cold water in a small bowl. Let it bloom until the gelatin is soft, about 5 minutes. Squeeze out any excess water from the gelatin and then dissolve it in the ½ cup Champagne as above.) Remove the saucepan from the heat and stir in the remaining ½ cup Champagne. Line a shallow 4-inch container (such as a storage container or small cake pan) with plastic wrap (this helps with unmolding). Pour the gelatin mixture into the lined container. Let cool in the refrigerator, uncovered, for at least 5 hours or until it has gelled. Unmold it and cut into whatever small shape you desire or break up with a fork to resemble a granita. Store, covered, in the refrigerator.

To shuck each oyster, place on a flat and sturdy surface, using a kitchen towel to keep the oyster stable and keeping the deep, or cupped, side down. Gently push the tip of an oyster knife into the hinged portion on the pointed end of the shell. Once firmly in place, leverage or lift the top shell until you hear or feel a pop. Slowly move the oyster knife around the top of the shell to release. Run the oyster knife under the bottom of the meat of the oyster to release it from the muscle holding it to the bottom shell, keeping the oyster level to reserve as much of the liquor (or juice) as possible. Leave the oyster in the bottom shell. Inspect each oyster for errant bits of shell. Keep cold on ice until ready to serve.

Serve the oysters over crushed ice or a bed of coarse sea salt. Garnish each oyster with some of the caviar, the Champagne gelée, and micro sorrel. ★

Crab Salad with Grapefruit, Fennel, and Apples

Serves 2

This salad is all about fresh, high-quality ingredients and a beautiful presentation. A regular weeknight supper doesn't call for an artfully sauced plate, but this is a good excuse to go all out. Squeeze bottles with fine tips are the best, and most fun, way to create perfect dots and precise streaks. They are inexpensive and widely available at art supply stores or online. Peekytoe crab is a colloquial name for Atlantic rock crab—the best ones are found in and around Maine's Penobscot Bay. Because the crabs are too delicate to ship live, they are steamed and then picked—often by the crabber's wife—as soon as they come off the boat. You will want to pick through the meat one more time at home to get rid of any errant shell fragments, but you do not need to cook it. Though peekytoe crab is beloved in restaurant kitchens, it can be tricky to find in grocery stores or retail seafood markets. If that's the case, blue crab will work just as well.

For the Crab Salad

¼ pound cooked peekytoe crabmeat

1 tablespoon Homemade Mayonnaise (page 246)

1 tablespoon small diced young fennel

1 tablespoon small diced Gala apple

2 grapefruit segments, thinly sliced

A few fresh chives, thinly sliced

A few fresh tarragon leaves, thinly sliced

Freshly squeezed lemon juice

Kosher salt

Freshly ground pepper

For the Fennel Puree

1 small bulb fennel, diced small

2 shallots, diced small

2 tablespoons butter, diced

Kosher salt

¼ cup Pernod

For the Grapefruit Emulsion

½ cup freshly squeezed grapefruit juice

3 tablespoons grapeseed oil

For the Garnishes

4 grapefruit segments

Gala apple, diced small

D'Avignon radish, diced small

Fennel fronds picked from stem

Celery leaves picked from stem

Micro mustard leaves

To make the crab salad: Pick through the crab with your fingers and remove any errant shells. Cut the crab into a small dice; you want the pieces to be the same size as the apple and fennel. In a small mixing bowl, combine the crab, mayonnaise, fennel, apple, grapefruit, chives, and tarragon. Season with lemon juice and salt and pepper. Taste and adjust if needed. The salad is best if mixed just before you are ready to serve, but you may make it up to 2 hours in advance and keep it, covered, in the refrigerator.

To make the fennel puree: In a medium sauté pan, cook the fennel and shallots in 1 tablespoon of the butter over low heat until aromatic. Season with salt and add the Pernod. Continue to cook until the liquid is reduced by three-fourths, then add enough water to barely cover the fennel. Cook until soft, about 20 minutes. While still hot, transfer to a blender and puree until smooth. Add the remaining 1 tablespoon butter and incorporate completely. Strain through a fine-mesh sieve and cool. Transfer to a squeeze bottle until needed. The fennel puree can be made up to 2 days in advance and kept in the refrigerator.

To make the grapefruit emulsion: Blend the grapefruit juice in a blender on high speed. Slowly add the grapeseed oil through the hole in the lid until fully incorporated. Transfer to a squeeze bottle until needed; this can be made several hours before serving.

To serve, place a small scoop of the crab salad on each plate. Alternately dress each plate with squeezes of the fennel puree and grapefruit emulsion. Decorate each plate with the garnishes as desired. ✻

Root Vegetable Consommé with Celery Root Agnolotti

Serves 2

This recipe creates a delicious, aromatic vegetable stock, and you can enjoy the leftovers all winter. Freeze the remaining stock in half-pint or pint containers and use it in any recipe that calls for vegetable stock, or as a wintry, vegetarian alternative to chicken stock. If you don't want to shape all of the pasta dough into agnolotti, you can cut the leftover portion into strips and wrap tightly. It will keep for a few days in the fridge or indefinitely in the freezer. It would be delicious with any leftover Beet Green Pesto (page 121) from the squab recipe.

For the Consommé

1 medium carrot

1 small yellow onion, peeled

1 stalk celery

1 small celery root, peeled

1 small rutabaga, peeled

1 bulb fennel

2 garlic cloves, peeled

2-inch piece fresh ginger, peeled

1 tablespoon olive oil

1 star anise

4 whole allspice

1/8 teaspoon coriander seeds

1/8 teaspoon mustard seeds

1/8 teaspoon fennel seeds

1/8 teaspoon whole black peppercorns

1 sprig fresh tarragon

1 sprig fresh basil

1 sprig fresh mint

1 sprig fresh parsley

2 bay leaves

For the Agnolotti

2 tablespoons butter

2 shallots, diced

1 celery root, peeled and diced

2 cups heavy cream

Juice of 1/2 lemon

Kosher salt

Freshly ground pepper

Freshly grated nutmeg

1 recipe (4 discs) Fresh Pasta Dough (page 244), rolled out and cut into 2-inch squares

For Serving

Minced fresh herbs, such as parsley, chives, micro sorrel, and tarragon

2 thumbelina carrots, blanched and cut in half

1 radish, sliced

1 stalk celery, blanched and sliced

Extra virgin olive oil

To make the consommé: Roughly chop the carrot, onion, celery, celery root, rutabaga, fennel, garlic, and ginger. Heat the oil in a 12-inch sauté pan over medium heat. Add the vegetables and cook until browned, about 10 minutes. You may need to cook in batches to avoid overcrowding the pan. Place the vegetables in an 8-quart stockpot.

Add the star anise, allspice, coriander seeds, mustard seeds, fennel seeds, and peppercorns to the same sauté pan and cook until fragrant, then transfer to the stockpot. Add the tarragon, basil, mint, parsley, and bay leaves to the stockpot. Cover the vegetables with 12 cups cold water and bring to a simmer over medium heat. Reduce the heat to low and simmer for 1 hour or until vegetables are soft. Strain through a fine-mesh sieve lined with cheesecloth. Do not push the cooked vegetables through the strainer as this will make the consommé cloudy. Cover and cool in the refrigerator overnight, or for at least 12 hours. Once the consommé is chilled, skim off any oil from the top with a spoon.

To make the agnolotti filling: Melt the butter in a 2-quart saucepan over low heat. Add the shallots and celery root and cook until softened, 5 minutes. Add 2 cups water, the cream, and 1 tablespoon of the lemon juice, then season with salt and pepper. Increase the heat to medium and bring to a simmer. Lower the heat and cook until the celery root is just tender, 20 to 30 minutes. Remove the celery root and shallots from the saucepan with a slotted spoon and place in the bowl of a food processor. Add 1/2 cup of the cooking liquid and process until smooth. Add more cooking liquid if needed; you want the consistency of cream cheese. Add a squeeze of lemon juice and adjust the seasoning with salt, pepper, and a few gratings of nutmeg.

To fill the pasta dough: Place 1 teaspoon of filling in the middle of each square. Use a pastry brush to moisten the edges of the pasta with cold water, then roll from the top to the bottom, leaving the top 1/4 inch of pasta exposed. Press the ends of the tube to seal. You will have more pasta dough and filling than you need for this recipe; you can make and form all the agnolotti up to this point and keep extra servings, wrapped well, in the freezer, where they will keep for several weeks.

To cook the agnolotti: Bring a large stockpot of salted water to a boil over high heat. Drop in the pasta and cook until they float to the surface, about 3 minutes if freshly made or 5 minutes if frozen. To serve, warm the consommé over low heat. For each serving, place 4 or 5 agnolotti in a shallow bowl and add 1 cup of consommé. Garnish with the herbs, carrots, radish, celery, and a few drops of olive oil. ✶

Squab with Beets and Beet Green Pesto

Serves 2

This is a delicious, unexpected, and colorful special-occasion dish. It consists of seared squab breasts served alongside the legs, which have been filled with a mousselike stuffing made from the liver and tenderloins. I love squab for its slightly gamey taste—it has a pleasant richness not apparent in domesticated birds. However, if you can't find squab, you could prepare this recipe with quail, Cornish game hens, or even a simple chicken. If you're unsure about breaking down the birds, ask your butcher to do it for you. If he or she doesn't have squab livers, chicken livers are an easy-to-find substitute that will create an equally delicious stuffing for the legs.

Depending on where you live, there's a chance you will be able to find a colorful assortment of beets at your local farmers' market, even in February. If available, use a combination of red and gold beets for maximum visual impact. Most people don't think to cook with beet greens, but they can be delicious, especially when they are young and tender. The beet green pesto is a gorgeous, deep-emerald color with a slightly earthier taste than traditional basil pesto. The leftover pesto would be delicious on pasta; it will keep in a small, airtight container in the freezer for several weeks.

2 (1-pound) whole squabs

2 squab livers, thoroughly dried

Kosher salt

Freshly ground pepper

1 large egg white

1 tablespoon heavy cream

Pinch of Insta Cure #1 (see "Curing Salt", page 16)

1 tablespoon Clarified Butter (page 246)

Beet Green Pesto (recipe follows)

Roasted Beets (recipe follows)

Prepare each squab: Remove both breasts from the cage and remove the small tenderloins on each breast. Remove and reserve the wings and legs. For each leg, french the end of the leg bone and remove the thigh bone. Set aside the breasts and legs. (Save the cage of the bird and all scraps and bones for stock.)

Place the breasts on a rack set over a baking sheet and refrigerate, uncovered, for 1 hour. This will dry out the surface of the skin for crispier skin when the breasts are seared.

To make the stuffing for the legs, combine the livers, tenderloins, salt, and pepper in the bowl of a food processor fitted with the metal blade and pulse to puree. While the processor is running, add the egg white and cream through the feed tube. Puree until completely smooth; the consistency should be like mousse. Pass through a fine-mesh strainer into a bowl to remove any bits that are not pureed. Season the stuffing with salt and pepper, as well as a

pinch of Insta Cure to retain color. Transfer the stuffing to a piping bag or a 1-quart resealable bag. Refrigerate until set, 1 hour or up to several hours. (Chilling the stuffing will make it easier to work with.)

Season the legs with salt and pepper. For each leg, pipe the stuffing into the leg where the thigh bone was. Wrap the skin and the flesh around the stuffing and wrap in plastic wrap. Twist the plastic around the leg so it resembles a lollipop with the bone sticking out at one end.

Fill the crock of a slow cooker with water, cover, and heat to 150° F. Place the legs in a resealable plastic bag and tightly seal. Poach in the water bath for 45 minutes, or until the internal temperature reaches 150° F. Remove the legs from the bag and discard the plastic wrap. Place a large pan over medium heat and add the butter. Sauté the legs, turning them, until golden and crispy. Remove and keep warm. Season the breasts with salt and pepper and sear, skin side first, until the skin turns golden brown, about 3 minutes. Flip and sear the other side, approximately 1 minute for medium rare or longer if you prefer medium. Let rest for 5 minutes and then slice for serving.

To assemble the dish: Paint or smear a stripe of the pesto down one side of your plate. Slice the leg into rounds and slice the breast in half lengthwise. Arrange the squab and beets around the pesto and garnish with more pesto. ⋆

Roasted Beets
Makes enough for 2 servings

1 pound small beets (golden and red or pink), scrubbed and trimmed, greens reserved for pesto

1 tablespoon red wine vinegar

1 teaspoon honey

Kosher salt

Freshly ground pepper

Preheat the oven to 300° F.

Place the beets in a roasting pan. Add 1 cup water, the vinegar, and honey. Season with salt and pepper and cover with parchment-lined foil. Bake for 2 to 3 hours, depending on the size of the beets. To test for doneness, pierce a beet with a knife; if the beet offers little resistance it is done.

Remove the beets from the liquid and let cool slightly. With a clean cloth, rub the skins free. Allow to cool completely, then dice into ½- to 1-inch cubes. ⋆

Beet Green Pesto
Makes ½ cup

Kosher salt

¼ pound beet greens, ribs removed

2 garlic cloves, peeled

2 tablespoons pine nuts

¼ cup finely grated Parmigiano-Reggiano cheese

Squeeze of lemon juice

1 tablespoon extra virgin olive oil

Bring 2 quarts water seasoned with 1 tablespoon salt to a boil in a 4-quart saucepan over medium to high heat. Prepare an ice bath for shocking the vegetables: Combine 2 cups water and 2 cups ice in a medium bowl. Blanch the greens by dropping them into the boiling water for 1 minute. Remove with a spider or slotted spoon and plunge into the ice bath. Drain and dry the greens thoroughly by wringing them out in paper towels or a kitchen towel. Next, blanch the garlic and pine nuts in the boiling water for 3 minutes. You do not need to place these in the ice bath. Dry the garlic and nuts thoroughly.

Combine the blanched greens, garlic, and nuts with the cheese, lemon juice, and a pinch of salt in a blender with 1 teaspoon ice or very cold water. Add the oil and puree until smooth. Check for seasoning and adjust as necessary. Store in an airtight container in the refrigerator. The pesto should be made the day of serving and kept cold; otherwise the color will fade. ⋆

Squab with Beets and Beet Green Pesto

Chocolate Soufflés and Rose Macarons

Chocolate Soufflés

Serves 2

A soufflé can make some home cooks nervous, as they worry about what will happen if it falls. My advice is to try this recipe anyway: A deflated soufflé is not quite as pretty as a perfectly puffy one, but it tastes just as delicious. If you have a convection oven, use it here, as the circulating hot air helps the soufflés rise consistently. However, a conventional oven can produce the same results if you raise the temperature slightly. I recommend using the highest quality chocolate you can find—one with at least 66 percent cacao. Valrhona, Callebaut, and Cacao Barry are all good brands. Look for cocoa powder labeled "Dutch process"; it produces better results for baking. You can top the warm, baked soufflés with freshly whipped cream, as we suggest below, or vanilla ice cream. Or, just enjoy the rich chocolate flavor on its own.

For the Soufflés

1 tablespoon butter, melted

3 tablespoons superfine sugar, plus extra for dusting

1 large egg yolk

2 tablespoons all-purpose flour

1 teaspoon cocoa powder

¼ teaspoon pure vanilla extract

Kosher salt

½ cup milk

¾ teaspoon instant espresso powder

¼ cup chopped chocolate (66 percent cacao)

¾ cup egg whites (from approximately 6 large eggs)

Pinch of cream of tartar

For the Whipped Cream

½ cup heavy cream

3 tablespoons granulated sugar

⅛ teaspoon pure vanilla extract

To make the soufflés: Prepare 2 deep ramekins (about 4 inches in diameter and 2 ½ inches tall) by brushing the insides with the melted butter and dusting with superfine sugar.

In a stainless-steel mixing bowl, whisk together the egg yolk and sugar until light yellow and thick. Add the flour, cocoa powder, vanilla, and a pinch of salt and mix well.

In a small stainless steel saucepan, combine the milk and espresso powder. Place over low heat until just simmering. Remove from the heat and add a small amount of the hot milk mixture to the yolk mixture, stirring constantly, until incorporated. Add the remaining milk mixture to the egg mixture and continue to stir until incorporated. Return everything to the saucepan and cook over low heat, stirring constantly, until the mixture has the texture of pudding, about 8 minutes. Place the chopped chocolate in a large bowl. Remove the custard mixture from the heat and pour it over the chocolate, stirring until melted and incorporated. Cover and set aside at room temperature for up to 1 hour. Or, refrigerate the custard for up to several hours; in this case, let the mixture return to room temperature before using.

Preheat a convection oven to 400° F or a conventional oven to 425° F. In a clean stand mixer bowl fitted with the whisk attachment, whip the egg whites on high speed until ripples form in the whites. Slowly add the cream of tartar and a pinch of salt. Whip until the whites form soft peaks. The whites should be stiff, shiny, and moist; they should not look dry.

Fold the whites into the chocolate mixture in three additions. Use a rubber spatula and scoop up from under the egg whites to maintain their volume.

Divide the mixture among the prepared ramekins. Once filled, run your thumb around the inside rim of each ramekin about ½ inch down; this will help the soufflé rise straight up. Bake for 8 to 10 minutes in a convection oven or 10 to 12 minutes in a conventional oven, until the soufflés have risen and a crust has formed on the top. Opening the oven during baking is not recommended, but it will not ruin your soufflé—just be careful to gently close the oven after opening.

To whip the cream: In the bowl of a mixer fitted with the whisk attachment, whip the cream until soft peaks form. Add the sugar and vanilla and continue to whip until the sugar is dissolved. Refrigerate until ready to serve.

As soon as the soufflés are baked, serve immediately with a spoonful of soft whipped cream. ⋆

Rose Macarons

Makes 18 macarons

French macarons—delicate, melt-in-your mouth, almond meringue sandwich cookies—are not to be confused with coconut macaroons. They come in a wide variety of flavors; here, we've used a few drops of rosewater to give them a subtle floral note. Be careful to avoid overdoing it with the rosewater, or else the macarons will end up tasting like your grandmother's perfume. Most rosewater used for cooking is clear, so if you want pink macarons, as pictured here, add a drop of red food coloring to the meringue batter. Macarons have become quite popular in the United States in recent years. If you don't want to make your own, there's a good chance you can buy them at a local bakery, gourmet foods store, or farmers' market. If you're up for a bit of a project, they are fun to make at home. They require some patience and precision, but if you love to bake, they will make an impressive addition to your repertoire. You can make both the meringues and the buttercream frosting in advance and then assemble the macarons shortly before serving. The meringues will keep in an airtight container in the freezer, and the buttercream can be refrigerated for several days.

¾ cup almond flour

1 cup confectioners' sugar

2 large egg whites

¼ cup granulated sugar

2 drops rosewater

Rosewater Buttercream (recipe follows)

Sift the almond flour and confectioners' sugar together twice. In the bowl of a stand mixer fitted with the whisk attachment, whip the egg whites and granulated sugar on medium speed until semi-stiff and shiny, about 10 minutes. Fold the almond flour and confectioners' sugar by hand into the egg whites until incorporated. Add the rosewater.

Line a baking sheet with parchment paper. Put the batter into a piping bag fitted with a ½-inch round tip. On the parchment paper, pipe 2-inch circles, placing them 1 inch apart. (You can trace 2-inch circles with a pencil on the paper to ensure the correct size of each macaron.) One tablespoon of batter should be enough for each circle. Let the batter dry for 30 minutes at room temperature, so that it forms a "skin" before baking.

Preheat the oven to 325° F. Place the baking sheet in the oven and immediately reduce the heat to 200° F. Bake the macarons for 10 to 15 minutes. If they remove easily from the parchment and do not stick, they are done. Let them cool, then transfer to a rack until you are ready to assemble. (You can make the macarons in advance: Once cooled, store in an airtight container in the freezer for up to 2 weeks or at room temperature for a day or two. These are very sensitive to humidity, so keep them tightly sealed. You may also wish to add a silica gel packet or other dessicant to your sealed container.)

To assemble the macarons, pipe the buttercream onto the flat side (or bottom) of a macaron. (You can also do this with a small offset spatula.) Top with another macaron to make a sandwich. Repeat until all the macarons are filled. Store in an airtight container. (These will keep for a couple of days, but it is best to store them unstuffed as the filling may cause the macarons to become soggy over time.) *

Rosewater Buttercream
Makes 2 cups

1 cup granulated sugar

3 large egg whites

1 cup (2 sticks) plus 1 tablespoon butter, at room temperature

½ teaspoon pure vanilla extract

Pinch of kosher salt

A few drops of rosewater

Place the sugar and egg whites in a heatproof bowl. Place the bowl over a saucepan of lightly simmering water and whisk by hand or with a hand mixer for about 10 minutes, until the mixture is hot to the touch, about 140° F. Transfer to the bowl of a stand mixer fitted with the whisk attachment and whip on high until doubled in volume.

While the meringue is whipping, cut the butter into small pieces. With the mixer on medium speed, slowly add the butter pieces, 2 pieces at a time, fully incorporating before adding more. Reduce the speed to low and add the vanilla, salt, and rosewater. Scrape the bowl to ensure that all the butter is completely incorporated. Transfer to an airtight container until needed. (It will keep, covered, in the refrigerator, for up to 5 days. Let it come to room temperature and whip again before using.) *

The Rites of Spring
A Lamb Fête

Serves 6

Preserved Meyer Lemon Collins

Lamb Tartare | **Italian Wedding Soup**

Lamb Pot au Feu: Lamb Sweetbreads, Lamb Merguez Sausage,

Pan-Roasted Rack of Lamb, Slow-Roasted Leg of Lamb | *Syrah*

Baked Sheep's Milk Ricotta | **Charred Pomegranate Popsicles**

For me, cooking good food is only part of the equation. I believe that a dish has to be served with the same generosity of spirit with which it was prepared, and in an environment that complements the ingredients and techniques involved. Creating the right dining atmosphere is essential, in my restaurants and in my home entertaining. But I don't adhere to any hard-and-fast rules for creating a perfect "look"—and you shouldn't, either. I want the meals that I prepare—from each individual dish, to the progression of courses, to the silverware and the centerpieces—to reflect my personality. Instead of worrying what's on-trend or expected, use what you love. For me, this usually means seasonal flavors on the plate and a complementary, but not completely matching, array of tableware and decorative elements.

Floataway Café, which was the setting for this early spring celebration of the lamb, is a reflection of the cuisine and the atmosphere that Clifford and I like best. Since opening Floataway in 1998, we've been serving a menu that can most accurately be described as Mediterranean by way of northern California. It's the kind of seasonal, ingredient-driven cuisine we fell in love with when we were in culinary school in the 1980s. Using the best and freshest ingredients to cook the food you love is a formula that never goes out of style.

This meal celebrates the lamb, one of my favorite symbols of spring. I've created a fresh, seasonal menu with a Mediterranean inflection. The meatball soup, for example, is based on an Italian wedding soup, and the dessert of baked sheep's milk ricotta with honey could be found in a Greek taverna. This meal honors both guests and ingredients. The flavors are pure and delicious, with the various preparations of lamb complementing the fresh baby vegetables. And it uses the entire animal, a gesture that is financially and environmentally responsible as well as respectful to the kill.

I serve this meal on all-white or neutral plates to highlight the bright colors and textures. All of our plates at Floataway come from Heath Ceramics, a San Francisco–based company that has been designing and manufacturing all of its products in California since 1948. The design is impeccable, a perfect blend of form and function. Use what looks best to you, but keep it simple and let the early-spring flavors take center stage.

Preserved Meyer Lemon Collins

Preserving Meyer lemons is a fantastic way to lengthen the season on these sweet, thin-skinned gems. I suggest preserving lemons to have in your cold pantry as a staple. They are delicious chopped as a relish for grilled fish, pureed in a vinaigrette for salad, or mixed into mayonnaise for sandwiches. The salty acidity they contribute to this cocktail—a riff on the classic Tom Collins—is a perfect match to the floral notes of the gin, and the rosemary garnish provides a pleasant, herbaceous accent. It's a refreshing way to begin an early-spring meal.

Preserved Meyer Lemons (recipe follows)

Fresh rosemary sprigs

Simple Syrup (page 186)

Gin (preferably Oxley dry gin)

Club soda

For each cocktail, muddle ½ preserved lemon with 1 sprig rosemary and 1 ounce simple syrup in a cocktail glass. Add 2 ounces gin and ice and stir with a cocktail spoon. There is no need to shake. Strain into a tall glass with fresh ice, garnish with rosemary, and top with a splash of club soda. ∗

Preserved Meyer Lemons
Makes 5 preserved lemons

If you do not have a cool room in your house to store the lemons while they are fermenting, then place on the top shelf of your refrigerator.

5 Meyer lemons

½ cup kosher salt

½ cup granulated sugar

Clean the outside of each lemon well under warm water. Quarter the lemons, from top to bottom, almost all the way through, leaving them connected at the bottom. Sprinkle the exposed flesh liberally with ¼ cup of the salt and ¼ cup of the sugar and reshape.

Cover the bottom of a sterilized glass quart jar with a sprinkle of salt. Place the lemons in the jar (they should fit snuggly), sprinkling liberally with salt and sugar between each lemon. Top with the remaining salt and sugar and seal the jar. Store in a dark cabinet at cool room temperature, gently agitating the jar daily, for 30 days. At this point the lemons are ready for use, or you may store them in the refrigerator, where they will keep for at least a couple of months. ∗

Lamb Tartare

Serves 6

If you enjoy beef tartare, why not try a similar preparation with lamb? For this recipe, you must begin with the freshest, best-quality meat you can find. Ideally, you should purchase the lamb directly from a farmer you know and trust, and then butcher the lamb yourself, using all the parts for this menu. This is not as daunting as it sounds, since a lamb is much smaller than a pig. Otherwise, try to find a butcher who can supply a high-quality, humanely slaughtered young animal and ask him or her to break the animal down into primal cuts for you. Be sure to remove all sinew and connective tissues (also known as silverskin) to ensure a pleasant mouthfeel. Lamb actually doesn't have a great deal of intramuscular fat, so the walnuts add a pleasant, fatty roundness to the tartare. I like to serve it with a fresh, crusty baguette, either baked at home (page 242) or store-bought.

1 (12-ounce) boneless lamb loin or 12 ounces lamb tenderloins

¼ cup walnuts

6 cornichons, minced

2 shallots, minced

1 tablespoon minced fresh mint

1 tablespoon Dijon mustard

1 tablespoon olive oil

Juice of ½ lemon

Kosher salt

Freshly ground pepper

1 Baguette (page 242)

Micro greens, for garnish

Quick Pickles (page 97), made with baby turnips and carrots in place of greens, for garnish

Remove the fat and silverskin from the loin of lamb and discard. Chop the meat finely with a sharp knife: For the best result, first cut into thin slices across the grain, then slice the rounds into strips about ⅛ inch thick, then finally slice into small cubes. Keep the meat cold in a chilled bowl in the refrigerator while preparing the garnishes.

Toast the walnuts in a dry nonstick pan over low to medium heat, occasionally shaking the pan, until fragrant, about 5 minutes. Let cool completely. Chop finely.

Add the walnuts, cornichons, shallots, mint, mustard, oil, and lemon juice to the chopped lamb in the chilled bowl. Taste and season with salt and pepper. Cover and refrigerate until serving. (The tartare can be prepared up to 1 hour before serving, but we recommend serving as quickly as possible. After the meat is mixed with garnishes it will begin to discolor if allowed to sit too long.)

Slice and toast the baguette and serve with the tartare, garnished with micro greens and quick pickles. ★

pasta & gr~

ziti, veal m~

sautéed

papr~

loc~

a sel~

Italian Wedding Soup

Serves 6

The meatballs for Italian wedding soup are usually made out of ground beef, veal, and/or pork. Here, we've given the traditional Italian-American recipe a spin by making lamb meatballs. I love the spiciness of the mustard greens with the savory meatballs, but you could easily substitute another leafy green vegetable such as cabbage, kale, or spinach. This soup is fantastic with freshly made, hand-cut pasta. However, if you don't have a pasta roller or you don't want to make your own pasta from scratch, use store-bought egg noodles instead. Cook them separately beforehand, and add them to the soup at the end.

For the Lamb Meatballs

1 pound lean ground lamb

1 large egg, beaten

¼ cup unseasoned bread crumbs

2 tablespoons chopped fresh mint

Zest of 1 Meyer lemon, finely grated

Kosher salt

Freshly ground pepper

¾ cup all-purpose flour

1 to 2 cups vegetable oil, for shallow frying

For the Pasta

2 discs (half recipe) Fresh Pasta Dough (page 244), rolled out and cut into 1-inch strips

For the Soup

1 tablespoon olive oil

1 sweet onion, coarsely chopped

3 garlic cloves, thinly sliced

1 sprig fresh thyme

Pinch of crushed red pepper flakes (optional)

1 cup fresh field peas, pink-eyed peas, or frozen small field peas

1 bunch young mustard greens, torn

4 cups Lamb Stock or Chicken Stock (page 244 or 245)

3 sprigs fresh flat-leaf parsley, stems removed, chopped, for garnish

Kosher salt

To make the meatballs: Combine the lamb, egg, bread crumbs, mint, and lemon zest in a large bowl. Season with salt and pepper and mix well by hand. Roll the mixture into balls about the size of golf balls, making about 18 balls at 1 ounce each. Place the flour in a small bowl and roll each ball in the flour. Tap off any excess flour.

Heat about ½ inch of oil in a 12-inch sauté pan over medium heat. Cook the lamb balls in the hot oil in batches. (You don't want to crowd the pan and reduce the heat; they should all fit across the bottom of the pan in one layer. You are looking for a slow, gentle shallow fry.) Cook the meatballs, using tongs to turn them so they cook evenly on all sides, until golden brown, 5 to 7 minutes. To test to see if they are done, insert a small knife into the middle of a meatball; if the blade comes out hot, they are done (or insert a meat thermometer into a meatball; it should register 155° F). Set aside at room temperature for serving.

To make the soup: Heat the oil in a saucepan over medium heat. Add the onion and garlic and sauté until translucent, a couple of minutes. Reduce the heat to low and add the thyme and red pepper flakes, if using. Add the peas and cook over low heat for 10 minutes, stirring occasionally. Add the mustard greens and stock and bring to a simmer. Add the fresh pasta and cook over low heat until tender, 2 to 3 minutes. Carefully place the meatballs in the saucepan and cook until heated through. Adjust the seasoning with salt.

Serve the soup in individual bowls, being sure to include 3 meatballs and some pasta in each. Garnish with the chopped parsley leaves and stems. ∗

Lamb Pot au Feu

Serves 6

Pot au feu—literally, "pot on fire" in French—is one of my all-time favorite comfort dishes. The term normally refers to beef stew, but can apply to any slow-roasted cut of meat, served in a rich broth with vegetables. At Bacchanalia, we serve this dish as Lamb Five Ways: a composed plate of sweetbreads, kidneys, lamb sausage, roasted rack of lamb, and slow-cooked leg of lamb, accompanied by fresh spring vegetables in a lamb stock. This makes for an impressive presentation and a delightful mix of tastes and textures, fitting for a meal that celebrates the whole lamb. However, you could make an equally wonderful, simplified version of Lamb Pot au Feu with just one or two cuts of meat. For instance, you could prepare the slow-roasted leg of lamb and serve it by itself with the vegetables and the broth, or do the leg with sweetbreads, or the leg with sausage—there are dozens of possibilities. Try as many or as few of these components as you want, using the leg or the rack as your base.

Kosher salt

1 bunch (about 12) young carrots, peeled

2 young fennel bulbs, cut into 2-inch pieces

4 young leeks, cut into 2-inch pieces

½ cup fresh or frozen green peas

½ cup baby butter beans

½ recipe Lamb Sweetbreads (page 138; optional)

Freshly ground pepper

1 teaspoon olive oil or Clarified Butter (page 246)

Lamb Merguez Sausage (page 138; optional)

Pan Roasted Rack of Lamb (page 139; optional), sliced

Slow-Roasted Leg of Lamb (page 139; optional), sliced

1 quart Lamb Stock or Chicken Stock (page 244 or 245)

A few fennel blossoms

A few watercress leaves

Fleur de sel

To blanch the vegetables: Season an 8-quart pot filled with 4 quarts of water with 1 tablespoon salt and bring to a boil over medium to high heat. Prepare an ice bath for shocking the vegetables: Combine 2 cups water and 2 cups ice in a medium bowl. Blanch the vegetables in batches: Drop the carrots in the boiling water and cook for about 3 minutes, until barely tender but not mushy. Use a spider or a slotted spoon to immediately transfer the carrots to the ice bath. Repeat with the fennel, leeks, peas, and beans. As soon as each vegetable is cooled, remove it from the ice bath and place on a clean dish towel to dry.

Remove the sweetbreads from their liquid and pat dry. Season with salt and pepper. Heat a sauté pan over medium heat. Add a slick of the oil or clarified butter and cook the sweetbreads, turning, for 3 to 4 minutes, until crispy on the outside.

Preheat the oven to 200° F. Arrange the cooked sweetbreads, sausage, rack of lamb slices, and leg of lamb slices on baking sheets and keep warm in the oven.

In a saucepan, heat the stock and season with salt and pepper. Add the blanched vegetables and warm.

Divide the warm lamb sausage, rack and leg slices, and the vegetables from the broth among serving bowls. Adjust the seasoning of the broth and ladle over the meat and vegetables. Garnish with the fennel blossoms and watercress leaves. Sprinkle with fleur de sel and serve immediately. ★

Lamb Sweetbreads
Serves 6

Most people are more familiar with veal sweetbreads, but I think that lamb sweetbreads are just as delicious; they have a fantastic flavor and very little gaminess. These are an optional addition to the pot au feu (page 137)—this recipe yields double what you will need for that dish. Leftovers are delicious reheated as a topping for pasta or polenta; you can also drain, dry, and pan-fry the sweetbreads. To properly prepare the sweetbreads, allow yourself a couple of days.

½ cup kosher salt

1 pound lamb sweetbreads

¼ cup grapeseed oil

½ carrot, chopped

1 rib celery, chopped

½ small onion, chopped

1 sprig fresh tarragon

1 sprig fresh thyme

1 garlic clove, crushed

¼ cup dry vermouth

4 cups Chicken Stock (page 244)

Two days before serving, prepare a salty, icy bath for the sweetbreads: Fill a large bowl with 1 quart water, 4 cups ice, and the salt. Place the sweetbreads in the bowl, cover, and soak overnight in the refrigerator.

Discard the water and rinse the sweetbreads under cold running water. Place paper towels on a baking sheet, lay out the sweetbreads, and cover with more paper towels. Top with another baking sheet, put a 5-pound weight or cans on top, and refrigerate for 12 to 24 hours.

Dry the sweetbreads well and chop into 1-inch pieces, cleaning away any of the blood lines and membranes. Heat the oil in a medium sauté pan over medium heat. Add the sweetbreads and sauté until light brown on both sides, about 10 minutes. Add the carrot, celery, onion, tarragon, thyme, and garlic. Add the vermouth and scrape up any browned bits on the bottom of the pan. Simmer until the liquid is reduced by half, about 5 minutes. Add the stock, bring to a simmer, and remove from the heat.

Transfer the sweetbreads to a cooling rack set over a baking sheet and refrigerate until chilled, about 1 hour. Strain the cooking liquid through a fine-mesh strainer into a bowl or container, cover, and refrigerate until chilled. (The sweetbreads and liquid should chill separately to reduce the risk of overcooking the sweetbreads. Also both will cool more quickly when separated.) After both are chilled, add the sweetbreads to the liquid, cover, and refrigerate until ready to use. (The cooked and cooled sweetbreads will keep in the refrigerator for up to 3 days.) *

Lamb Merguez Sausage
Makes 5 pounds or 15 links

This Spanish-style sausage, spiced with smoked paprika and cayenne pepper, can be served as part of the pot au feu (page 137), on its own, or as a substitute for pork sausage in a variety of dishes. The sausage can also be made into patties without casings and cooked in a pan with a little olive oil. This recipe will make more than you need for the pot au feu but leftovers will keep well refrigerated or frozen.

3 large red bell peppers

2 teaspoons olive oil

4 pounds lamb leg or shoulder meat, well chilled

1 ¼ pounds pork fatback, well chilled

8 garlic cloves, finely chopped

5 tablespoons kosher salt

3 tablespoons chopped fresh thyme leaves

4 teaspoons finely grated lemon zest (about 2 lemons)

1 teaspoon smoked paprika

1 teaspoon Insta Cure #1 (see "Curing Salt," page 16)

½ teaspoon cayenne pepper

1 package hog casings, for 5 pounds sausage
(about 6 feet in length)

Preheat the oven to 400° F.

Rub the bell peppers with 1 teaspoon of the oil and place on a baking sheet. Roast for 20 to 30 minutes, until blistered. Transfer to a paper bag to cool. Discard the skin and seeds. Finely dice the flesh and set aside.

Carefully remove the sinew and connective tissue from the shoulder or leg meat with a sharp knife; it is important to remove any silverskin or sinew so it does not get caught in the grinder and cause a "smear." Cut the lamb into 2-inch cubes. Cube the fatback into 1- to 2-inch pieces. Place the cubed meat and fat in a resealable plastic bag, keeping them as separate as possible, and put in the freezer for 10 to 15 minutes.

Using a meat grinder fitted with the medium grinding plate, grind half of the meat into a large bowl. Change to a fine grinding plate and grind the remainder of the meat with all of the fatback into the same bowl. In a separate small bowl, combine the diced peppers, garlic, salt, thyme, lemon zest, paprika, Insta Cure, and cayenne. Combine well, then add to the bowl with the meat mixture and incorporate well by hand; the mixture should be pastelike. Cure the sausage mixture, soak the casings, and stuff the sausages according to the instructions on page 103.

When you are ready to cook the sausage, use kitchen shears to snip the links apart. Heat the remaining 1 teaspoon olive oil in a 12-inch sauté pan over medium heat. Add the links, reduce the heat to low, and cook the sausage slowly, turning, until browned and the internal temperature reaches 150° F, about 15 minutes. ★

Pan-Roasted Rack of Lamb

Serves 6

Traditionally you would never find this elegant cut in a peasant dish like the pot au feu (page 137), but I like the way it elevates the other simple and more casual preparations of the lamb into something quite spectacular. However, you might prefer to prepare this on its own. A simple rack of lamb needs very little to accompany it: some spring vegetables, a salad with mint, and you are done. Look for a rack of spring lamb with 6 to 8 rib bones. I find the lamb from Jamison Farm to be exceptional. Over the past thirty years, Sukey and John Jamison have diligently and lovingly controlled the process from breeding to harvest, resulting in meats that taste extraordinary.

1 (1- to 1 ½-pound) rack of lamb

Kosher salt

Freshly ground pepper

1 tablespoon olive oil

1 garlic clove, crushed

1 sprig fresh rosemary

Preheat the oven to 400° F.

Use a sharp knife to remove most of the fat cap from the rack of lamb and discard. Dry the rack with paper towels and season with salt and pepper. Heat a 10-inch sauté pan over medium heat. Add the oil, garlic, and rosemary. Add the lamb rack, fat side down, and sear until golden brown, carefully basting with the hot oil in the pan as it sears; this should take about 3 minutes. Turn the rack over and brown the other side. Place the rack in a roasting pan and roast for 10 minutes, or until a meat thermometer registers 145° F for medium rare. Let the meat rest for at least 15 minutes before slicing. Serve 1 lamb rib per pot au feu. ★

Slow-Roasted Leg of Lamb

Serves 6

This recipe's technique is what the French would call "in the style of the baker's wife." It comes from the days when a tough joint of meat was cooked slowly over aromatics in the dying embers of the wood-burning bread ovens. It is a perfect and fitting component for the pot au feu (page 137), but it would also make a perfect stand-alone Sunday supper if you threw a few roots and taters into the pan during cooking. I prefer to brine a leg before roasting it; it's not absolutely necessary, but if time allows, a two-day brine will help keep your leg of lamb both moist and flavorful.

1 (4- to 5-pound) leg of lamb, untrimmed

1 cup plus 2 tablespoons kosher salt

6 sprigs fresh rosemary, stems removed

½ cup fresh mint

8 garlic cloves

1 tablespoon granulated sugar

1 teaspoon freshly ground pepper

½ cup olive oil

½ cup freshly squeezed lemon juice (about 3 lemons)

4 Preserved Meyer Lemons (page 130), cut in half

Two days before you plan on serving, brine the lamb: Dissolve 1 cup salt in 1 gallon of cold water. Place the lamb in a large container and pour the brine over. The lamb should be completely submerged. If it is not, make additional brine using the same ratio of 1 cup salt to 1 gallon water. Cover the container and refrigerate for 2 days.

Preheat the oven to 500° F. Remove the meat from the brine and dry well. Cut slits through the fat, 2 inches apart, to form a crosshatch pattern, being careful not to cut into the meat.

In the bowl of a food processor fitted with the metal blade, combine the rosemary, mint, garlic, sugar, pepper, and remaining 2 tablespoons salt. Process until roughly chopped. Press this mixture into the slits cut into the leg. Place the leg of lamb in a roasting pan and roast for 20 minutes.

Turn the oven down to 225° F. Mix the lemon juice with the oil. Add the preserved lemon halves to the roasting pan and pour the lemon juice mixture over the lamb. Continue to roast for 6 to 8 hours, checking the lamb frequently after 4 hours. The lamb is done when the meat is fall-off-the-bone tender. ★

Baked Sheep's Milk Ricotta

Serves 6

This is a simple, rustic, and incredibly delicious dessert—one of my personal favorites. Continuing with the lamb theme, we use sheep's milk ricotta as the base for a slightly sweet, eggy custard that we then bake in individual ramekins. Sheep's milk ricotta is not too difficult to find—most Italian or Greek ricottas are made from sheep's milk. There are a few excellent domestically made options as well. Bellwether Farms in Sonoma County, California, and Old Chatham Sheepherding Company in upstate New York both make fresh ricotta from a blend of cow's and sheep's milk. I love sheep's milk for its tangy flavor—it is slightly higher in acid and lower in fat than ricotta made from cow's milk. However, this dish will work just as well with a cow's milk ricotta. Though the bee pollen is technically an optional garnish, I encourage you to seek it out. It is highly nutritious and has a pleasantly unusual, almost dusty, flavor and texture.

1 tablespoon softened butter

4 large eggs

½ cup granulated sugar, plus more for dusting

2 tablespoons honey

1 teaspoon kosher salt

1 pound fresh sheep's milk ricotta

¼ pound honeycomb, for garnish (optional)

2 teaspoons bee pollen, for garnish (optional)

Preheat the oven to 350° F. Prepare six ramekins, each sized 3 ½ inches in diameter and at least 2 inches in height, by rubbing with the butter and dusting with sugar.

In the bowl of a stand mixer fitted with a whisk attachment, combine the eggs, sugar, honey, and salt on low speed until all of the sugar has been incorporated. Whisk on high until the mixture has increased in volume slightly and is a pale yellow. Place the ricotta in a large bowl and fold in the egg mixture in thirds.

Spoon the custard into the prepared ramekins and place the ramekins in a baking dish. Fill the dish with warm water to come halfway up the sides of the ramekins. Bake for 25 minutes, until browned on the top and slightly puffed in the center. Place the custards on a baking sheet and heat the broiler. Place the ramekins 4 to 5 inches below the broiler and broil until the tops are browned, about 2 minutes. Serve immediately, garnished with a spoonful of honeycomb and a pinch of bee pollen if you like. ⋆

Charred Pomegranate Popsicles

Makes 10 to 16 popsicles

We serve this as a palate cleanser at the end of the meal. The sweet smokiness of the charred pomegranate is refreshing and delightfully unexpected. If you like pickled watermelon rinds, serving a few on the side would make the perfect tart, crunchy garnish. If you do not have a juicer, juice the seeds in a blender; just be sure to let the juice sit for a few hours, until the foam and cloudiness settles, before pouring into the popsicle molds. You could use POM Wonderful juice or another bottled pomegranate juice as a shortcut, but your finished popsicles won't have the same smoky flavor from the grill. Finally, although gourmet popsicles are enjoying a moment right now, you don't have to invest in your own set of popsicle molds if you don't think you would use them much. This recipe would be delicious prepared as a granita: Pour the liquid into a shallow pan or baking dish, put it into the freezer, and scrape the surface with a fork every half hour until it reaches the desired consistency.

6 pomegranates

¼ lemon

Pinch of kosher salt

1 cup Simple Syrup (page 186)

Light a charcoal grill or place a grill pan over high heat.

Tear the pomegranates in half and place, torn side down, on the grill or grill pan. Grill until the surface is charred, about 15 minutes. When the pomegranates are cool enough to handle, hold over a bowl and hit the exterior of the pomegranate with the back of a spoon to knock the seeds into the bowl.

Juice the pomegranate seeds using a juicer. Transfer to a glass or ceramic container, cover, and refrigerate for 1 hour; this allows the pith to settle, clarifying the juice.

Carefully pour the clarified juice out of the container, leaving the sediment in the container. You should have about 3 cups. Add a squeeze of fresh lemon and a pinch of salt. Add the simple syrup. (If you have more or less than 3 cups of juice, the ratio of pomegranate juice to simple syrup is 3 to 1. So if your pomegranates yield only 2 cups of juice, use ⅔ cup simple syrup.)

Pour into 12 (5-ounce) popsicle molds fitted with popsicle sticks and freeze for at least 6 hours. This can be done several days in advance. ⋆

Hunting Eggs on the Farm

An Easter Supper

Serves 12 to 20

Spring Forward Cocktail

Deviled Eggs in the Shell | **Slow-Roasted Porchetta**

Potatoes Boulangère

Braised, Pureed, and Raw Beets with Spring Leaves and Herbs

Radishes with Cultured Butter and Salt

Fresh Pea and Fennel Salad | **Roasted Asparagus and Farm Egg Emulsion**

Thyme Onion Rolls | *A Crisp Sauvignon Blanc*

Angel Food Cake with Macerated Strawberries and Poached Rhubarb

Spring at Summerland Farm arrives hopeful, vibrant, and early. By April we are ready to harvest our spring delicacies and arrange them on a plate. English peas and strawberries are among our favorites, but they are just the beginning. There is not a more colorful season in our world, with the jonquils bursting into bloom and so many fresh, bright roots ready to pull from the warm earth of the garden.

And the eggs! In the winter, our hens take a pseudo-sabbatical from laying. Come April, they redouble their efforts. Their prolific habits create the perfect conditions for an Easter egg hunt—no dye or plastic eggs needed. Many of our guests bring their children to the farm for Easter, and the young ones delight in hunting for freshly laid eggs in the hen house.

This is the buffet we serve every Easter, with little variation. It celebrates all that we love about spring: The flavors, textures, and colors play off one another perfectly. I never tire of this repertoire. In fact, by the end of winter, I find myself counting the weeks until it is time to prepare the Easter spread.

Many of these dishes can be prepared or partially assembled in advance, allowing for a leisurely Easter Sunday. Clifford and I like nothing more than sleeping a bit later than usual, awaking to the aroma of the slow-roasting porchetta. By the time the guests arrive, we are ready to pour the adults a refreshing spring cocktail and turn the children loose to search for eggs.

We set our table for this late-afternoon feast outside, using a 1940s-era relic from the Star Provisions meatpacking plant. It was once the table in the employees' break area, and had been bolted to the floor when we arrived in 1999 to turn the space into our present-day Star Provisions. We pulled up a variety of wicker chairs, some brought from the house, and others borrowed from the restaurants. In the center of the table, we planted antique packing boxes with nasturtiums, moss, and ferns. We used Judy Jackson plates from New York and Alex Marshall pottery from northern California; Green Glass Company glassware made from recycled wine bottles; and Belgian linen napkins from Libeco in a lovely, complementary shade of grass green.

As a simple touch, I like to set out a glass trifle bowl filled with crushed ice that is studded with crisp D'avignon radishes (also called French radishes), for guests to pluck out and dip into cultured butter and fleur de sel. This menu never feels like work or a chore. It is seamless in its simplicity and is delicious hot, room temperature, or even cold.

Spring Forward Cocktail

This delicious, low-octane cocktail is both economical and seasonal, in that it utilizes the cooking liquid from the Poached Rhubarb (page 163). If you are not making the rhubarb, you could substitute pink grapefruit juice. We like to use Tito's vodka here—a clean and smooth-tasting spirit distilled in Texas. This is a perfectly refreshing start to a spring meal.

1 hibiscus tea bag

Rhubarb poaching liquid (see page 163)

Tito's vodka

Lemon bitters, preferably Fee Brothers

**Rhubarb stalks, for garnish
(reserved from Poached Rhubarb, page 163)**

To make the tea, place 1 hibiscus tea bag in a heatproof pitcher or cup, add 2 cups boiling water, and let steep for 6 to 8 minutes. Remove the tea bag and let the tea cool slightly. Place in the refrigerator to cool completely, about 1 hour. (You can make the tea a day in advance.)

For each cocktail, in a pint cocktail mixing glass filled with ice, combine 1 ounce tea, 1 ounce rhubarb poaching liquid, 1 ½ ounces vodka, and 2 drops bitters and stir well. Fill a tall 10-ounce glass with fresh ice and strain in the cocktail. Garnish with the rhubarb stalk. ⋆

Deviled Eggs in the Shell

Makes 24

Deviled eggs—a Southern staple—always make an appearance on our spring menus. We devised this appetizer to showcase our lovely colored eggs. Serve the deviled eggs from an egg carton (pasteboard is best) to keep them upright—this is also the best way to stabilize and store the egg shells as you prepare the filling. We "top" the eggs used in the mayonnaise (below), Roasted Asparagus (page 158), and Angel Food Cake (page 162) to reserve enough shells for this serving idea. Topping can easily be accomplished with an egg topper—a handy little kitchen tool that knocks a crack in the top of a raw egg.

For the Eggshell Cups

24 large eggs

1 tablespoon distilled vinegar

For the Eggs

10 large eggs

1 cup Homemade Mayonnaise (page 246), plus more as needed

1 teaspoon Dijon mustard

½ teaspoon white wine vinegar

½ teaspoon paprika

¼ teaspoon cayenne pepper

Kosher salt

Juice of 1 lemon

Freshly ground pepper

Chopped fennel fronds, for garnish

Small basil leaves, for garnish

To make the eggshell cups: Place 1 raw egg in an egg carton with the smaller end facing up. Place the bottom of an egg topper over that end. Gently pull the top ball of the egg topper and release it so the spring in the egg topper allows metal to contact the egg shell. If you do not have an egg topper, use the tip of a small sharp paring knife to run a crack around the top of the shell until you are able to lift the top off. Once the top has been removed, carefully pour out the raw egg. Repeat to make 24 cups. (The raw eggs can be stored in the refrigerator for up to a week.)

Put 8 cups warm tap water in a large bowl and add the vinegar. Carefully place the shells in the water-vinegar bath and let soak for 10 minutes. The shells should not be submerged for longer than 20 minutes or they will discolor. Carefully peel the membrane from the inside of each shell. I find that my fingers are the best tool for this: Simply gently roll the membrane between your index finger and the shell. Store the shells in the egg cartons to allow to dry completely. (The dried egg shells will keep indefinitely.)

To cook the eggs: Place the 10 eggs in a pot large enough to hold them in a single layer and cover with cold water. Bring to a boil over medium heat. As soon as the water comes to a boil, put a lid on the pot, turn off the burner, and let stand for 10 minutes. Combine 2 cups of ice and 2 cups of water in a bowl to form an ice bath. After 10 minutes, transfer the eggs to the ice bath to stop them from cooking (the colder the ice bath, the easier the eggs will be to peel). Once cooled, peel and separate the yolks and whites.

In a blender, combine ½ cup of the mayonnaise, the cooked yolks, the mustard, 1 tablespoon water, the vinegar, paprika, and cayenne and blend on low speed until smooth. The mixture should have the consistency of store-bought mayonnaise. If it is too stiff, add another tablespoon of water or mayonnaise. Season with salt to taste. Transfer to a pastry bag fitted with a medium round tip. (Alternatively, you may use a resealable plastic bag and cut a ¼ inch off one corner to form a makeshift piping bag.) Refrigerate until final egg assembly. (The yolk mixture will hold in the refrigerator for up to 24 hours.)

Pass the cooked egg whites through a fine-mesh strainer into a bowl and add the remaining ½ cup of the mayonnaise and the lemon juice. Mix well and season with salt and pepper. Transfer to a pastry bag and refrigerate until final egg assembly. (The white mixture is best prepared the same day.)

To assemble the deviled eggs, use egg cartons to keep the shells stable. Pipe the egg white mixture about halfway up each shell. Next, pipe in the yolk mixture, filling another one-quarter of the way up the shell. Garnish with the fennel fronds and basil and serve. ∗

Slow-Roasted Porchetta

Serves 12, with leftovers

This leg of pork is the culmination of many years of perfecting an age-old technique: slow-roasting heritage pork overnight for a late Easter lunch the next day. Aside from the long, slow roasting, two things help make this a spectacular dish: first is the quality of the meat, with the skin left intact; second is the brining. We use local Berkshire hogs in our restaurants. Unlike industrial pigs, heritage breeds have not been genetically selected to grow fast and lean. Instead, they have a greater amount of intramuscular fat, resulting in a sweet, flavorful meat. In sourcing heritage breed hogs from a farmer we trust, we know that we're getting an animal that has been raised and processed with care. No matter what kind of pork you use, be sure to brine it. The brining seasons the meat while highlighting its natural flavors. It also helps to break down the muscular fibers, resulting in a more tender finished product. You can also add aromatics to the brine such as bay leaf, celery leaves, raw onion, garlic, coriander seeds, and black peppercorns—these are all optional. This dish can also be prepared with a pork shoulder or butt, but the presentation won't be as dramatic, and you won't get the terrific crispy crackling. The actual effort involved in the cooking is minimal, and the aroma of the pork roasting is sublime.

9 cups kosher salt for brining, plus 1 tablespoon for the spice mixture

1 (15-pound) whole leg of pork, bone-in, skin-on

1 cup fennel seeds

2 tablespoons crushed red pepper flakes

8 garlic cloves

2 cups freshly squeezed lemon juice (about 10 lemons)

2 cups spicy olive oil, such as Arbequina

One week prior to cooking, brine the pork: You can ask your butcher to brine the leg for you, or do it yourself: Dissolve 3 cups salt in 2 gallons cold water in a 5-gallon bucket. After the salt is dissolved, add ice to bring the water up to the 3-gallon mark to ensure that the brine is very cold. Place the whole leg in the brine and refrigerate for up to a week. (If refrigerator space is a consideration, a sturdy 5-gallon bag, sealed tightly, would also work.) I like to change the brine every couple of days, using up to 9 cups of salt.

The night before serving the pork, preheat the oven to 450° F. Remove the leg from the brine and allow it to air dry, or pat dry with paper towels. With a sharp paring knife, make parallel incisions about 1 inch apart the length of the pork through the skin and fat of the leg almost to the meat. Repeat, covering the entire skin side of the leg with the incisions.

Lightly toast the fennel seeds in a dry large nonstick pan over medium heat until just fragrant; let cool. In a food processor, pulse the cooled fennel seeds, red pepper flakes, garlic, and the 1 tablespoon salt until roughly chopped. Generously press the spice mixture into the incisions in the leg.

Place the leg of pork in a roasting pan and roast for 45 minutes. The pork should be deep golden brown in color and very aromatic. Mix the lemon juice with the oil and pour over the browned pork leg. Turn the oven down to 225° F and continue to roast for about 12 hours. Baste with the pan juices every few hours, if you like, or just leave it to cook. In the morning I will baste a few times. Check the pork frequently after 11 hours; the meat should fall off the bone and the skin should be a deep golden brown. Reserve 1 cup of the pan juices for the vinaigrette for the Fresh Pea and Fennel Salad (page 156) if you like.

To serve, remove the crackling skin and then pull the meat with a fork into long pieces. Drizzle the pork with the remaining pan juices, or serve the jus on the side. Serve the crackling skin, cracking it into pieces if you wish, as a garnish with the pork (some think it the best part). ★

Clockwise from top left: Slow-Roasted Porchetta | Potatoes Boulangère
Roasted Asparagus and Farm Egg Emulsion | Braised, Pureed, and Raw Beets with Spring Leaves and Herbs

Potatoes Boulangère

Serves 12

My Georgia grandmother, Mae B. Stiles, was both environmentally aware and health conscious long before these qualities became fashionable. Her environmentalism was pragmatic—her goal was to create no waste. She burned, composted, buried, and recycled. I was amazed at her dedication to this task. She even recycled her vegetable poaching liquids, using them as her drinking water. As a child, this practice horrified me.

I do remember one of her dishes fondly: a casserole of sliced potatoes, not necessarily thin, with white onions and country ham. This was baked in a casserole dish with chicken broth and whole milk until all the components were soft and the top was golden brown. My grandmother served it as a main dish.

I think my affection for the dish we now call Potatoes Boulangère ("baker's wife's potatoes") stems from this food memory. The recipe, which I have developed over time, replaces the milk of my grandmother's casserole with a rich chicken stock. And, although we usually do not do it in the restaurants, at home I have been known to stud the potatoes with a little ham, for memory's sake.

1 teaspoon olive oil

3 sweet onions (such as Vidalia), sliced

8 garlic cloves, thinly sliced

Kosher salt

8 fresh thyme sprigs, stemmed, plus more for garnish

Freshly ground pepper

4 cups Chicken Stock (page 244)

10 medium Yukon gold or other waxy potatoes, peeled

½ cup (1 stick) cold butter, cubed

Preheat the oven to 350° F.

In a large sauté pan over low heat, combine the oil, onions, and garlic and sprinkle with salt. Cook until translucent, about 10 minutes, being careful not to brown the onions. Add the thyme and adjust the seasoning with salt and pepper.

Warm the stock in a medium saucepan over low heat. Thinly slice the potatoes by hand or using a mandoline with a safety guard. In a 9 x 13-inch casserole, alternately layer the potatoes and cooked onions, overlapping the slices slightly in each layer. For each layer, season with salt and pepper, add a little warm stock to cover them, and dot with a few cubes of butter.

Bake, uncovered, for about 2 hours, or until the potatoes are fork tender. If the potatoes are browning too quickly, cover with parchment and aluminum foil, removing the parchment and foil for the last 15 minutes of cooking. This dish is best served warm but will reheat well. Garnish with more thyme leaves just before serving. ⋆

Braised, Pureed, and Raw Beets with Spring Leaves and Herbs

Serves 12

When I first started cooking in the early eighties, beets were a hard sell, even in San Francisco. Diners seemed to equate them with the taste of soil and the texture of rubber. Negative associations with canned beets may have been the culprit. Today, beet salads are a bestseller in our restaurants. Beets grow year-round at Summerland Farm, but the young beets that we harvest in the spring are the sweetest and most tender. This salad combines cooked beets in both whole and pureed form as well as an assemblage of raw spring vegetables. It tastes as wonderful as it looks. For the garnishes, we like to highlight whatever is in season; the list below is simply a suggestion. We intentionally place the garnishes in a random fashion, and finish the dish with olive oil, salt, and pepper. Use your imagination, and your garden—or your local farmers' market—for inspiration.

Braised Beets and Beet Puree

3 to 4 pounds (30 to 40) mixed baby beets, washed and trimmed of roots and greens

Kosher salt

Freshly ground pepper

1 tablespoon red wine vinegar

1 tablespoon honey

1 ½ teaspoons olive oil

For the Vinaigrette

1 tablespoon honey

1 shallot, finely diced

1 teaspoon diced crystallized ginger

2 tablespoons grapeseed oil

Kosher salt

Freshly ground pepper

For the Garnish

Thinly sliced small chioggia (candy-striped) beets, small radishes, small carrots, spring onion or scallion, and/or small fennel bulb

Fresh herb leaves such as fennel fronds, Thai basil, red ribbon sorrel, baby mint, and/or nasturtium

Drizzle of extra virgin olive oil, preferably a fruity type such as Castelas or Château Virant

Fleur de sel

Freshly ground pepper

To braise the beets: Preheat the oven to 300° F. Place the beets in a baking dish that is large enough to fit them in a single layer. Season with salt and pepper, toss, and add 1 cup water, the vinegar, and honey. Cover the baking dish with a piece of parchment paper and then cover that with a sheet of aluminum foil, crimping it around the edges of the dish.

Braise for 1 to 2 hours, depending on the size of the beets. The beets are done when they can be easily pierced with a paring knife. Remove the beets from the liquid and allow them to cool slightly before peeling. Reserve the braising liquid.

While the beets are still warm, rub off the skins with a clean kitchen towel or paper towels; you may want to wear disposable gloves to keep the beets from staining your hands. Allow the beets to cool completely. Reserve 2 whole beets for the puree. Depending on the size of the remaining beets, slice, quarter, or halve them into bite-sized pieces. Set aside in a large bowl.

To make the puree: Place the reserved whole beets in a blender with ½ cup of the braising liquid, the oil, salt, and pepper. Blend until smooth. Check the seasoning.

To make the vinaigrette: Whisk the honey with 2 tablespoons of the braising liquid. Add the shallot and ginger and whisk. Slowly whisk in the oil to emulsify. Season with salt and pepper. Add the vinaigrette to the braised beets in the large bowl and toss.

To assemble, place a spoonful of puree on a large platter and pull it across the platter with the back of a spoon or offset spatula. Artfully place the cooked beets in a random fashion lengthwise down the platter and garnish with an assortment of fresh spring garnishes, roots, and leaves. Finish the platter with dots of vinaigrette salvaged from the bottom of the bowl, a drizzle of oil, and fleur de sel and pepper. *

Fresh Pea and Fennel Salad

Serves 12

Even the canned peas my mother served us when I was growing up could not squelch my affinity for these little gems. When young and freshly picked, peas barely need to be cooked. For a salad like this, you could simply slice through the pod and serve the whole pea. If fresh-picked peas are not available, frozen are perfectly acceptable. Indeed, I find that fresh peas in the shell that have aged a bit (often in transport or left too long on the vine) become woody and bitter. In that case I am an advocate of the frozen variety. I like to dress this simple salad, a perfect foil for the unctuous pork, with the pan drippings from that dish.

2 cups fresh peas, blanched (or raw if small), or frozen peas

4 small fennel bulbs, cored and thinly sliced, fronds reserved for garnish, plus 2 fennel bulbs for juice

¼ cup freshly squeezed lemon juice (1 to 2 lemons)

2 shallots, thinly sliced

1 teaspoon fennel pollen, plus extra for garnish

1 cup olive oil, or 1 cup pan drippings from the Slow-Roasted Porchetta (page 152)

Kosher salt

Freshly ground pepper

Combine the peas and sliced fennel in a medium mixing bowl and set aside.

To make the fennel juice, remove the fronds from the 2 whole bulbs, and cut the bulbs into pieces appropriate for your juicer tube. Push the stems and bulb through the juicer. If you do not have a juicer, then eliminate this step and double the lemon juice; the vinaigrette will still be delicious.

In another medium bowl, combine the fennel juice, lemon juice, shallots, and fennel pollen. While whisking, slowly add the oil and whisk until just combined. Season with salt and pepper. Add to the peas and fennel, toss well, and adjust the seasoning. Transfer to a serving bowl and garnish with the fennel fronds and a pinch of fennel pollen. Serve immediately. ⋆

Roasted Asparagus and Farm Egg Emulsion

Serves 12

Jumbo California asparagus, the young, sweet, and tender member of the lily family, has become our much-anticipated harbinger of spring. We order four or five containers (each is 1,200 pounds) of jumbo asparagus from a farmer in California who harvests and ships the same day. It's an exception to our preference for local produce, but the quality is unparalleled. By mid-March, our guests begin calling to find out when we will receive the first shipment. During the short season, our restaurants highlight the asparagus in amuse-bouches, side dishes, and even desserts. And not one peel or stem is discarded. Fresh asparagus can be eaten raw—without peeling or blanching—but it's also delicious roasted and served with a simple egg emulsion. The simplicity of this recipe demands that you use the best asparagus and eggs you can find.

2 pounds jumbo California asparagus

2 tablespoons olive oil

Kosher salt

Freshly ground pepper

1 cup (2 sticks) butter

4 large egg yolks

1 large egg

5 tablespoons freshly squeezed lemon juice

Preheat the oven to 400° F.

Remove the tough ends of the asparagus by breaking them—a simple snap of the stem offers the perfect breaking point. On a baking sheet, toss the asparagus with the oil and season with salt and pepper; arrange in a single layer. Roast for 10 minutes, until crispy outside but still al dente.

Meanwhile, melt the butter slowly in small saucepan over low heat; keep warm. In a blender, combine the egg yolks, whole egg, and lemon juice and blend on low. While the blender is running, slowly drizzle in the warm melted butter. The sauce should be the consistency of soft whipped cream. If the emulsion is too thick, you can add warm water to adjust the consistency. Season with salt and pepper.

To serve, arrange the warm asparagus on a platter and pour the emulsion over the top. ★

Thyme Onion Rolls

Makes 36 rolls

Dorothy, our baker, created these rolls for the burger we serve at Abattoir. The sweet yet savory soft roll has since become a favorite dinner roll from our bakery at Star Provisions as well. This recipe is easy to make at home, even if you aren't an expert baker, and the result is head and shoulders above frozen, store-bought rolls.

For the Sponge

1 ½ tablespoons dry yeast

½ cup warm water

1 cup warm milk

½ cup granulated sugar

2 cups bread flour
or high-gluten flour

For the Caramelized Onions

1 tablespoon olive oil

1 large white onion, thinly sliced

Kosher salt

For the Dough

½ cup honey

4 large eggs

4 cups all-purpose flour,
plus extra for dusting

1 tablespoon chopped fresh thyme leaves

2 teaspoons fine sea salt

½ cup (1 stick) soft butter,
plus extra for greasing the pans

To make the sponge: Mix the yeast, water, milk, sugar, and flour in a large bowl by hand until combined—this will be very loose. Let sit, uncovered, for 1 hour in a warm place, such as an upper shelf over your stove.

To make the caramelized onions: Place the oil and onions in a large, heavy-bottomed sauté pan over low heat. Lightly salt the onion to help draw out the moisture. Allow the onion to caramelize slowly, stirring frequently; it will take about 1 hour for the onion to become deep brown. The goal is to gain color without burning. Adjust the seasoning with salt, then set aside and let cool. Makes about ¼ cup.

To make the dough: In the bowl of a stand mixer fitted with a dough hook, combine the sponge, honey, and 3 of the eggs. Mix until thoroughly combined. Add the caramelized onion, flour, thyme, and salt and mix on low until a dough starts to form. Slowly incorporate the butter, 2 tablespoons at a time. Mix for 5 to 7 minutes, until a soft and sticky, but not tacky, dough forms.

Place the dough in a lightly oiled 6-quart bowl and cover with plastic. Allow to double in size at cool room temperature (about 68° F); this will take about 1 hour. (You can make the dough up to this point and store in the refrigerator for up to 2 days or continue with the recipe. If you refrigerate, allow the dough to rest at 68° F for 2 hours before the next step.)

Lightly butter three 9-inch pie pans. To shape the dough, turn it onto a lightly floured surface. Portion into about 36 (1 ½-ounce) pieces, each about the size of a golf ball. We use a scale to portion the dough, but you can eyeball it. Roll into balls by cupping the dough with the palm of your hand while sliding the side of your hand on the board and moving it in a circular motion, putting light pressure on the ball of dough.

Arrange 12 balls in each prepared pie pan as you work: 8 around the outer edge and 4 in the middle. Cover the filled pans with plastic and allow to rise for 45 minutes—they should double in size. (Before you allow the dough to rise you can freeze the pans of rolls, tightly wrapped in plastic. Before baking, allow the rolls to thaw and proof at room temperature until the rolls double in size, about 2 hours.)

Preheat the oven to 350° F. Meanwhile, prepare the egg wash by whisking the remaining egg with 2 tablespoons cold water. Brush the tops of the rolls lightly with the egg wash. Bake for 18 minutes, or until golden brown. Serve immediately, or keep at room temperature; the rolls reheat very well. ★

Thyme Onion Rolls

Angel Food Cake with Macerated Strawberries and Poached Rhubarb

Angel Food Cake with Macerated Strawberries and Poached Rhubarb

Serves 12

My northern grandmother, Anne B. Quatrano, was incredibly stylish, loved to cook, and served everything with flair. Thanks to the china collection she left me, Clifford and I were able to open the first location of Bacchanalia on a very tight budget. Her angel food cake was sublime, and has been a favorite of mine since I was a child. It was, and still is, the birthday cake of choice for everyone in my family. My grandmother cooled the cake by inverting the pan on a bourbon bottle (a wine bottle works too). This trick keeps the airy cake from falling or becoming dense. I cannot think of anything I would rather eat with just-picked strawberries and their juice.

2 cups sifted cake flour

1 teaspoon kosher salt

1 ½ cups granulated sugar

16 large egg whites, at room temperature

2 tablespoons freshly squeezed lemon juice

2 teaspoons cream of tartar

2 teaspoons pure vanilla extract

1 tablespoon finely grated lemon zest

Macerated Strawberries (recipe follows)

Poached Rhubarb (recipe follows)

Preheat the oven to 375° F.

Sift together the flour, salt, and ¾ cup of the sugar onto a piece of parchment paper. Sift again and set aside.

In the bowl of a stand mixer fitted with a whisk attachment, beat the egg whites on low until frothy, then add 2 tablespoons water, the lemon juice, cream of tartar, and vanilla. Gradually increase the mixer speed until the whites begin to mound. In ¼-cup increments, add the remaining ¾ cup sugar, ensuring that the sugar has been fully incorporated before adding more. Beat the whites until they are glossy and form soft peaks; be careful not to overmix. Remove the bowl from the mixer. Fold in the lemon zest.

Sprinkle one-third of the flour-sugar mixture over the egg whites and gently fold with a rubber spatula to incorporate. Repeat two times, making sure the flour-sugar mixture is evenly distributed.

Carefully transfer the batter to an ungreased, very clean 10-inch angel food or tube pan. Use a spatula or a knife to draw through the batter to remove any large air pockets (this method is preferable to banging the pan on the counter to remove air pockets).

Bake for about 45 minutes, until the cake is golden brown and springs back when touched. Allow the cake to cool in the pan, upside down on the neck of an empty wine bottle. Once cooled, run a paring knife around the edges and invert onto your cake stand. (The cake will keep, covered, at room temperature, for a day or two but it is always best the day it is made.) Serve slices of the cake topped with the strawberries and rhubarb. *

Macerated Strawberries

Serves 12

After peaches, strawberries are our next largest crop at Summerland. We plant up to four thousand plants each October, and enjoy the rewards in April and May. We prefer not to refrigerate the berries, so we pick them on the morning we plan to use them. We give them a quick rinse, drain, and mix them with sugar and lemon so they release their beautiful pink juices, which soak into the angel food cake.

2 pounds strawberries, rinsed, hulled, and quartered or halved, depending on size

3 tablespoons granulated sugar

Juice of 1 lemon (about 2 tablespoons)

In a large bowl, combine the strawberries with the sugar and lemon juice. Let them sit for 1 hour, so the strawberries release their liquid. (They will keep refrigerated, covered with plastic wrap, for 1 day.) *

Poached Rhubarb

Serves 12

Fresh rhubarb is tart and delicious. I prefer to poach it very lightly and serve it with both savory and sweet dishes in the spring. This quick poaching method retains the texture of the stalks while removing some of the bitterness. The poaching liquid, with its sweet tang, is also quite versatile. We save it to use it in the Spring Forward Cocktail (page 148) and in savory dishes as well.

4 to 6 large rhubarb stalks

1 cup freshly squeezed orange juice (2 to 3 oranges)

2 cups granulated sugar

½ cup white port

Juice of 1 lemon

To peel the rhubarb, grab the strings between your thumb and a sharp paring knife and pull down to the end of each stalk; repeat all the way around. Reserve the strings. Slice the peeled stalks lengthwise into ¼-inch-wide strips and then cut the strips into 2-inch-long pieces.

In a medium saucepan, combine the rhubarb strings, orange juice, sugar, port, lemon juice, and 1 cup water. Bring to a boil over medium to high heat and let simmer for 2 to 3 minutes. Remove the strings from the liquid and discard. Add the sliced rhubarb to the saucepan, reduce the heat to low, and cook for 1 minute. Transfer the rhubarb with a slotted spoon to a bowl; refrigerate until cool.

Over medium heat, continue to cook the poaching liquid until it is reduced in volume by one quarter. This should take about 10 minutes. Strain the poaching liquid through a fine-mesh strainer into a bowl and let cool. Add the rhubarb back to the liquid and store in the refrigerator, covered or in an airtight container, for up to 1 week. Reserve 1 cup of the poaching liquid and several of the spears of cooked rhubarb for the Spring Forward Cocktail (page 148), if you like. *

The Global South
A Campside Picnic

Serves 10

Abattoir Moscow Mule

Chicharrones | **Roasted Early Summer Squash Salad**

Spicy Pickled Vegetables | **Banh Mi**

Crispy Chickpeas with Cumin Salt | **Korean Beef Jerky**

Looking Glass Creamery Pack Square Cheese,
a brie-style cheese from Fairview, North Carolina, with Baguette (page 242)

Rabbit Rillettes | **Dry-Fried Green Beans**

Torrontes, Chenin Blanc, or Albariño

Fried Blueberry Hand Pies

May brings lovely, warm evenings to Summerland Farm, creating the perfect conditions for an outdoor cocktail party. A few years ago, Clifford and I bought an Airstream trailer. We dream of taking it on the road when we retire, but for now, it is parked at the edge of our garden, between the raised vegetable beds and the peach orchard. Though it sits only a hundred yards or so from the house, we always feel like we're on a mini camping vacation when we have cocktails or dinner by the Airstream. We've built a makeshift, portable "patio" out of wooden shipping pallets and furnished it with anodized metal deck chairs. The chairs are durable, rust-proof, and best of all, they complement the Airstream's silver-toned exterior! For evening entertaining, we string up homemade lanterns made out of votive candles and glass canning jars.

This meal is broadly inspired by Atlanta's cosmopolitan culinary offerings and in particular by the diversity of our own kitchens. Restaurants attract workers with diverse talents, tastes, and backgrounds, and mine are no exception. I want my staff to have the creative freedom to bring their heritage and influences into the kitchen. Their innovations shape our menus in ways that Clifford and I couldn't have imagined by ourselves. You can adapt this approach for your own entertaining as well. If you cook dishes that reflect who you are, you are more likely to enjoy the process. And your guests will feel and taste that love on the plate.

As much as we enjoy our Airstream, we're not suggesting that you need one of your own. You don't even need a farm. This kind of atmosphere can be re-created in your backyard, on your deck, or even on the rooftop of a city apartment. Here, I've presented the food in galvanized buckets, glass jars, on wooden serving planks, and even straight out of the cast-iron skillet. I serve the cocktails in copper mugs, which are the traditional vessel for a Moscow Mule. I also use melamine dinner plates from Thomas Paul and plastic Tervis tumblers. They round out the casual atmosphere and are practical for outdoor entertaining, as they don't chip or break. The best part of this meal is that it is comprised mostly of finger foods. In fact, if you're having guests over for drinks and you don't need to prepare an entire menu, any one or two of these items makes for an impressive cocktail snack. Some of the tastes are unexpected, but we've found them to be instant crowd pleasers, perfect for a warm-weather party under the stars.

Abattoir Moscow Mule

This is a classic cocktail, part of a family of drinks called "mules" or "bucks," made with liquor, ginger beer, and fresh citrus. The Moscow Mule was invented in California in the early 1940s and had spread across the country by the 1950s. It is traditionally served over crushed ice in a copper mug, but it's just as refreshing—if a bit less festive—in a highball or Collins glass. Making your own ginger beer is absolutely worth it. It doesn't take very long to assemble the ingredients, and you won't believe how fresh it tastes. If you don't have a soda charger or siphon, look for a high-quality bottled ginger beer or ginger ale. Our favorite is Fentimans Botanically Brewed Ginger Beer from England, which you can find online or in gourmet markets. Blenheim Ginger Ale, a spicy brand from South Carolina, is a Southern favorite.

Your favorite vodka

Freshly squeezed lime juice

Ginger Beer (recipe follows)

Lime zest

For each cocktail, fill a mug with crushed ice and add 1 ½ ounces vodka and ½ ounce lime juice.

Top with 2 ounces ginger beer and garnish with lime zest.

Ginger Beer
Makes 4 cups

2 pounds fresh ginger, scrubbed well

6 tablespoons raw honey

¼ cup freshly squeezed lime juice

Using a juice machine, juice the ginger and strain well. (Alternatively, you can chop the ginger, puree it in a food processor, and strain out the juice, pressing on the solids to extract all liquid.)

Combine the ginger juice with the honey, lime juice, and 2 generous cups water. Charge the mixture in a soda canister. ⋆

Chicharrones

Serves 20 as a snack

If you are a fan of Southern barbecue, chances are you're familiar with chicharrones—you just know them as "pork rinds" or "cracklins." *Chicharrones* is a Spanish word for the Mexican style of fried pork skins. Nothing tells your guests you love them quite like a light, crispy morsel of rich pig skin that you fried yourself! It's easier than you think to make chicharrones at home. While it isn't a quick process, most of the time is hands off. This recipe will be easiest if you have a food dehydrator. When you're seasoning the finished chicharrones, you could substitute crushed red pepper for the Korean red pepper flakes, but keep in mind that it is significantly hotter and doesn't have the same depth of flavor.

2 pounds pork rind

8 cups peanut oil or pork fat

Kosher salt

Korean red pepper flakes (optional)

Lime (optional)

To braise the rind: Lay the rind on a cutting board and scrape off all visible fat, sinew, and lean meat using a sharp knife. Cut into strips approximately 2 by 4 inches. Place the rind in a large Dutch oven or a slow-cooker with 1 cup water. Cover and cook on the very lowest heat possible, stirring occasionally and adding more water if necessary to make sure the skin does not stick. Cook for about 4 hours, until the rind is soft and supple and has released much of its moisture and gelatin. Drain the rind and transfer to a cutting board, exterior side down. While the rind is still warm, with a sharp knife scrape away any fat and/or gelatin that has released from the rind.

To dry the rind: Set the food dehydrator to 145° F with the fan on medium to medium high. (Alternatively, preheat the oven to 145° F. If your oven does not have a setting this low, set it to 200° F, but leave the oven door slightly ajar, about 2 inches if possible.) Set the skin on the drying racks (or, if using an oven, on stainless-steel cooling racks). Turn the rind over every 4 hours. Let the rind dry until it is brittle to the touch; this will take at least 8 hours and up to 24 hours. (The fully dried rind will keep for several weeks in an airtight container at room temperature.)

To fry the rind: Heat the peanut oil or pork fat in a large stockpot until a deep-fry or candy thermometer registers 350° F. In batches, fry the pieces in the oil until light and crispy. This should take only a minute or two, depending on the size of the pieces. Be sure not to put more than a few pieces in the pot at one time as they expand as much as eight times in size as they fry. Overcrowding also reduces the temperature of the oil, prohibiting the rind from expanding to the full desired size.

Use a spider or tongs to remove the chicarrones from the oil and place on a baking sheet lined with paper towels to drain. Season with salt and red pepper flakes, if using. Some like them with a squeeze of lime as well. ★

Roasted Early Summer Squash Salad

Serves 10

We plant squash in the winter in our hoop house (an unheated greenhouse that traps warmth from the sun), so by early spring, we are already harvesting young summer squash. The delicate vegetables need little cooking—they are tender and sweet on their own. Just a quick toss in a hot pan and then a garnish with fresh basil makes for a quick, delicious salad. This salad can be made up to several hours ahead of serving, but I would let it remain at room temperature instead of refrigerating it. For the squash, I like a mixture of small zucchini, pattypan, sunburst, ronde de Nice, and yellow crookneck. Try a selection of the varieties on offer at your local farmers' market.

2 tablespoons extra virgin olive oil

2 garlic cloves, peeled

2 pounds assorted small squash, cleaned and quartered

Kosher salt

Freshly ground pepper

Torn fresh basil, such as Thai, opal, or lemon

In a 12-inch cast-iron skillet, heat the oil and garlic over low heat. Cook until the garlic is fragrant, then remove it and discard. Increase the heat to medium high and add the squash. Sauté over medium to high heat for just a few minutes, until the squash starts to brown slightly. Remove from the heat and season with salt and pepper. Let cool. (The salad can be made up to a few hours ahead of time. Cover and keep at room temperature; do not refrigerate.) Toss the salad with the basil right before serving. ⋆

Spicy Pickled Vegetables

Makes four half-pint jars

This is a quick-pickled version of the spicy Korean fermented vegetables known as kimchi. Traditional kimchi is made with raw vegetables, which become tender over a long fermenting period. With this preparation, we blanch the chunkier vegetables so that they readily absorb the marinade. You can also substitute your favorite vegetables for the ones listed below.

1 tablespoon kosher salt

1 pound small carrots, peeled and halved

1 pound hakurei or young turnips, halved

1 pound d'Avignon radishes, halved (you may substitute cherry belle or Easter egg radishes)

½ cup roughly chopped peeled fresh ginger

½ cup roughly chopped shallots

¼ cup roughly chopped garlic

½ cup freshly squeezed lime juice (about 6 limes)

½ cup spicy bean paste

½ cup fish sauce (nam pla)

2 tablespoons shrimp paste

1 tablespoon Korean red pepper flakes

1 pound green onions (about 4 bunches), cleaned and cut into 2-inch lengths

Blanch each batch of vegetables in the same pot of boiling water: Season an 8-quart pot filled with 4 quarts water with the salt and bring to a boil over medium to high heat. Prepare an ice bath for shocking the vegetables: Combine 2 cups water and 2 cups ice in a medium bowl.

Blanch the vegetables starting with the carrots: Drop into the boiling water and cook for 2 to 3 minutes, remove with a spider or slotted spoon, and plunge into the ice bath. When cool, remove to a clean dish towel to dry. Blanch the turnips next, followed by the radishes.

In a large mixing bowl, combine the ginger, shallots, garlic, lime juice, bean paste, fish sauce, shrimp paste, and red pepper flakes. Mix well and adjust the seasoning. Add the blanched vegetables and the green onions and toss together until all are well coated. Cover the bowl with plastic wrap and marinate in the refrigerator for 2 hours. Transfer to pint or half-pint glass canning jars, place the lids on, and return to the refrigerator. (The pickled vegetables will keep well in the refrigerator for about 1 week.) ⋆

Banh Mi

Makes 20 sandwiches

The banh mi is a sandwich that dates to the French occupation of Vietnam in the early 20th century. It's a flavorful mash-up of ingredients—the traditional version includes pâté, ham, pickles, cilantro, and chiles on a fresh, airy baguette. In recent years, banh mi have developed something of a cult following in the United States. Popular fillings now include chicken, beef, tofu, vegetables, and pork belly, as we've used here. This is the version that we serve at Star Provisions, and it has become quite popular. The combination of sweet, unctuous, pickled, fresh, and spicy flavors is addictive. Banh mi aficionados agree that a super-fresh baguette is essential to the finished product; if you don't make your own bread, buy the freshest loaves you can find.

For the Sauce

1 cup soy sauce

²⁄₃ cup honey

¹⁄₃ cup fish sauce (nam pla)

2 tablespoons chopped fresh ginger

4 garlic cloves, peeled and smashed

1 jalapeño chile, halved

Juice of 4 limes (about ¾ cup)

For the Pork Belly

1 cup soy sauce

¹⁄₃ cup fish sauce (nam pla)

½ cup maple syrup

4 garlic cloves, crushed

2 jalapeño chiles, roughly chopped

¼ cup chopped or finely grated fresh ginger

¼ cup fresh cilantro leaves, chopped

¼ cup fresh basil leaves, chopped

1 (3-pound) piece pork belly, about 2 inches thick

For the Herb Salad

¼ cup fresh basil leaves

¼ cup fresh cilantro leaves

¼ cup fresh mint leaves

¼ cup thinly sliced red onion

For the Sandwiches

5 freshly baked Baguettes (page 242)

1 cup Homemade Mayonnaise (page 246)

1 cup Spicy Pickled Vegetables (page 171)

2 jalapeño chiles, thinly sliced

1 cucumber, peeled and thinly sliced

To make the sauce: Place the soy sauce, honey, fish sauce, ginger, garlic, jalapeño, and lime juice in a blender and pulse to combine; strain through a fine-mesh strainer into a bowl. The sauce can be made in advance: It will keep, covered in a pint-size glass jar, for up to 2 weeks.

To make the pork belly: Combine the soy sauce, fish sauce, ¼ cup of the maple syrup, the garlic, jalapeño, ginger, cilantro, and basil in a medium bowl. Place the pork belly in a large resealable storage bag, add the marinade, seal the bag, and rub the marinade around the pork belly. Let marinate for 8 hours in the refrigerator if time allows.

Preheat the oven to 300° F. Place the pork belly in a roasting pan and pour the marinade over the belly. Cover with parchment paper and then foil and slow-cook in the oven until fork-tender, about 4 hours. Remove the pork belly and set aside on a plate. Increase the oven temperature to 425° F.

Strain the cooking liquid from the roasting pan through a fine-mesh strainer into a 4-quart saucepan. Add the remaining ¼ cup maple syrup to the saucepan and cook over medium heat until reduced by one-fourth to a glaze consistency, about 10 minutes.

Put the belly back in the roasting pan, brush with the glaze, and bake, uncovered, for 15 minutes, until crispy and brown. Let cool slightly and slice against the grain into ¼-inch slices. (Or refrigerate for up to 4 days with sauce and slice cold.)

To make the herb salad: Combine the basil, cilantro, mint, and onion in a small bowl; set aside until ready to assemble.

To assemble the sandwiches: If you need to reheat the pork belly, place the slices on a baking sheet, brush with some of the sauce, and heat for 10 minutes in a 400° F oven. Slice each baguette into 4 (4-inch) sections. Split each section of baguette down the center, coat one side with mayonnaise, add a few slices of warm pork belly, top with pickled vegetables, herb salad, jalapeño slices, cucumber slices, and a drizzle of the sauce. ⋆

Clockwise from top left: Chicharrones | Roasted Early Summer Squash Salad and Crispy Chickpeas with Cumin Salt
Dry-Fried Green Beans | Crispy Chickpeas with Cumin Salt (made with fresh chickpeas)

Crispy Chickpeas with Cumin Salt

Serves 20 as a snack, about 4 cups

When planning the menu at Abattoir, we wanted a bar snack that was different but addictive. So we soaked, then slow-cooked chickpeas (aka garbanzo or ceci beans), let them dry completely, and deep-fried them until the skins started to come away from the pea. We dusted them with cumin salt and watched them disappear from bowl after bowl; our customers loved them as much as we did. When in season, we also fry fresh chickpeas in the pod. We snip about a ½ inch off the pointed ends of the pods to expose the pea before frying, which allows it to cook more evenly. Then you pull the peas out of their pods using your teeth, just like edamame. Either cooked or fresh, these peas are delicious.

1 pound dried chickpeas

2 bay leaves

1 sprig fresh thyme

3 garlic cloves, crushed

2 tablespoons kosher salt

8 cups peanut oil

1 ½ teaspoons ground cumin

Pick through the dried peas to remove any stones or other debris. Soak in a 2-quart bowl of cold water that covers the peas by at least 4 inches in the refrigerator for 8 hours.

Drain the peas and rinse thoroughly. Place in a 4-quart saucepan and fill with water, again to cover by 4 inches. Add the bay leaves, thyme, and garlic. Bring to a boil over medium to high heat and add 1 tablespoon of the salt. Reduce the heat to a very low simmer—you are looking for a slow cook with very little agitation of the peas. Skim off any foam that rises to the top. Cook the peas slow and low for 2 hours, or until the insides of the peas are creamy. Drain and discard the bay leaves, thyme, and garlic. Cool the peas on a baking sheet at room temperature. (At this point, you can cover and refrigerate the cooked peas for up to a week.)

Make sure the cooked peas are completely dry before frying. If possible, lay them out on a paper towel–lined baking sheet for an hour or so to air-dry completely. To fry the chickpeas, heat the oil in an 8-quart stockpot until a deep-fry or candy thermometer registers 350° F. In batches, carefully add the dry, cooked peas to the oil. A good method would be to use a spider or strainer to lower the peas into the hot oil 1 cup at a time. Fry peas until golden brown, about 5 minutes. The skins of the peas should start to separate and crisp.

In a large bowl, combine the remaining 1 tablespoon salt with the cumin. Once the peas are fried, toss them in the cumin salt immediately. Serve. *

Korean Beef Jerky

Serves 10

None of our picnics is complete without this playful dish, which is our version of Korean barbecue on the fly. It was dreamed up by our Abattoir chef, who is inspired by the dizzying array of international eats along suburban Atlanta's Buford Highway. Clifford and I have a longstanding weakness for Korean barbecue, so this dish is a favorite of ours as well. Instead of cooking strips of raw meat on a tabletop grill, as you would at a Korean barbecue restaurant, we present our guests with richly marinated slices of prepared jerky. The jerky is very tasty on its own, but you can make it into more of a hands-on appetizer by inviting your guests to create lettuce wraps. Serve the jerky and lettuce with a range of traditional garnishes such as Spicy Pickled Vegetables (page 171), Korean soybean paste, toasted sesame seeds, Korean red pepper flakes, sushi rice, sliced jalapeños, and slivered garlic. Be sure to start this dish the day before you plan to serve it, as the spice rub is best left on the meat for a full 24 hours. You should begin with the beef cut into a rectangular shape; your butcher would be happy to do this for you.

1 pound top round

For the Rub

3 tablespoons brown sugar

2 tablespoons ground coriander

2 tablespoons ground black pepper

1 tablespoon plus 2 ½ teaspoons kosher salt

1 tablespoon garlic powder

1 tablespoon dried oregano

1 ½ teaspoons ground ginger

1 ½ teaspoons cayenne

1 ½ teaspoons chili powder

1 ½ teaspoons curry powder

1 ½ teaspoons paprika

For the Glaze

1 cup soy sauce

¼ cup brown sugar

1 tablespoon sesame oil

1 tablespoon chopped garlic

1 tablespoon sesame seeds, toasted

1 tablespoon sherry

1 tablespoon freshly squeezed lime juice

1 tablespoon onion juice (optional)

For the Garnish

1 garlic clove, slivered (optional)

½ teaspoon sesame seeds, toasted (optional)

Freeze the meat for 1 hour to make it easier to slice.

Meanwhile, make the spice rub: In a small bowl, combine the brown sugar, coriander, pepper, salt, garlic powder, oregano, ginger, cayenne, chili powder, curry powder, and paprika.

Trim the meat into a neat rectangular shape, approximately 8 inches long by 4 inches wide by 1 ½ inches thick. Slice the meat against the grain into ¼-inch-thick slices. Rub with the spice mixture on both sides and lay flat on a baking sheet. Refrigerate, uncovered, for 24 hours.

Preheat the oven to 180° to 200° F (or set a food dehydrator to 140° F with the fan on medium). Lay the jerky slices on oiled drying racks in a single layer. Dry in the oven for 30 minutes (or in the dehydrator for 20 minutes). Flip the beef strips and let them continue to dry for another 30 minutes in the oven (or 20 minutes in the dehydrator). Let cool to room temperature. (You can store the jerky in an airtight container for up to several weeks.)

To make the glaze: Preheat the oven to 350° F. In a 2-quart saucepan over medium heat, combine the soy sauce, brown sugar, sesame oil, garlic, sesame seeds, sherry, lime juice, and onion juice (if using). Bring to a simmer to dissolve the sugar, then cook until thickened, about 10 minutes.

Place the jerky on a baking sheet and brush generously with the glaze. Bake until sticky, about 10 minutes. You can serve warm or at room temperature, garnished with the garlic slivers and toasted sesame seeds, if you like. ★

Rabbit Rillettes

Makes four 8-ounce jars

A confit of rabbit is less expected than duck confit, and it's exceptionally delicious. Rabbits tend to be quite lean, so poaching them in duck fat keeps the flesh moist and accentuates the mild flavor of the meat. If you do not have the time to prepare this recipe, but you'd like to serve something similar, potted chicken livers, a country terrine, or a pâté would all be good substitutions. I like to serve this with toast, red onion jam, and flaky sea salt.

2 whole rabbits, quartered

Kosher salt

Freshly ground pepper

4 cups rendered duck fat, homemade or store-bought

4 garlic cloves, peeled

Preheat the oven to 250° F.

Season the quartered rabbits with salt and pepper. In a large ovenproof stockpot or skillet with a tight-fitting lid, melt 1 tablespoon of the duck fat over high heat. Sear the rabbit until lightly browned on all sides. Reduce the heat to medium and add the garlic. Add the rest of the duck fat, covering the meat. Place the lid on the pan, or place a sheet of parchment paper on the surface then crimp a sheet of aluminum foil on top of that to seal the pan.

Place the pan in the oven and cook until the meat falls off of the bone, 3 to 4 hours. Let the meat cool to room temperature in the cooking liquid. Remove the rabbit from the cooking liquid and pick through the meat to remove and discard the bones. Strain the cooking liquid and duck fat through a fine-mesh strainer into a bowl. Reserve 4 tablespoons of the duck fat for sealing the top of the rillettes jars. (Save any leftover fat; it is delicious used to sauté potatoes.)

In a stand mixer fitted with a paddle attachment, mix the rabbit meat, slowly adding about 2 cups of the room-temperature cooking liquid and fat to the desired consistency. It should be like a thick spread such as pâté or room-temperature butter. Spoon the mixture into glass canning jars and pack down, leaving about 1 inch of space at the top. Refrigerate until chilled. Once cool we add a spoonful of melted duck fat to the top of each jar to keep the rillettes moist and prevent them from oxidizing. (The rillettes will keep for 3 to 4 weeks in the refrigerator.) Serve rillettes at room temperature with crusty bread. ★

Dry-Fried Green Beans

Serves 10

My mother used to make these green beans, and we always assumed she had burnt them by accident. (In fact, the name of this recipe is something of a euphemism.) I am still not sure that was not the case, but as an adult, I crave them. My staff made fun of these homely looking green beans until they tasted them. The sweet, caramelized, and crusty dark beans with crispy centers pair well with the lightly browned garlic, and the salt brings it all together. I make them whenever I have filet beans, snap beans, or pole beans—any fresh bean will work. They are excellent hot from the pan and also at room temperature. If you're entertaining, go ahead and make them a few hours ahead of time. As with the squash salad, just keep the cooked beans at room temperature rather than refrigerating them.

2 tablespoons olive oil

2 pounds fresh green or pole beans, ends trimmed

4 garlic cloves, thinly sliced

Sea salt

Freshly ground pepper

Heat a 12-inch cast-iron pan over medium to high heat. Add the oil and beans and sauté for 10 to 15 minutes, until dark brown, tossing frequently to ensure they don't burn. Reduce the heat to low, add the garlic, and cook for just a minute or so. The garlic will cook quickly; you just want it lightly browned, not burnt. Transfer the beans to a serving bowl and season with salt and pepper. ★

Fried Blueberry Hand Pies

Makes 12 pies

Every Southerner with a sweet tooth loves a hand pie. It's a half-moon-shaped pocket of dough wrapped around a fruit or custard filling, then baked or fried. You can pick it up and devour it in a few bites—no utensils necessary. Our pastry chef, Carla Tomasko, grew up in Ecuador, where the meat, cheese, and vegetable hand pies called empanadas are ubiquitous. Now, we make both savory and sweet hand pies at our restaurants. For these desserts, we used preserved blueberries that we had put up the year before. Depending on the season and availability of blueberries in your area, you can use fresh berries or preserves.

1 ½ cups all-purpose flour, sifted

1 teaspoon salt

¼ cup chilled lard or unsalted butter

2 cups blueberries, fresh (rinsed) or frozen

¼ cup granulated sugar

1 tablespoon freshly squeezed lemon juice

1 teaspoon cornstarch

Pinch of kosher salt

4 cups peanut oil

½ cup superfine sugar

Sift together the flour and salt into a large bowl. Incorporate the lard or butter into the flour using your hands. Once well incorporated, add ¼ cup cold water and mix; the dough will seem dry, but will come together into a ball when pressed together. Form a ball with the dough, wrap in plastic wrap, and let rest for 15 minutes (or refrigerate for up to 2 days until ready to use).

Meanwhile, if you are using fresh or frozen blueberries, place a 4-quart saucepan over medium heat, add the blueberries, granulated sugar, lemon juice, cornstarch, and salt and cook just until the blueberries start to soften, about 5 minutes. Remove the blueberries with a slotted spoon and simmer the cooking liquid for 5 minutes. Return the blueberries to the syrup and let cool completely before assembling the pies. (Alternatively, you could use 2 cups of a blueberry preserve that you have put up at an earlier date.)

On a lightly floured surface, roll out the dough to an ⅛-inch thickness and cut out twelve 5-inch rounds. To assemble, place 2 tablespoons of the filling in the middle of each dough round. Brush the edge of each round with water, fold in half, and crimp the edges together with a fork to seal. (You can freeze the uncooked pies, tightly covered with plastic wrap, for up to several weeks, then fry them straight from the freezer.)

To fry, heat the oil in a large stockpot until a deep-fry or candy thermometer registers 350° F. In batches, slip the pies into the oil, being very careful not to splash. Do not fry more than 6 pies at a time to avoid reducing the temperature drastically. Fry until golden brown, about 5 minutes. Drain on paper towels and dust with superfine sugar. These pies are great warm or at room temperature. If you are serving them at room temperature, do not hold them covered or they will become soggy. ★

★

June

Here Comes the Bride

A Masked Tea Party

Serves 50

Sweet Tea Cocktail | *Prosecco*

Date Relish and Parmesan on Baguette | **Farm Egg Tea Sandwiches**

Caramelized Onions, Olive Soil, and White Anchovies on Dark Bread

Watermelon Radish and Cultured-Butter Tea Sandwiches

Cucumber and Herbed Goat Cheese Tea Sandwiches

Lobster Brioche Rolls

Country Ham and Preserves on Buttermilk Biscuits

Salt-and-Pepper-Cured Beef Tenderloin Crostini

White and White Cookies | **Mr. and Mrs. Cupcakes**

Peach Semifreddo

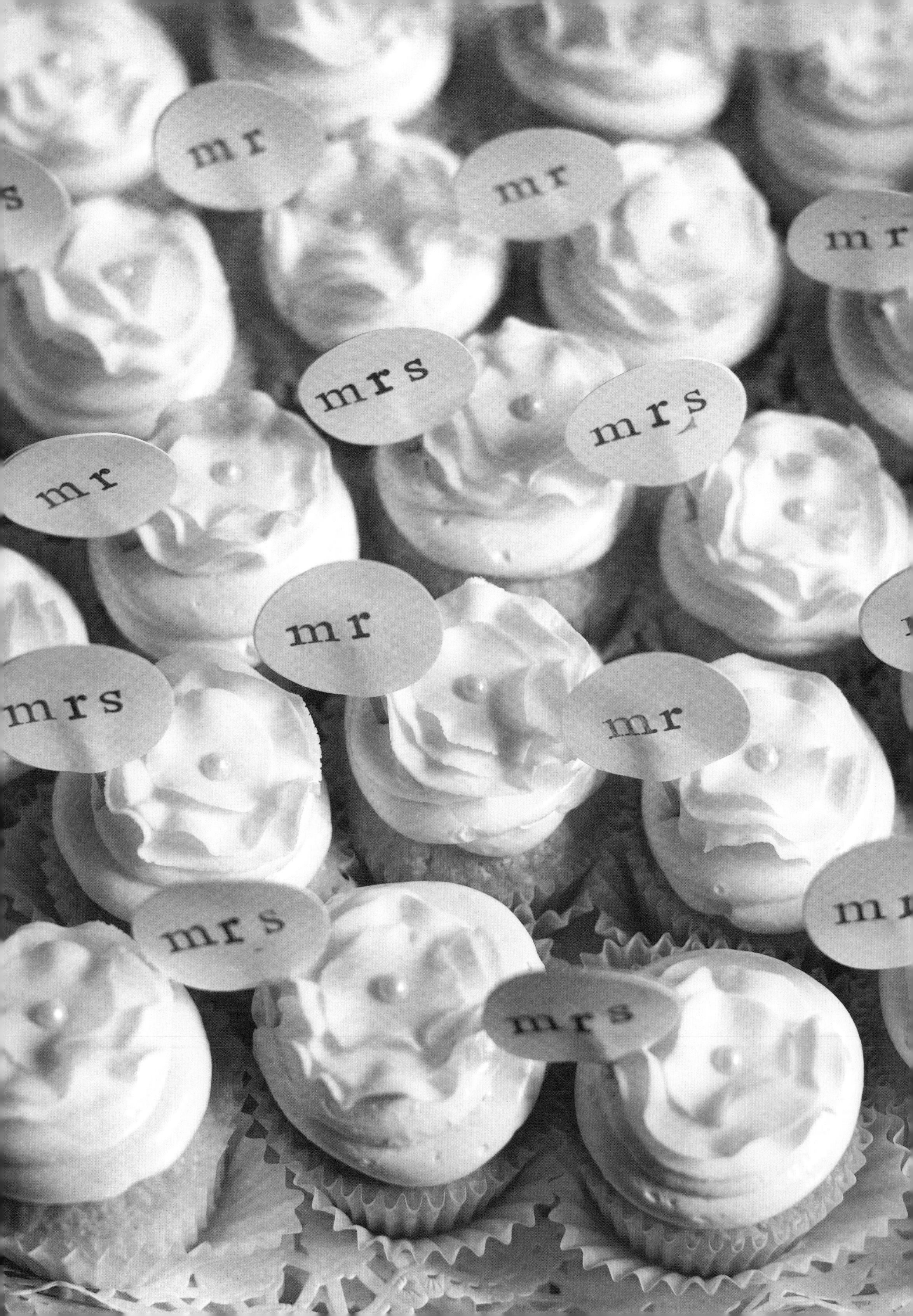
mr
mr
mrs
mrs
mr
mr
mrs
mr
mrs
mrs

As luck would have it, we had six wedding engagements among our employees last year—and most of them were to fellow staff members! (The restaurant business demands long hours and late nights, and as a result, many of us, myself and Clifford included, find our mates on the line or in the front of the house.) Because their engagements came so close on the heels of one another, I thought it would be fitting to celebrate them all at once with a tea party at Summerland Farm.

We designed invitations and gave ten to each couple, to invite their family and friends. I rounded out the crowd with the managers and kitchen staffs of each of our restaurants, allowing the couples' families and "work families" to come together. It was a diverse bunch, with many parents and siblings traveling from afar to converge on the farm. And (to no one's surprise) the guests let loose, and quite the party ensued.

When I plan an event—even if it's just a small dinner party—I think of the menu, table setting, and overall atmosphere as inseparable. For this party, the visual aspects were particularly important. I asked all of the guests to wear white, which matched the decorations and the desserts. It also provided a striking effect with the animal masks that the guests were invited to wear for photographs. The masks were dramatic and almost a bit creepy, like something from another era. I brought a sofa from the house out to the garden—which I often do for summer entertaining—and asked Brian Woodcock, our talented photographer-friend from Atlanta, to shoot portraits of the couples.

The food was classic tea party fare with some updated flavors. A menu like this lends itself to a variety of summer events, from a graduation lunch to a semi-formal afternoon wedding. We served on stylish, recycled-paper plates from a Japanese company called Wasara, and the drinks in reusable plastic, stemless glasses from Govino. The finger-food-only menu eliminated the need for flatware, and each guest was given a linen hemstitched luncheon napkin to combat errant bits of egg salad or chunks of lobster.

We prepared all of the food in advance—most of the sandwich fillings keep well in the refrigerator for a day or two—and assembled the sandwiches just before the party, letting them come to room temperature. By the time the guests arrived, the sandwiches were fresh and ready to go. And just as importantly, so were the hosts.

Sweet Tea Cocktail

In the South, you can't have a garden party—or any summer get-together, for that matter—without sweet tea. This is a sweet tea–based cocktail with a kick of white whiskey. The white whiskey has a smooth, clean flavor, perfectly suited to a daytime cocktail.

For the tea, we use Harney & Sons, but any orange pekoe tea will work. We suggest a ratio of one ounce of bagged tea to a gallon of water. In the summer, the easiest brewing method is to combine the tea and water in a large glass jar or pitcher, cover the top, and leave it in the sun for a few hours. If you don't have time to make sun tea, you can of course pour hot water over the tea bag. Or, if you have a cold-brewing device, such as a Toddy, you could put it to use in this recipe. After making a great deal of iced tea in our restaurants, we've discovered a couple of tricks for optimal flavor. When we remove the tea bag from the water, we never use our hands, because it can lend an unpleasantly bitter flavor to the finished tea. Instead, we use tongs or a slotted spoon. Second, we never squeeze the bag back into the tea when we remove it, as we find that also causes bitterness.

For the engagement party, we served these cocktails in plastic stemless wineglasses from Govino. They are great for a large party, as they don't break and can be washed and used again. And if a few glasses do happen to wander off, they are easily replaceable. However, for a smaller crowd or a slightly more formal event, you could use "real" stemless wineglasses, highball glasses, or mint julep cups.

Brewed orange pekoe tea, cooled

Whiskey (preferably American Spirit white whiskey)

Simple Syrup (recipe follows)

Freshly squeezed lemon juice

Lemon slices, for garnish

To make one cocktail, combine 3 ounces tea, 1 ½ ounces whiskey, ¾ ounce simple syrup, and ½ ounce lemon juice in a tall cocktail shaker filled with ice. Shake vigorously and pour into a tall glass filled with fresh ice. Garnish with a slice of lemon. ∗

Simple Syrup
Makes 2 ⅔ cups

2 cups granulated sugar

Heat the sugar and 2 cups water in a medium saucepan over medium heat, stirring, until the sugar is dissolved. Do not bring to a simmer. Remove from the heat, let cool slightly, and store in a lidded glass container in the refrigerator, where it will keep for up to a few weeks. ∗

Date Relish and Parmesan on Baguette

Makes 24 sandwiches

Combining nutty, salty Parmesan cheese with a sweet fruit like dates is a classic, winning combination. The cumin and coriander add a pleasing earthiness to the date relish, which you can make a few days ahead. Top with shards of the best Parmesan cheese you can find— if you have a choice, opt for Parmigiano-Reggiano. If you are preparing this entire menu, these can be the first sandwiches you assemble. They sit well without spoiling, and the flavors are best at room temperature. As with all of these sandwiches, fresh, high-quality bread makes a huge difference. If you aren't going to bake your own baguettes, seek out the freshest ones you can find (ideally, baked that morning) from a local bakery.

1 tablespoon olive oil

1 large onion, sliced

2 cups dates, pitted

½ teaspoon ground cumin

½ teaspoon ground coriander

2 ½ cups tawny port

Kosher salt

¼-pound chunk of Parmesan cheese

2 Baguettes (page 242), cut into 48 round slices

Extra virgin olive oil, for drizzling

Baby arugula

Heat the olive oil in a shallow saucepan over medium-high heat. Add the onion and sauté until it begins to color, about 5 minutes. Add the dates, cumin, and coriander and cook for 2 minutes. Add the port, scraping any browned bits from the bottom of the pan. Cook until the port is reduced by half; the mixture should be sticky and clear. Remove from the heat and cool slightly. Transfer the date-port mixture to the bowl of a food processor and pulse just until smooth. Add salt to taste. (The relish can be covered and refrigerated for up to 3 days.)

Allow the date relish to come to room temperature. Use a vegetable peeler to shave the cheese into curls.

To assemble each sandwich, smear the date puree on one slice of baguette and top with a few curls of cheese. Drizzle with extra virgin olive oil, top with a sprig or two of arugula, and close with another slice of baguette. *

Farm Egg Tea Sandwiches

Makes 24 sandwiches

The quality of the eggs makes all the difference in these egg salad sandwiches. I know I've said it before, but it's worth repeating: In any dish where eggs are the main ingredient, it's essential to use the best ones you can find. Eggs from pasture-raised chickens are higher in protein and have the most richly colored, nearly orange yolks. They also tend to be more flavorful than commercially raised eggs from caged hens. Almost any farmers' market will have at least one vendor selling fresh, local eggs, and they're often available at natural foods stores as well. The couple of dollars' difference you will pay per dozen is well worth it for a healthier, fresher, better-tasting egg.

This egg salad is especially delicious on our homemade old-fashioned white bread (page 243). If you are going to try one bread recipe, this is it. The milk and honey lend a slight sweetness, and the finished loaf is pleasantly dense, with a bit of "bounce." If you want, you can cut the bread into shapes with a biscuit cutter or a cookie cutter before you assemble the sandwiches. Circles, stars, or hearts would all be lovely—just be mindful of a size that is easy to pick up and eat in two or three bites.

10 large eggs

½ cup Homemade Mayonnaise (page 246), plus more as needed

10 cornichons, diced

1 tablespoon minced fresh parsley

Juice of 1 lemon

1 teaspoon white wine vinegar

½ teaspoon smoked paprika

¼ teaspoon cayenne

Kosher salt

Freshly ground pepper

1 loaf White Bread (page 243)

Small celery leaves

Small watercress leaves

Fresh chives, cut into 1-inch lengths

To hard-cook the eggs, place in a saucepan large enough to hold them in one layer and cover with cold water. Bring to a boil over medium heat. As soon as the water comes to a boil, put a lid on the pot and turn off the burner. Let stand for 10 minutes.

Combine 2 cups ice and 2 cups cold water in a bowl to form an ice bath. Transfer the eggs to the ice bath to stop them from cooking. The colder the ice bath, the easier the eggs will be to peel. Once cooled, peel away the shells and finely chop the eggs.

Make the salad in a large mixing bowl: Combine the chopped eggs, mayonnaise, cornichons, parsley, lemon juice, vinegar, paprika, and cayenne. Season with salt and pepper. Add more mayonnaise if you like a smoother filling. Taste and adjust for seasoning.

Cut the bread into 24 slices of 1/4-inch thickness. (Freezing the bread for about 15 minutes makes slicing easier.) Trim the crusts or leave them on, as you like. Cut the slices into rectangles 2 inches by 1 inch. You should have 48 rectangles.

To assemble each sandwich, put 1 tablespoon of egg salad on one slice of bread, top with celery and watercress leaves and chives, and cover with another slice of bread. ⋆

Clockwise from top left: Farm Egg Tea Sandwiches | Caramelized Onions, Olive Soil, and White Anchovies on Dark Bread
Watermelon Radish and Cultured-Butter Tea Sandwiches | Cucumber and Herbed Goat Cheese Tea Sandwiches

Caramelized Onions, Olive Soil, and White Anchovies on Dark Bread

Makes 24 open-faced sandwiches

The bold ingredients in this sandwich would work best on a dark bread, such as a pumpernickel or a homemade dark rye (page 243). Don't be afraid to make the olive soil! Most of the time required to prepare it is totally hands-off. You can turn your oven to the lowest temperature setting and let the olives dehydrate overnight. They add visual interest to the open-faced sandwich, as well as a pleasant kick of salt that contrasts beautifully with the sweetness of the caramelized onions. The white anchovies, called *boquerones* in Spain, are lightly cured in salt and then marinated in vinegar and olive oil. You can buy them in jars or by the pound in specialty stores. If you have leftover olive soil, it would be delicious on pastas, salads, or pizzas.

1 pound pitted Kalamata olives, rinsed and drained

½ loaf Dark Bread (page 243)

¾ cup Caramelized Onions (recipe follows)

24 cured white anchovies, drained on paper towels

Extra virgin olive oil, for drizzling

24 (1-inch) sprigs fresh thyme (preferably lemon thyme)

To make the olive soil: Preheat the oven to 120 to 140° F. (Alternatively, use a food dehydrator set between the 120 and 140° F settings for 6 to 12 hours.) Use paper towels to blot excess oil from the olives. Line a baking sheet with a cooling rack and place the pitted olives on the rack. The olives should not touch the bottom of the pan; air needs to circulate around the olives in order to properly dry them.

Place the pan in the oven and dry the olives for 8 to 12 hours. If your oven does not go below 200° F, then turn the oven off after 1 hour and leave the oven door closed for the remaining 11 hours. The oven should be warm enough to remove all the moisture, but you want to be careful to avoid cooking the olives. The olives should be shriveled and dry to the touch when done. (The olives can be dried ahead of time and keep well for months in an airtight container at room temperature.)

Once the olives are completely dry and cool, transfer to a food processor and pulse to create the soil; you are looking for a consistency of fine potting soil. (The olive soil will keep well in an airtight container for several days.)

To assemble the open-faced sandwiches: Cut the bread into 12 slices of ¼-inch thickness. (Freezing the bread for about 15 minutes makes slicing easier.) Trim the crusts or leave them on, as you like. Cut the slices into rectangles 2 inches by 1 inch. You should have 24 rectangles.

For each open-faced sandwich, smear a teaspoon of the caramelized onion puree in the middle of one slice of bread, top with an anchovy fillet, a drizzle of olive oil, and a sprig of lemon thyme. ★

Caramelized Onions
Yields about 2 cups

2 tablespoons olive oil

4 large white onions, thinly sliced

Kosher salt

Place the olive oil and onions in a large, thick-bottomed sauté pan on medium to low heat. Add 1 teaspoon salt to help draw out the moisture, which will quicken the caramelization. The goal is to gain color without burning the onions: Cook on low, stirring often, for about 1 hour, until the onions are a deep brown color. Adjust the seasoning with salt and cool slightly.

Transfer the caramelized onions to a food processor or blender and puree until smooth. Transfer to a bowl, cover with plastic wrap, and refrigerate until ready to use, up to 3 days. ★

Watermelon Radish and Cultured-Butter Tea Sandwiches

Makes 24 sandwiches

The simplest of the tea sandwiches on this menu also happens to be my favorite. All you taste is the cool fat of the butter and the crunchy heat of the radish, so look for the best of both. I suggest using Watermelon radishes because they are strikingly beautiful when sliced—as their name suggests, they have a green outer ring surrounding a vibrant, hot-pink interior. But practically any kind of radish would work for this sandwich: the cylindrical, red-and-white d'Avignon; the purple, red, or white Easter Egg; or the classic Scarlet Globe. I find most radishes to be spicier in the summer, which I like. But you can choose a variety that dials the heat up or down, depending on your preference. I strongly recommend using a cultured butter—often labeled "European-style"—for these sandwiches. Its higher fat content is a pleasant contrast to the heat of the radishes, and the added culture gives a richer, tangier flavor. If you've never used cultured butter before and you aren't sure what to look for, try the version from Vermont Creamery, which is widely available in grocery stores across the country.

1 loaf White Bread (page 243)

12 Watermelon radishes or 20 cherry belle or d'Avignon radishes

4 tablespoons French-style cultured butter, softened

1 teaspoon fleur de sel

48 leaves (from 1 bunch) watercress

Cut the bread into 24 slices of ¼-inch thickness. (Freezing the bread for about 15 minutes makes slicing easier.) Trim the crusts or leave them on, as you like. Cut the slices into rectangles 2 inches by 1 inch. You should have 48 rectangles.

Slice the radishes very thinly using a mandoline or sharp knife.

To assemble each sandwich, spread a thin coating of butter on 2 slices of bread. Layer one slice with 2 or 3 slices shaved radish, sprinkle with salt, and garnish with 2 watercress leaves. Top with the second slice of buttered bread. ⋆

Cucumber and Herbed Goat Cheese Tea Sandwiches

Makes 24 sandwiches

The combination of cucumber and cream cheese is a classic tea-sandwich filling. Here, we've made it more flavorful with the addition of herbed goat cheese and fresh fines herbes, while keeping some of the cream cheese for spreadability. Look for a creamy goat cheese rather than a crumbly one—if the cheese is packaged in a log or a small tub, it will spread better when combined with the cream cheese.

2 seedless cucumbers

1 cup (about 8 ounces) fresh goat cheese

1 cup (about 8 ounces) cream cheese, softened

2 teaspoons chopped fresh dill

2 teaspoons chopped fresh chives

1 teaspoon chopped fresh tarragon

1 teaspoon chopped fresh chervil

Kosher salt

Freshly ground pepper

1 loaf White Bread (page 243)

Scrub the outside of the cucumber, peel if the skin is thick, and thinly slice using a mandoline or a sharp knife.

In a stand mixer fitted with the paddle attachment, combine the goat cheese, cream cheese, and herbs on low speed; season with salt and pepper.

Cut the bread into 24 slices of ¼-inch thickness. (Freezing the bread for about 15 minutes makes slicing easier.) Trim the crusts or leave them on, as you like. Cut the slices into rectangles 2 inches by 1 inch. You should have 48 rectangles.

To assemble each sandwich, spread a generous 1 tablespoon of the cheese mixture on a slice of bread. Top with 2 or 3 slices of cucumber and add a top slice of bread. ⋆

Clockwise from top left: Lobster Brioche Rolls | Country Ham and Preserves on Buttermilk Biscuits
Peach Semifreddo | Salt-and-Pepper-Cured Beef Tenderloin Crostini

Lobster Brioche Rolls

Makes 32 sandwiches

Lobster rolls are a New England classic, and they are still my favorite things to eat when I visit my father in Connecticut in the summer. In New England, there are two basic varieties of lobster roll, and the debate that rages between their respective proponents is reminiscent of Southerners defending their regional styles of barbecue. Almost all lobster rolls are served on a toasted, buttery brioche bun, but the difference is in the preparation of the lobster meat itself. It can either be mixed with butter and served warm, or tossed with mayonnaise and served cold. I am staunchly opposed to reheating cooked lobster meat, so I fall in the "cold-with-mayonnaise" camp. The quality of the lobster meat will determine the quality of this sandwich. Use fresh lobster, never canned or frozen. If you have time, it's absolutely worth the effort to make your own brioche buns, but if you can't, the best substitute would be to slice a fresh, store-bought loaf of brioche and fold the slices into buns, buttering each one liberally before toasting.

3 (1¼-pound) lobsters

1 cup Homemade Mayonnaise (page 246)

2 ribs celery, peeled and finely chopped

1 teaspoon minced fresh tarragon,
plus whole leaves for garnish

Freshly squeezed lemon juice

Kosher salt

Freshly ground pepper

Brioche Rolls (page 242)

2 tablespoons Clarified Butter (see page 246)

Prepare the lobster: Bring a large pot of water to a rapid boil. Meanwhile, to humanely kill each lobster, insert a sharp knife between the eyes of a lobster and cut straight down the length of the body, stopping at the tail. Cut the tail off the body. Remove the claws by grasping with a kitchen towel and bending them back while twisting. To keep the tail from curling when cooking, insert a skewer into the flesh of the cut side and push it through to the end of the tail. (Discard the bodies or reserve to make lobster bisque. The bodies can be frozen for up to 2 months in a resealable bag.)

Add the claws and tails to the boiling water; you may have to cook the claws and tails separately if your pot is too small. The tails will take 3 to 5 minutes to cook and the claws 5 to 7 minutes, depending on the thickness of the shells. They are done when the shells are a deep orangey red color. Prepare an ice bath while the lobsters are cooking: Combine 4 cups ice with 4 cups water in a large bowl. Plunge the lobster pieces into the ice bath immediately after removing them from the boiling water. Cool completely.

Carefully crack the shells of the claws and remove the flesh with a knife or lobster pick. To remove the flesh of the tail, squeeze the tail to release the meat and pull through the cut

side. Finely chop all of the lobster meat. You should have approximately 1 pound.

To make the salad: combine the chopped lobster, mayonnaise, celery, and minced tarragon in a medium bowl. Mix well and season with lemon juice, salt, and pepper. Taste and adjust the seasoning, if needed. Cover the bowl with plastic wrap and refrigerate until ready to serve. (The lobster salad can be prepared up to 2 hours in advance, but it will become watery if it sits any longer.)

To assemble the sandwiches: cut the rolls apart (as they will have baked together on the baking sheet). The rolls that were on the outer edge of the baking sheet will have an outer crusty edge; I like to trim this off so that all the rolls will toast evenly. Make a slit in the top of each roll from end to end three quarters of the way through the roll. In a 14-inch nonstick pan, melt 1 tablespoon of the clarified butter over low heat. Working with half of the rolls, brown both sides in the pan, turning. Repeat with the remaining butter and rolls. Push open the slit in the top of the roll and insert 1½ tablespoons of lobster salad. Garnish each roll with a tarragon leaf. ✴

Country Ham and Preserves on Buttermilk Biscuits

Makes 32 sandwiches

This is another recipe with a short list of simple ingredients whose quality makes all the difference. The combination of sweet fruit and salty ham on a fresh, fluffy biscuit is irresistible. I encourage you to make your own strawberry preserves. If you've never made them before, you will be impressed by the fresh, ripe taste and texture of the finished product. The old-fashioned French method we suggest here takes four days from start to finish, but it requires very little hands-on time. If you are not inclined to can your own preserves, look for a brand made in small batches using fresh, whole fruit. For the country ham, we always use Benton's from Madisonville, Tennessee, which is available by mail order.

2 pounds (3 pints) strawberries, rinsed and hulled

2 cups granulated sugar

32 Buttermilk Biscuits (page 244)

4 tablespoons butter, softened

32 thin slices of country ham or prosciutto, about 1 pound

To make the strawberry preserves: Combine the strawberries and sugar in a medium bowl and cover with plastic wrap. Let stand at room temperature for 12 to 24 hours to macerate.

Transfer the strawberries to a 4-quart saucepan and bring to a boil over medium heat. Reduce the heat to low and simmer gently for 5 minutes. Remove from the heat and let cool. Transfer to a glass bowl, cover with plastic wrap, and refrigerate for 12 to 24 hours.

The next day, repeat the process of simmering the strawberries gently for 5 minutes, cooling, and refrigerating for 12 to 24 hours. Repeat this process one more time. Do not stir during the repeated cooking in order to keep the strawberries intact. After the third cooking, put the preserves in 2 pint-size jars that have been sterilized. Refrigerate for up to 3 months.

To assemble each sandwich: Cut a biscuit in half and spread with a thin layer of butter. Fold a slice of country ham or prosciutto on the bottom half and top with a teaspoon of preserves. Cover with the top half of the biscuit. ★

Salt-and-Pepper-Cured Beef Tenderloin Crostini

Makes 48 sandwiches

Here's a secret: Most chefs aren't crazy about beef tenderloin. In general, they believe its so-so flavor is undeserving of the inflated price tag. However, if you cure a beef tenderloin before cooking it, it's a different story. This salt-and-pepper cure forms a delicious, pleasantly crunchy crust that contrasts nicely with the medium-rare interior. It's fair to call this the least feminine of the tea sandwiches on this menu—when we served them at the engagement party, the male guests in particular couldn't get enough of them! A bonus: All of the components can be prepared in advance, and leftover aioli and pickled onions would be delicious on practically any kind of sandwich.

For the Pickled Red Onions

3 cups red wine vinegar

3 cups granulated sugar

1 tablespoon allspice

1 tablespoon kosher salt

2 teaspoons black peppercorns

2 star anise

2 cloves

4 fresh or dried bay leaves

5 red onions, very thinly sliced

For the Balsamic Aioli

3 large egg yolks

1 large egg

4 garlic cloves, peeled

Juice of 2 lemons

2 tablespoons balsamic vinegar

2 cups canola or peanut oil

Kosher salt

Freshly ground pepper

For the Cured Beef

2 tablespoons kosher salt

2 tablespoons cracked black pepper

2 tablespoons fresh thyme leaves, roughly chopped

1 (3-pound) tenderloin of beef, trimmed

1 tablespoon olive oil

For the Sandwiches

2 Baguettes (page 242), cut into 48 slices

Fleur de sel

Cracked black pepper

48 small sprigs fresh thyme

To make the pickled red onions: In a 4-quart saucepan, combine the vinegar, sugar, allspice, salt, peppercorns, star anise, cloves, and bay leaves. Bring to a boil over medium heat, then lower to a simmer and cook for 5 minutes. Add the onions to the simmering liquid, in batches if necessary, and cook for 1 minute. Transfer the onions with a spider or slotted spoon to a bowl and let stand for 5 minutes or until cooled slightly. Bring the vinegar back to a simmer and repeat, cooking the onions for 1 minute, then removing to the bowl to cool for 5 minutes. Repeat one more time, then let the onions cool completely. This process allows the onions to pickle without overcooking so they remain crisp. Cool the pickling liquid in the refrigerator, uncovered. When cool, add the onions, cover, and store in the refrigerator. (The pickled onions will keep for several weeks in the refrigerator.)

To make the balsamic aioli: Place the egg yolks and whole egg in the bowl of a food processor and pulse. Add the garlic and pulse until chopped, then add the lemon juice and vinegar. With the machine running, slowly add the oil through the feed tube until the mixture thickens. If it becomes too thick, add a teaspoon of water. Season with salt and pepper. Cover and refrigerate until ready to use. (The aioli can be made up to 2 days in advance.)

Make the cured beef: Combine the salt, pepper, and thyme and rub on all sides of the tenderloin. Place on a stainless-steel rack over a baking sheet and refrigerate, uncovered, for 24 hours.

Coat a grill grate or grill pan with the oil and prepare for high heat. Cook the tenderloin on all sides until the internal temperature reaches 120 to 125° F for medium rare, or to your preference. Let the meat rest for at least 20 minutes at room temperature before serving. (If you wish to hold it longer, wrap the meat and keep it in the refrigerator, where it will keep for up to 3 days—although this will be best if you serve the day you cook. Remove the meat from the refrigerator about 1 hour before serving in order to bring it to room temperature.) Cut the tenderloin into ¼-inch slices.

To assemble each open-faced sandwich, place a slice of beef on top of 1 slice of baguette. Add a small dollop of aioli (about ½ teaspoon), and small spoonful of pickled onions. Sprinkle with fleur de sel and cracked black pepper and top with a sprig of thyme. ★

White and White Cookies

Makes 12 cookies

Inspired by the largely white color scheme of this party, we created a riff on the classic black-and-white cookie—an iconic staple of New York's Jewish delis: half plain white icing and half white chocolate icing. This is an easy recipe to follow and yields a cakey, crumbly cookie. If you do want to make a black and white cookie, simply substitute regular chocolate for the white chocolate. This recipe can easily be doubled for a crowd.

For the Cookies

½ cup granulated sugar

4 tablespoons European-style, high-fat butter (preferably Plugra), softened

¼ cup crème fraîche or sour cream

2 tablespoons heavy cream

1 large egg

½ teaspoon pure vanilla extract

1 cup all-purpose flour

⅜ teaspoon baking soda

⅛ teaspoon kosher salt

For the Icing

2 cups confectioners' sugar

3 tablespoons whole milk, plus extra if needed

1 tablespoon freshly squeezed lemon juice

2 teaspoons light corn syrup

2 ounces white chocolate, chopped

Preheat the oven to 325° F. Line a 12 x 18-inch baking sheet with parchment paper. Use a pencil to trace 2-inch circles evenly spaced on the parchment paper (3 across and 4 down), and then spray with nonstick cooking spray.

To make the cookies: Beat the granulated sugar and butter in a stand mixer fitted with the whisk attachment on medium speed until light and fluffy, about 5 minutes. In a separate medium bowl, combine the crème fraîche, cream, egg, and vanilla and whisk lightly. Add this to the sugar-butter mixture and beat on medium speed until incorporated. Combine the flour, baking soda, and salt in a small bowl, then add to the batter. Beat on medium speed until smooth, 2 to 3 minutes.

Spread 2 tablespoons of batter onto each 2-inch circle on the prepared baking sheet. Bake the cookies for 10 to 12 minutes, until a toothpick inserted in a center comes out clean. Remove to a cooling rack. Cool completely before icing.

To make the icing: Mix the confectioners' sugar, milk, lemon juice, and corn syrup in a medium bowl. Transfer half to a separate bowl. To melt the white chocolate, place in a glass or ceramic bowl and heat in a microwave oven on medium power for 20 seconds; repeat if needed. Add the melted white chocolate to one portion of the icing and combine thoroughly, adding milk if needed to adjust the consistency; it should be loose, almost pourable.

Spread the plain white icing on half of each cookie and allow to set, about 10 minutes. Spread the white chocolate icing on the other half of each cookie and allow to set. The cookies may be made in advance but are best served the same day. Once the icing has set they can be stored in an airtight container. ★

Mr. and Mrs. Cupcakes

Makes 12 cupcakes

This is our best-selling cupcake at Star Provisions: a moist, white cake topped with cream cheese frosting. We typed "Mr." and "Mrs." using an old-fashioned, typewriter-style font, cut an oval shape around the letters, and affixed them to toothpicks to create miniature flags. You could do the same thing with a wedding date, initials, graduation year, or birthday. And while the simplicity of the white cupcake is elegant, you can always add a few drops of food coloring to the icing if you're serving the cupcakes at a child's birthday, or if your party has a particular color scheme. The two tricks to achieving a moist cupcake are the addition of crème fraîche (or sour cream) and not overbaking. Remove the cupcakes from the oven as soon as the tops look set, as they can overcook quickly and become dry. This recipe can easily be doubled for a crowd.

For the Cupcakes

1 ½ cups all-purpose flour

1 cup granulated sugar

1 ½ teaspoons baking powder

½ teaspoon kosher salt

½ cup (1 stick) butter, at room temperature

½ cup crème fraîche or sour cream

1 large egg, at room temperature

2 large egg yolks, at room temperature

1 teaspoon pure vanilla extract

For the Cream Cheese Frosting

8 ounces cream cheese, at room temperature

1 cup (2 sticks) butter, at room temperature

5 cups confectioners' sugar, sifted

Pinch of kosher salt

1 teaspoon pure vanilla extract

Preheat the oven to 325° F. Line a 12-cupcake pan with white paper liners.

To make the cupcakes: In the bowl of a stand mixer fitted with the whisk attachment, combine the flour, granulated sugar, baking powder, and salt and mix on low until combined. Add the butter, crème fraîche, egg, egg yolks, and vanilla. Mix for about 30 seconds on medium speed. Stop and make sure everything on the bottom has been combined; if not, scrape the bowl and mix for another 20 seconds.

Use a # 20 ice cream scoop or a ¼-cup measure to scoop the batter into the lined cups of the cupcake pan. Bake for about 20 minutes, until the tops spring back when touched or a toothpick inserted in a center comes out clean. Let cool completely before frosting. (Since there is no oil added to the batter of these cupcakes, they will not stay moist long and therefore are best if consumed the day they are baked.)

To make the cream cheese frosting: Combine the cream cheese and butter in the bowl of a stand mixer fitted with a whisk attachment. Beat well on high for at least 5 minutes, until no lumps remain, stopping the mixer often to scrape down the bowl. Add the confectioners' sugar, 1 cup at a time, beating well and stopping the mixer to scrape down the bowl as needed. Add the salt and vanilla extract. (The frosting can be made up to several days in advance; bring it to room temperature and whip until smooth before using.)

Place the frosting in a piping bag fitted with a medium star tip. Pipe in a circular motion to frost each cupcake; you can also hand ice with the back of an offset spatula. ＊

Peach Semifreddo

Makes 25 small cups, about 4 ounces each

This dessert is incredibly easy and makes a beautiful presentation. It comes together quickly, requires few ingredients, and is gluten free—an added bonus these days when you're entertaining a crowd with diverse dietary needs. We macerate fruit instead of cooking it, using granulated sugar and just a bit of lemon juice. This way, the fruit releases its own juices instead of soaking up cooking liquid or simple syrup. If fresh peaches are not in season, it works just as well with any kind of berry. If you freeze it in advance, let it sit long enough to become partially softened before serving.

For the Macerated Peaches

6 peaches, peeled, pitted, and finely diced

Juice of 1 lemon

½ cup granulated sugar

For the Meringue

1 cup egg whites (about 9 eggs)

Pinch of cream of tartar

¾ cup granulated sugar

For the Whipped Cream

1 quart heavy cream

½ cup granulated sugar

Pinch of kosher salt

Fresh mint leaves, for garnish

To make the macerated peaches: Mix the peaches, lemon juice, and sugar together in a medium bowl and let macerate at room temperature for 30 minutes, stirring occasionally to dissolve the sugar. Drain and set aside, reserving the juice and fruit separately.

To make the meringue: In the bowl of a stand mixer fitted with a whisk attachment, whip the egg whites on medium speed until foamy. Add the cream of tartar. Mix 1 minute on medium speed, then increase the speed to high and gradually add the sugar. Continue to whip on high speed until the meringue is glossy and triples in volume. Cover and refrigerate for up to 2 hours.

To make the whipped cream: In the bowl of a stand mixer fitted with a whisk attachment, mix the cream on low speed, then add the sugar and salt. Turn up to high speed and mix until soft peaks form; it should take 5 minutes. Cover and refrigerate for up to 2 hours.

To assemble the semifreddo: If the meringue looks spongy, whip again until glossy. In a large bowl, fold the meringue and whipped cream together. Add the drained peaches gradually in three parts and gently fold. Do not overfold! You are looking for gentle streaks of peach throughout the semifreddo.

Fill 25 (4-ounce) glass cups or small disposable containers with the semifreddo. Freeze for 1 hour. These are best if just slightly frozen, so try to serve just after 1 hour of freezing. If frozen for longer, allow the cups to sit at room temperature for 10 minutes before serving. Drizzle some of the reserved juice from the peaches on top just before serving. Garnish each cup with a mint leaf. ⋆

Red, White, and Blue

Independence Day on the Lake

Serves 20

Watermelon Sangria

Pickled Georgia White Shrimp | **Gazpacho Salad**

Dottie's Skillet Cornbread

Preserved Chanterelle Mushrooms

Todd's Wood-Grilled Summer Sausage | *Cabernet Franc*

Honey-Roasted Peaches with Chamomile Ice Milk

Citrus Shortbread Cookies

Clifford and I both grew up near the ocean: he on the island of Oahu, Hawaii, and I in Fairfield, Connecticut. Both of us loved the beach so much that we would spend virtually the whole summer in the water. When we migrated in our early thirties from Long Island (where, in addition to cooking, we had been quite the beach bums) to northwest Georgia, we experienced quite a shock. The sand and the sea—and the summer holidays they symbolized to us—suddenly felt worlds away. Our first couple of years in Georgia, the Fourth of July came and went without much fanfare on our part. I have always adored fireworks, but somehow the displays in town weren't the same as the waterside celebrations I remembered from my childhood.

Then this past year, we were invited to Chef Drew Belline's family boathouse on Lake Rabun in northeast Georgia. Lake Rabun is deep, cool, and peaceful—everything I want in a midsummer escape. The boathouses on the lake remind me of the camps that line New York's Finger Lakes. The journey is easy, and the day is slow and long. Clifford and I subscribe to a "travel with food" philosophy, so we come prepared to feed.

Friends come and go, filling their plates and stomachs. We relax on the deck, which we decorate with hand-stitched flags in abstract patterns of red, white, and blue—our take on Independence Day bunting. We wait for the sun to fall below the horizon so that the fireworks can begin. The lake is filled with boats overflowing with spectators. The night is clear and the bursts of light, reflected on the water, are spectacular. Now I know I have found just the right place to spend the Fourth of July in Georgia.

This menu is simple, fresh, and colorful—perfect for midsummer entertaining. And most of the dishes taste best cold or at room temperature, which is perfect for entertaining a crowd. Use the best produce you can find, as the seasonal flavors—corn, tomatoes, watermelon, peaches—are meant to be the stars of this meal. I keep the presentation very simple for most of the dishes and encourage guests to help themselves. For example, we pack the corn into large glass jars (you can find similar, inexpensive styles at Anchor Hocking) and drop a generous pat of butter on top, letting it melt down over all the ears. Instead of dinner plates, we use white pie plates from Hall China, a West Virginia–based company that's been in business since 1903. The size and depth of the plates allow for ample servings and work equally well at the table or on a lap. In keeping with the all-American theme, we use mess kit flatware from an Army surplus store.

Watermelon Sangria

Serves 20

Melons are cool reward on long, hot summer days. In the South, we like to eat our melons with a little salt—or drink them with a little wine, as in this sangria. Between our own harvest at Summerland Farm and the melons raised by some of our local organic suppliers, we end up with quite an assortment. I love the names of the heirloom varietals—Moon and Stars, Sorbet Swirl, Yellow Canary, Crimson Sweet, Charentais, Sugar Baby, and muskmelon—almost as much as the taste of their sweet flesh. You should feel free to use whatever kind of melon you have on hand in this recipe, or a combination. If you have a mini melon baller, you might use it to scoop the melon instead of cubing the flesh. To make the melon water, you could use the trimmings that are left over after making the melon cubes or balls. The finishing touch comes from tonic water, whose characteristic flavor comes from quinine. Derived from the cinchona tree, quinine adds a little residual bitterness to balance the sweetness here. Q Tonic makes a delicious tonic water that can be purchased online.

For the Melon Water

1 heirloom watermelon (about 8 pounds), peeled, seeded, and roughly chopped

¼ cup white wine vinegar or Champagne vinegar, or to taste

Kosher salt

For the Sangria

3 (750 ml) bottles pinot grigio

1 ½ cups Cointreau

6 cups cubed and seeded watermelon

Pinch of kosher salt

10 fresh mint leaves, torn, plus sprigs for garnish

1 (16-ounce) bottle tonic water

To make the melon water: Puree the chopped watermelon in a blender until smooth. Strain through a fine-mesh strainer lined with cheesecloth to separate out the liquid. It may take an hour or so for the liquid to drip through. Discard the solids. Season to taste with up to ¼ cup vinegar and salt. You should have at least 3 cups of melon water. The melon water can be made a day or two in advance.

To make the sangria: In a large pitcher, combine 3 cups melon water, the wine, Cointreau, and 4 cups of the watermelon cubes. Allow to macerate for approximately 30 minutes. Add the salt and mint.

Serve the sangria in chilled glasses over ice with a splash of the tonic to finish. Garnish each glass with one of the reserved melon cubes and a mint sprig. ⋆

Pickled Georgia White Shrimp

Makes 12 half-pint jars

Each week shrimpers arrive at our restaurant loading dock with sweet, delicious head-on Georgia white shrimp. A few years back, I started pickling shrimp as I remembered my paternal grandmother used to do. The dish became wildly popular—perhaps too popular. There was a time when my staff would have stuffed me into a jar if I had asked them to pickle another shrimp! We now reserve this delicacy for special occasions, like the Fourth of July, which begins with iced jars of simply pickled shrimp on the boathouse deck. Try to prepare the shrimp around 8 hours before you plan to serve them, so that they have enough time to soak up all the flavor of the pickling liquid. You will need 12 half-pint jars at the ready for this recipe. I like to use Weck jars, which have glass lids and rubber gaskets—they are functional, reusable, and quite attractive. Of course, regular Ball jars work well too. Pequin chiles are a small (about 1/3 inch long) chile with a faint smoky, citrus heat.

For the Pickling Liquid

2 teaspoons fennel seeds

2 teaspoons coriander seeds

2 teaspoons mustard seeds

2 cups white vinegar

2 cups granulated sugar

15 to 20 dried pequin chiles

2 teaspoons Tellicherry black peppercorns

2 fresh bay leaves

2 teaspoons kosher salt

For the Court Bouillon

1 leek, trimmed of dark green tops and roots, cut in half, and rinsed well

1 large carrot, cut into 2-inch pieces

1 onion, quartered

1 cup white wine

12 whole black peppercorns

1 fresh bay leaf

1 sprig fresh thyme

1 sprig fresh parsley or a handful of parsley stems

1 small handful of celery leaves

1 tablespoon kosher salt

1 lemon, cut into quarters

For the Shrimp

2 pounds Georgia white shrimp, heads removed, peeled, and deveined

1 teaspoon coriander seeds

2 bulbs fennel, thinly sliced, fronds reserved

2 sweet onions, thinly sliced

2 lemons, thinly sliced and seeds removed

12 fresh bay leaves

20 dried pequin chiles

To prepare the pickling liquid: Pour the three kinds of seeds together into a dry skillet set over medium-high heat. Toast the seeds, shaking the pan often so that they do not scorch, for 1 to 3 minutes, until fragrant.

In a 4-quart stockpot, combine the toasted seeds with 2 cups water and the vinegar, sugar, chiles, peppercorns, bay leaves, and salt. Place over low heat and stir until the sugar is completely dissolved. Remove from the heat. Cover and let the pot sit for at least 1 hour to allow the aromatics to steep. Strain the liquid, discarding the aromatics, and let it cool. (You may prepare the pickling liquid up to 3 days in advance; cover and refrigerate.)

To prepare the court bouillon: Combine the leek, carrot, onion, and 4 quarts water in an 8-quart stockpot and bring to a boil over high heat. Reduce to a simmer and add the wine, peppercorns, bay leaf, thyme, parsley, celery leaves, and salt. Squeeze the lemon into the bouillon and drop in the quarters as well. Simmer for 15 minutes.

To make the shrimp: Add half of the shrimp to the court bouillon. Prepare an ice-water bath: Combine 2 cups ice and 2 cups cold water in a large bowl. Once the court bouillon comes back to a simmer, about 2 minutes, transfer the shrimp with a skimmer to the ice water bath to stop the cooking. Repeat with the remaining shrimp, making sure the court bouillon comes back to a simmer in between batches. Drain the shrimp well and pat dry with paper towels. You may discard the used court bouillon, or use it for poaching fish or, strained, as a base for a fish or shellfish soup.

Toast the coriander seeds in a dry skillet as done with the other seeds for the pickling liquid. Among 12 half-pint jars, evenly distribute the shrimp, fennel slices and fronds, onions, lemons, bay leaves, chiles, and toasted coriander seeds. Pour enough of the pickling liquid into each jar so that the solids are all submerged. Put the lids on the jars and refrigerate. We like to let the filled jars chill for at least a few hours before serving, but no more than 8 hours, in order to let the flavors marry. ✳

Corn on the cob with butter

Clockwise from top left: Gazpacho Salad | Dottie's Skillet Cornbread | Preserved Chanterelle Mushrooms | Moon and stars watermelon

Gazpacho Salad

Serves 20

In the South, the punishing summer heat and humidity are made (almost) bearable by the abundance of fresh, colorful produce in season. These are the months that we wait for all year at our restaurants, when our menus and tables are full of clean, bright, crisp ingredients. This salad of summer offerings, inspired by the chilled Spanish soup, is a perfect example of what fills our garden in June and July: tomatoes, peppers, cucumbers, cucumbers, and cucumbers. Cucumbers are the zucchini of the Southern sun—they grow like weeds, even taking over space from the other plants. We love the Lemon cucumber for its soft and sweet flesh, the Marketmore for its abundance, the Soyu Long for its bright flavor and seedless interior, and the Crystal Apple for its crisp, white flesh. Of course, any cucumber will do, but using a variety adds dimensions of textures and flavors to this simple summer salad.

4 pounds assorted cucumbers

4 pounds assorted heirloom tomatoes

4 garlic cloves, peeled

2 cups Tomato Water (recipe follows)

6 tablespoons white balsamic vinegar

¼ cup freshly squeezed lime juice (2 to 3 limes)

Dash of maple syrup

Sea salt

2 pounds red onions, sliced

2 pounds banana peppers, sliced into rounds

Extra virgin olive oil

6 fresh basil sprigs, leaves torn into pieces

Lardo (recipe follows), frozen (optional)

Peel and seed the cucumbers, reserving the peel and seeds. Cut the cucumbers into ½-inch-thick slices and set aside. Cut the tomatoes in half, squeeze to remove the seeds and pulp, reserving them. Slice the tomatoes into ½-inch pieces and set aside.

In a blender, combine the peels, seeds, and pulp from the cucumbers and tomatoes with the garlic, tomato water, vinegar, lime juice, and maple syrup. Blend until the mixture resembles a puree. Season with salt to taste. Strain through a fine-mesh strainer lined with cheesecloth. We typically let this drip for several hours in our coolers to

ensure that all of the liquid has been collected. Compost the solids. Cover the mixture and refrigerate for at least 1 hour or up to overnight—allow the liquid to settle and clarify. Skim off the foam that forms at the top. (This will keep for 3 to 4 days in the refrigerator, covered.)

In a large bowl, combine the sliced cucumbers and tomatoes with the sliced onions and peppers. When ready to serve, pour the tomato-cucumber liquid over the vegetables. Drizzle with oil and sprinkle with the basil and sea salt to taste. Lastly, if you like, use a vegetable peeler to make 12 to 14 thin curls of the lardo to garnish the salad. ★

Tomato Water

Makes 2 cups

Tomato water is a terrific by-product made from the trimmings of tomatoes used in other recipes. You can also use "seconds," cracked and bruised tomatoes that are not fit to be sliced for the plate. The water can be used as a dressing for salads, a sauce for crudos, a base for soups and succotash, or frozen and scraped with a fork for a granita. It also makes a terrific light summer Bloody Mary. It is a staple in our cold pantry.

2 pounds tomato trimmings or seconds, roughly chopped

¼ cup fresh basil leaves, torn into pieces

3 tablespoons white balsamic vinegar, or more to taste

Kosher salt to taste

Place all the ingredients in a blender or a food processor and process on high speed for 30 seconds.

Line a colander or strainer with a double layer of cheesecloth, set over a bowl, and pour in the contents of the blender. Transfer the colander and the bowl to the refrigerator. Allow it to drip and settle overnight.

The next day, remove and discard the cheesecloth and compost the solids. The liquid in the bowl is your tomato water. Taste and add more salt or vinegar if needed. (The tomato water will keep, covered in the refrigerator, for up to 5 days, longer if sealed in a vacuum bag.) ⋆

Lardo

Makes 5 pounds of lardo

Lardo is simply cured pork fat. We use it as the crowning touch in the Gazpacho Salad, but you could leave it out and just drizzle on a bit more extra virgin olive oil. You can purchase lardo from a specialty butcher, gourmet market, or even online. But if you are game for attempting to cure your own, it is a rewarding project. Just keep in mind that it takes a couple of months to cure. To ensure safe curing, it's important to use a scale so that your measurements are precise.

This recipe yields much more lardo than you need for the Gazpacho Salad. It keeps for several months in the refrigerator and can easily be frozen to preserve for longer periods. It is terrific when shaved over grilled bread with fresh tomatoes, pizza, tomato bruschetta, or a summer salad. You may want to freeze the lardo for an hour or so before serving to facilitate slicing the curls with a vegetable peeler.

93 grams kosher salt

70 grams granulated sugar

12 grams fennel seeds, ground

6 grams Insta Cure #2 (see "Curing Salt," page 16)

5 grams coriander seeds, ground

5 grams black peppercorns, ground

1 gram crushed red pepper flakes, ground

8 grams fresh garlic, chopped

3 grams fresh thyme, chopped

5 pounds Berkshire pork fatback, skin removed

In a large bowl, combine all the ingredients except the pork fat and mix well. Place the pork fat in a 2-gallon resealable plastic bag. Pack the curing mixture around the fat in the bag. Try to press out and eliminate as much air from the bag as possible before sealing it. A trick to remove the air: Submerge the bag in a vessel of water, keeping the open end above the water line; this will push all the air out before you seal the bag. Be careful not to let any water into the bag.

Let the fat cure for 18 days in the refrigerator. Remove the fat from the bag, rinse thoroughly under cold water, and dry. Wrap the fat in a thin layer of cheesecloth and tie with butcher's twine, which protects it while still allowing it to breathe. Hang the lardo between shelves in the refrigerator for another 45 days to finish the curing process. This will keep, wrapped in plastic, for a few months in the refrigerator or indefinitely in the freezer; we also find it is much easier to shave with a peeler when frozen. ⋆

Dottie's Skillet Cornbread

Serves 20

This recipe was perfected over time by one of our most beloved employees, Miss Dorothy ("Dottie") Copenhaver. Over the past decade, Dottie has played a variety of roles in our kitchens and is now the head baker for all of our restaurants. Dottie's cornbread highlights how very fine ingredients will come together beautifully in a simple preparation. We use Cruze Farm buttermilk from Tennessee, which creates an unctuous tang and subtle smoothness when added to the sweet, finely ground cornmeal from South Carolina's Anson Mills. The hot grease and butter form a lacy crust on the bottom that is the perfect foil for the soft interior. The resulting cornbread is sublime. Dottie does not add any sugar to hers—the only way to make cornbread, most Southerners would argue.

4 cups finely ground cornmeal (preferably Anson Mills)

4 teaspoons baking powder

1 teaspoon baking soda

1 teaspoon kosher salt

6 eggs, beaten

4 cups fresh buttermilk

2 tablespoons lard or bacon grease

2 tablespoons Clarified Butter (see page 246), plus more for finishing

Place three 8-inch cast-iron skillets in the oven and preheat to 400° F.

Sift together the cornmeal, baking powder, baking soda, and salt in a large bowl. In a separate medium bowl, mix the eggs and buttermilk, then stir into the cornmeal mixture, making sure to combine thoroughly.

Divide the lard and clarified butter among the hot skillets and let melt; if needed, return the skillets to the oven but only until the butter and lard are melted. Once melted, pour the excess lard and butter from the skillets into the batter and stir well with a wooden spoon.

Immediately divide the batter among the hot skillets and return to the oven. Reduce the oven temperature to 350° F. Bake the cornbread, uncovered, for approximately 20 minutes. To test for doneness, insert a toothpick in the middle of each skillet; if it comes out dry, the cornbread is done. Cut each pan of cornbread into 8 wedges and serve immediately, topped with butter. (Alternatively you may store the cornbread at room temperature for a couple of days. To reheat, brush the top with clarified butter and place in a 350° F oven for 10 to 15 minutes.) ∗

Preserved Chanterelle Mushrooms

Makes 2 quart jars or 4 pint jars

When we have a moist, cool spring, the Georgia mountain chanterelles pop up in force as the weather warms. We forage in the woods surrounding Lake Rabun for these delicate, nutty treasures and do little more than clean them gently and hit them with warm extra virgin olive oil, lemon juice, salt, pepper, and oregano. The result is perfect. To preserve mushrooms to consume later, we go a few steps further.

2 pounds chanterelle mushrooms

4 cups extra virgin olive oil

Kosher salt

Freshly ground pepper

2 large shallots, finely chopped

4 garlic cloves, thinly sliced

3 sprigs fresh thyme

1 fresh bay leaf

2 tablespoons sherry vinegar

½ cup dry sherry wine

With a paring knife, trim the mushroom ends and scrape the stems, removing the outer layer of skin. Wash the mushrooms three times in cold clear water, gently tossing so as not to bruise the flesh. Allow to air dry thoroughly on paper towels; if possible place them in front of a table fan to speed up the drying process. Cut the dry mushrooms lengthwise into quarters, or sixths if they are large.

In a large (preferably 14-inch) sauté pan, heat 2 tablespoons oil over medium heat until lightly smoking. Add one-fourth of the mushrooms and cook until golden brown, about 15 minutes. Remove and drain on a plate lined with paper towels. Repeat, adding another 2 tablespoons oil and another one-fourth of the mushrooms to the pan. Repeat two more times to sauté all the mushrooms. Place the hot, drained mushrooms in a heatproof bowl and season with salt and pepper.

Add the shallots and garlic to the hot skillet you cooked the mushrooms in, reduce the heat to low, and sweat until translucent, about 5 minutes. Return the mushrooms to the pan and add the thyme and bay leaf. Add the vinegar, scraping up any browned bits, then add the wine and toss to coat the mushrooms. Cook until the liquid has been absorbed by the mushrooms, about 15 minutes. Add the remaining oil (about 3 ½ cups) to cover the mushrooms. Heat the oil to 145° F, or until just hot to the touch. Remove from the heat and allow to cool to room temperature.

Spoon the mushrooms and oil into quart or pint jars, cover, and refrigerate. They will be best after standing for a day and will keep for up to 2 weeks in the refrigerator. ∗

A Variety of Tomatoes: Beams Yellow Pear, Green Grape, Black Cherry, Yellow Gooseberry, Red Fig, and Sweet Pea

Todd's Wood-Grilled Summer Sausage

Todd's Wood-Grilled Summer Sausage

Makes 5 pounds sausage or 16 links

In 2004 we began seriously making charcuterie at Star Provisions for Bacchanalia and Floataway Café. We added a special walk-in cooler for production and another for aging. Todd Immel began working with us and, through his knowledge and love of the curing process, pushed our charcuterie program to the next level. Now we produce some of the best fresh and dry-cured sausage in the country. This summer sausage is a quick fresh sausage that can easily be replicated at home. When curing meat, precise measurements are essential to the quality and safety of the finished product, so this is a time to get out your kitchen scale. I believe you will agree the results are worth the extra effort. When working with raw meat for sausage, it's important to keep all of your equipment—bowls, grinding plates, utensils—and meat cold throughout the process. This ensures the safest and best possible result. We keep our grinding tube, plate, and blade in the freezer until ready to use. If you don't have a meat grinder, this work can be done by a reliable butcher.

1 package hog casings, for 5 pounds sausage (about 6 feet in length)

3 pounds pork shoulder, cut into 1-inch cubes, partially frozen

¾ pound beef top round, cut into 1-inch cubes, partially frozen

1¼ pounds pork fatback, cut into 1-inch cubes, partially frozen

Seasoning Mixture

12 grams dextrose

6 grams Insta Cure #1 (see "Curing Salt," page 16)

35 grams salt

7 grams freshly ground pepper

7 grams juniper seeds, ground

6.6 grams mustard seeds, ground

4.5 grams dried marjoram, ground

4 grams paprika

3.4 grams mace

2.8 grams garlic powder

2 grams caraway seeds, ground

For Serving

Hoagie Rolls (page 243)

Grainy mustard

Half-Sour Pickles (recipe follows), split lengthwise

Soak the casings in cool water in the refrigerator for 12 to 24 hours; we like to change the water at least twice during the soaking period. Rinse the casings thoroughly after soaking, holding each open and running cool water through it to rinse completely.

Combine the pork and beef in a large bowl. Put one-third of the pork and beef mixture through the grinder using the medium grinding plate. Place the ground meat in a large bowl. Add the fatback to the remaining cubed meat. Attach the fine grinding plate (changing the grinding plate produces a nice textural contrast). Put the meat and fatback mixture through the grinder, then combine with the medium-ground meat.

In a small bowl, mix all the seasoning ingredients with ½ cup cold water to form a paste. (Rather than adding the seasonings to the ground meat directly, this is a better way to ensure that the seasonings are evenly distributed.) Add the paste to the ground meat and fat mixture and mix thoroughly by hand until it becomes sticky and pastelike.

Put the sausage mixture into 2 gallon-size resealable plastic storage bags; make sure to remove as much of the air as possible to prevent oxidation. A trick to remove the air: Submerge the bag in a large bowl of water, keeping the open end above the water line; this will push all the air out before you seal the bag. Be careful not to let any water into the bag. You can also use a vacuum-seal bag, if you have one. Refrigerate for at least 12 hours, or up to 24 hours.

For this step a sausage stuffing tube would help: This is a tube that fits onto the end of your meat grinder and keeps the casing open as the grinder presses the mixture in. Also, there is an attachment for grinders available for stand mixers that has a tube that will hold the casings while the grinder pushes the sausage into the casing. (You should not stuff the sausage directly into casings as you are grinding, though; the sausage needs to cure overnight before going into the casings.) Use the sausage grinder or grinder attachment without the blade and die and with the stuffing tube attachment. Fit the casings onto the stuffing tube and then push the sausage into the casings. Once a length of casing is full, create links every 5 inches by twisting the sausage a few times in one direction and/or using butcher's twine to tie it off, remembering to tie off each end first. Repeat the process with the other casings until all the mixture is used. Prick the air pockets in the sausage with a needle.

Hang the sausages in the refrigerator. We set up a dowel with cans or boxes at either end to support it, and drape the sausage over the dowel. Keep a pan underneath to catch any drips. Alternatively, place the sausage links on a stainless-steel drying rack set over a baking sheet. Let cool in the refrigerator for at least 12 hours to allow the sausages to rest and bring the temperature of the fat down (smoking the sausages immediately after filling them would cause the loss of too much fat).

To smoke the sausages: Light a charcoal grill and allow the fire to burn down to embers (or heat a gas grill on the lowest temperature). Add an aluminum pan of soaked wood chips to the embers and allow them to begin to smoke. Add the sausage to an upper shelf of the grill if possible and cover the grill. Smoke the sausages over low heat until they reach an internal temperature of 155° F. Depending on the temperature of your grill, this should take approximately 1 hour; begin checking the internal temperature of the sausage after 30 minutes. Allow to cool at room temperature. The sausages are fully cooked at this point. (If not being served immediately, the sausages can be wrapped and refrigerated for up to 10 days or frozen for several months.)

To serve the sausages, grill over a wood fire or pan sear over medium heat until golden brown and heated through, about 10 minutes. We like to serve the sausages hot-dog style, with our homemade hoagie rolls, grainy mustard, and Half-Sour Pickles. ∗

Half-Sour Pickles
Makes 4 quarts

We never have a shortage of cucumbers when they are in season. We also like to preserve them for the times when they aren't, so we turn to the Southern tradition of making pickles. These are our favorites. They can be made with any cucumber, but the pickling variety works best.

¼ cup pickling salt

5 pounds small pickling cucumbers

6 garlic cloves, unpeeled

6 dill heads or sprigs of fresh dill

2 tablespoons dill seeds

4 small fresh or 4 small dried chiles, such as pequin

1 tablespoon coriander seeds, toasted

1 tablespoon Tellicherry black peppercorns

12 fresh bay leaves

Combine 8 cups water and the pickling salt in a pickle crock or thick-walled ceramic vessel with a lid. Stir well to dissolve the salt.

Wash the cucumbers and remove the stem ends. Crush the garlic cloves with the flat side of a knife. Add the cucumbers to the salted water, then add the garlic, dill, dill seeds, chiles, coriander seeds, peppercorns, and bay leaves. Stir gently to distribute the spices evenly.

Place a weight or ceramic plate in the crock to keep the cucumbers submerged in the brine. Cover the crock with the lid or plastic wrap and store at room temperature (68° F) for 3 to 5 days. Check the crock once a day and use a spoon to remove any bubbles or scum that have formed on the top. Taste the pickles after 3 days and if you prefer them to be more sour, let brine for 1 or 2 more days. Once the pickles are sour, they should be stored in the refrigerator. They will keep for several weeks in a sealed container. ∗

Honey-Roasted Peaches with Chamomile Ice Milk

Serves 20

Peaches were our first crop at Summerland Farm, and they are still our most prolific. Since we do not use pesticides on our trees, the fruit is not always beautiful, but it is always delicious. The annual yield varies depending on the weather, but there have been summers when we've harvested hundreds of pounds of peaches. We attempt to use each and every peach we harvest, which can sometimes overwhelm our pastry chef! (Our customers, though, have never complained.) This preparation is the perfect end to a summer day on the lake. We wrap the peaches in foil packets and tuck them around the edges of the grill to roast as the embers are dying. Chamomile and peach is a perfect combination. We add the crunch of granola for a little texture at the end. You can make the ice milk and granola up to several weeks in advance.

10 ripe peaches, halved, stones removed

6 tablespoons wildflower honey

6 tablespoons butter

Chamomile Ice Milk (recipe follows)

1 cup Granola (page 246)

Prepare a grill for indirect heat or preheat the oven to 400° F.

Cut 20 (10-inch) squares of foil and parchment paper. Place half a peach on a square of parchment on top of a square of foil. Drizzle with 1 teaspoon of the honey and place 1 teaspoon of the butter on top. Fold the parchment and foil over the peach half and crimp the edges to seal. Repeat for all peach halves. Place the foil bundles of peaches around the edges of the mostly burnt-out embers of the fire and allow to slow roast for 10 to 15 minutes. (Alternatively, you can roast the peaches in the oven for about 15 minutes.) The peaches are done when bubbling and tender. Serve immediately, placing a scoop of ice milk in each warm peach half and adding a sprinkle of granola on top. ⋆

Chamomile Ice Milk

Makes 3 quarts

10 cups local organic whole milk

1 ¾ cups granulated sugar

¼ cup dried chamomile flowers

1 teaspoon pure vanilla extract

Pinch of kosher salt

In a 4-quart saucepan, combine the milk, sugar, chamomile, vanilla, and salt and place over medium heat, being careful not to boil and scorch the milk. Once the mixture is hot, remove from the heat and cover, allowing the chamomile to steep for 15 minutes. Taste to be sure it is infused to your liking; you can steep for longer depending on your preference.

Strain the mixture through a fine-mesh strainer into a bowl (discard the chamomile) and let cool. Churn in an ice cream maker according to the manufacturer's directions. ⋆

Citrus Shortbread Cookies

Makes about 24 cookies

This treat is not only one of my personal favorites, but has become our best-selling cookie at Star Provisions. The base of the cookie is wonderfully buttery and simple. The dough can be cut into a wide assortment of shapes and iced for any number of occasions. We love the citrus undertones with the buttery roundness of the cookie, but the zests are optional and can be left out if you prefer a classic, unadulterated shortbread. We bake shortbread cookies slowly in order to keep them from spreading or developing color. You want the delicate taste of sweet butter in every bite.

For the Cookies

1 pound (4 sticks) cold butter, cubed

1 cup granulated sugar

1 ½ teaspoons kosher salt

4 cups all-purpose flour

Finely grated zest of 1 lime

Finely grated zest of 1 lemon

Finely grated zest of 1 orange

For the Icing

3 cups confectioners' sugar

¼ cup cold milk

Red and blue paste food coloring

To make the cookies: Preheat the oven to 225° F. Line two baking sheets with parchment paper.

In a stand mixer fitted with the paddle attachment, cream together the butter, sugar, and salt on low until light and smooth. Slowly add the flour and zests and continue to mix on low until all the ingredients are combined.

Lightly flour a rolling pin and your work surface. Roll out the dough to a ¼-inch-thick sheet. With your favorite 2 ½-inch cookie cutter (such as a star for the Fourth of July), cut out shapes. The dough will allow a second rolling without getting tough, so you can reroll your scraps once and cut out more shapes to avoid any waste. Place the cookies on the parchment-lined baking sheets. (You can make the cookies in advance up to this point: We wrap the entire baking sheets, loaded up with cookies, in plastic wrap, to help them keep their shape. Pull out a length of plastic wrap, place the baking sheet on top of the plastic, and wrap the plastic over and under from both directions until the sheet is completely sealed. The cookies will keep in the freezer for up to 2 weeks. Once shaped it is best to keep the cookies flat so freeze them directly on the baking sheet. This will also make it quite easy to bake when you are ready. (They will bake up nicely going straight from the freezer to the oven, just increase the baking time by 5 to 10 minutes.)

Bake for 65 minutes, until firm; they should not have any color. Transfer immediately to a wire rack and let cool completely before icing, or enjoy without icing.

To make the icing: Combine the confectioners' sugar and milk in a bowl and mix until smooth. Divide the icing into thirds, placing 2 portions into separate small bowls or cups. Mix dots of the red paste food coloring into one bowl and blue paste food coloring into the other bowl until you like the colors. Coloring paste is very dense and powerful, so a little goes a long way. We use a toothpick or bamboo skewer to add small amounts. One bowl of the icing should remain white, uncolored.

Once the cookies are cool you are ready to ice: We use a pastry bag or squirt bottle with a fine tip to outline the cookie with a small bead of colored icing, then fill in the area with the same color icing with a pastry bag or squirt bottle with a fine tip, using a clean toothpick or skewer to push the icing around to cover the area completely. Alternate the colors so you have all three represented for the red, white, and blue cookies. Place on a rack for 1 hour to let the icing set slightly so it will not smudge when moved or packed. The iced cookies will keep for a couple of days stored in a sealed container at room temperature. ★

The Dog Days of Summer

A Fig Feed

Serves 4

Fig Fest Cocktail

Crostini of Fig, Caramelized Onions, and Lonzino

Wood Oven–Roasted Whole Foie Gras | *Sauternes*

Branzino Steamed in Fig Leaves with Fig Butter and Pecans

Poached Shrimp, Melon, and Chile Soup | *Viognier*

Chicken Roulades with Fig Stuffing

Summer Vegetable Succotash (page 246) | *A Dry Riesling*

Crottin de Chavignol Cheese, Tupelo Honey, and Celeste Figs

Yogurt Parfait with Fig Gelée and Peanut Brittle

Fig Clafoutis

There are days in August when I think it could not possibly get any hotter in Atlanta. Fortunately, because of the elevation, it is usually a few degrees cooler at Summerland Farm. And the farm offers another welcome respite from the late-summer heat: fresh figs. Hundreds of pounds of them, in fact. When I was a child and we came to the South, figs were an unusual treat. I remember eating them only when we visited Summerland Farm.

Generations ago, my ancestors planted figs on the property, and some of those trees are still yielding fruit. Clifford and I continued the tradition by cultivating even more varieties. We currently grow the Brown Turkey and Celeste figs that are so popular throughout the South, as well as the Kadota—with its lime-green exterior giving way to sweet, red flesh—and Clifford's current favorites, the LSU Gold and LSU Purple varieties, developed by Dr. Ed O'Rourke at Louisiana State University.

All of our figs have thrived despite the sometimes-unpredictable weather in our part of the state, and they are generous with their fruit in the summer. There are plenty of figs for us to share with the birds—who don't ask our permission to swoop down and take them—and with our dogs, who love to bite them from the lower branches and pop the sweet, tender fruit in their mouths.

As an icon of summer in the Deep South, the fig is less clichéd than the peach, but no less beloved. It has been celebrated by Southern cooks for generations and immortalized in fiction. Stories by Flannery O'Connor, Katherine Anne Porter, and Eudora Welty—who put up her own fig preserves every summer—feature figs and fig trees as supporting characters.

A few years ago, Clifford and I donated an evening at Summerland Farm in an Atlanta charity auction. To our delight, a group of local chefs went in together and purchased the dinner. We were flattered that our colleagues wanted to share this experience, so we set about dreaming up a special menu that would really blow them away. They asked to schedule the dinner in August, a typically slow month for Atlanta restaurants. Immediately I thought of the fig, my summer standby. As much as I relish the taste of figs by themselves, I also love them for their versatility. They play the supporting role beautifully in both sweet and savory dishes.

Before our fellow chefs-cum-dinner-guests arrived, I set a table by the fig tree at the edge of our herb garden. (We grow a variety of herbs in raised beds and in oversized galvanized tubs a few steps from the house, with a large fig tree standing sentinel at one end.) We served cocktails in silver mint julep cups, but other than that, I kept the tableware simple and earthy to let the figs shine. I balanced fresh figs on top of ceramic mustard pots for a playful centerpiece. Salt-glazed stoneware plates, beige linen napkins with muted stripes, and wooden coasters created an atmosphere that felt grounded yet special. Our guests agreed. This is a menu I would happily serve again. Thinking about it almost makes me long for August—until I remember the heat! ⋆

Fig Fest Cocktail

If you'd like to have a "house" cocktail up your sleeve for summer and fall entertaining, this is it. It is more like an aperitif: relatively low in alcohol and perfect for sipping on a hot summer evening. The combination of ingredients is unexpected, but you and your guests will be pleasantly surprised by the results. Tinctures, like shrubs (see the Orange Shrub in January's Red-Eyed Cocktail, page 92), are an excellent and relatively simple way to preserve the taste of a fruit at the peak of its flavor. This preparation is particularly well suited to figs, especially the Brown Turkey variety, as they tend to overripen quickly. Prepare the tincture a week before you plan to serve the drink, and it will keep for several months. We serve the Fig Fest Cocktail over crushed ice in a mint julep glass for a special touch, but a highball glass will work as well.

Fig Tincture (recipe follows)

Tawny port (preferably Warre's Otima)

Calvados

Lemon verbena sprigs (optional)

To make one cocktail, in a pint cocktail mixing glass filled with ice, stir together 1 ½ ounces fig tincture, 1 ounce port, and ½ ounce calvados. Strain into a glass of crushed ice. Garnish with a sprig of lemon verbena, if you like. ★

Fig Tincture
Makes 1 ½ cups

Sorghum is a grassy plant historically grown throughout the South for the sweet syrup it yields when the stalks are crushed and boiled down like sugar cane. Look for it at farmers' markets or online. You may substitute molasses, maple syrup, or honey depending on your preference.

6 figs, halved (preferably the Brown Turkey variety)

1 cup vodka

2 tablespoons sorghum syrup

In a large bowl, use a muddler to mash the figs. Stir in the vodka and syrup. Pour the mixture into a clean pint jar. Store in a cool, dark place, such as your kitchen cabinet or pantry, for a week to allow the flavors to meld.

Strain the tincture through a sieve, pressing on the solids slightly to release all the juice. Discard the solids. Pour the liquid into a clean pint jar or bottle, cap, and refrigerate. (The tincture will keep for at least several months.) ★

Clockwise from top left: Fig Fest Cocktail | Wood Oven–Roasted Whole Foie Gras
Crottin de Chavignol Cheese, Tupelo Honey, and Celeste Figs | Branzino Steamed in Fig Leaves with Fig Butter and Pecans

Crostini of Fig, Caramelized Onions, and Lonzino

Makes 12 crostini, serves 4

If you are the adventuresome sort and like to dabble in science projects, then making lonzino will be right up your alley. It is our fastest and simplest charcuterie recipe. The whole process takes approximately 7 weeks for aging, but the actual prep time is less than 30 minutes. The end result will depend greatly on the quality of the pork, so try to find a nice, locally raised, heritage-breed loin. Curing meat is an exact science, so we do recommend that you weigh all the ingredients with a scale instead of measuring by volume.

You will have lonzino left over after assembling the crostini. It will keep for several months in your refrigerator and can be used in numerous ways: in salads and sandwiches, as a pizza topping, or on an antipasto plate. If you are not up to the challenge, there are many artisan charcuterie producers throughout the country and it is not hard to find an exceptional domestic or imported lonzino (in this case, ask your butcher to thinly slice the lonzino for you). Thin slices of prosciutto would be delicious with the crostini as well.

For the Lonzino

1 (4-pound) pork loin with fat cap

90 grams kosher salt

70 grams granulated sugar

6 grams Insta Cure #2 (see "Curing Salt," page 16)

5 grams ground black peppercorns

5 grams fennel seeds, toasted and ground

5 grams coriander seeds, toasted and ground

7 grams fresh garlic, finely chopped

1 gram crushed red pepper flakes

3 grams fresh thyme leaves, chopped

3 grams fresh rosemary leaves, chopped

For the Crostini

1 loaf sourdough bread or similar crusty artisan bread

1 tablespoon extra virgin olive oil, plus extra for drizzling

Fleur de sel

Caramelized Onions (see page 192)

10 fresh figs (preferably the Kadota variety), stems removed, and sliced

12 leaves baby arugula, for garnish

To make the lonzino: Place the pork on a cutting board and, with a sharp knife, clean the meat of connective tissue. Leave the fat cap intact. In a small bowl, combine the salt, sugar, Insta Cure, pepper, fennel, coriander, garlic, crushed red pepper, thyme, and rosemary; mix thoroughly. Reserve half of the mixture in a resealable plastic bag in the refrigerator. Rub the other half on the pork loin, then seal in a 2-gallon resealable storage bag, rolling around the meat to remove as much air as possible before sealing. (Note: If the loin is too long to fit into the resealable bag, cut it into two equal pieces.) Refrigerate for 9 days.

After 9 days, remove the meat from the bag; there will be some residual liquid in the bag, simply discard it with the bag. Apply the remaining cure mixture to the pork. Seal again in a new 2-gallon resealable storage bag and refrigerate for another 9 days. Remove the loin from the bag, rinse well, and allow it to dry in the refrigerator, uncovered, for at least 12 hours.

Wrap the loin in cheesecloth and tie the ends. Using a meat hook or butcher's twine, hang it in the refrigerator: We typically tie it to the underside of a shelf with enough room for the loin to hang freely with airflow around all sides. If you don't have room for hanging, you can place the wrapped loin on a stainless-steel drying rack with a drip pan below it or a cooling rack fitted inside a baking sheet. Let the pork age in the refrigerator for 3 to 4 weeks. By the end of the process, the loin should lose 30 percent of its original weight and be firm to the touch all the way through. The lonzino will keep well sealed in the refrigerator for up to 3 months.

To assemble the crostini: Cut the bread into 3/4-inch-thick slices, brush with the oil, and sprinkle with fleur de sel to taste. Toast the bread or grill it. Spoon 1 tablespoon of the caramelized onions on each slice. Use a sharp knife to cut the lonzino into thin slices; you will need approximately 24 slices. Top each piece of bread with 2 or 3 slices of fresh fig and 2 slices of lonzino. Garnish with the arugula and more oil and fleur de sel and serve. ∗

Wood Oven–Roasted Whole Foie Gras

Serves 4 to 6

This was a decadent accident that we came up with one August night when cooking at home for a group of Atlanta chefs. We had a lobe of foie gras and the wood-burning oven was very hot, so we decided to try roasting it whole. The result was visually stunning and absolutely delicious. We loved the smoky flavor imparted by the wood oven, but a very hot gas or electric oven would work as well. Of course, foie gras is quite expensive. But if you are willing to splurge, you won't regret it. To really get your money's worth, save the juices and rendered fat from the pan after roasting. They will keep in the refrigerator for at least a week, giving you time to enjoy a luxurious sauté of vegetables, chicken, or seafood cooked in foie gras drippings. As foie gras goes, this is a simple preparation. But you will need to plan a day ahead to marinate the foie gras in the sweet wine.

1 whole lobe (1 ½ pounds) foie gras

1 (375 ml) bottle sweet or dessert wine

1 tablespoon kosher salt

Freshly cracked pepper

1 pound fresh figs (12 to 14), stems removed and halved

4 sprigs fresh rosemary

4 sprigs fresh thyme

Place the foie gras in a baking dish and generously douse with the wine. Season with the salt and refrigerate, covered with plastic wrap, for 12 to 24 hours.

Allow the foie gras to come to room temperature (about 1 hour). Preheat a wood oven or conventional oven to 500° F.

Re-season the foie gras with a sprinkling of salt and pepper. Pour off any remaining wine marinade and reserve. Score the lobe on the diagonal, at ⅛-inch intervals, to make a cross-hatch pattern. Line a roasting pan with the fresh figs, and rosemary and thyme sprigs, then set the foie gras on top. Brush the foie gras with the reserved marinade and add about ¼ cup to the bottom of pan. Roast for about 15 minutes. Keep a careful eye on it and rotate and baste with the marinade and rendered fat from the pan every 2 minutes. If the foie gras appears to be browning too quickly, loosely tent the top with aluminum foil. After about 15 minutes, the internal temperature should reach 135° F. Present immediately to your guests in the roasting pan for them to admire, then transfer to a warm platter and garnish with the figs and sprigs of herbs from the pan. ⋆

Branzino Steamed in Fig Leaves with Fig Butter and Pecans

Serves 4

Here we make use of fig leaves (which our trees produce in copious amounts) as a vessel for steaming fish. The leaves impart some of the herbaceous flavor of the garden while protecting the delicate fish from the heat. Not many people realize that fig leaves can be used much as grape leaves are; if tender and young, they are quite tasty when cooked. You can also substitute leaves of grapevine, cabbage, collard, or chard. Branzino is a European sea bass, but any kind of bass would work well in this recipe. If you do not have a bamboo steamer, I've offered an alternative preparation. But I encourage you to get one! They are very inexpensive and easy to find at kitchen supply stores, Asian markets, and online.

12 to 15 small fig leaves, washed well

For the Fig Butter

**1 pound fresh figs
(preferably the Brown Turkey variety),
stems removed and halved**

¼ cup pecan or grapeseed oil

1 pound (4 sticks) butter, softened

Kosher salt

For the Toasted Pecans

**½ cup pecan pieces
(preferably the Elliott variety)**

1 tablespoon butter

Pinch of kosher salt

Pinch of sugar

For the Branzino

4 (3-ounce) branzino fillets, with skin intact

Kosher salt

Freshly ground pepper

1 lemon

1 garlic clove, crushed

1 sprig fresh rosemary

1 sprig fresh thyme

1 fresh bay leaf

To blanch the fig leaves: Bring a 4-quart pot of water to a boil. Meanwhile, create an ice bath by combining 2 cups ice and 2 cups cold water in a large bowl. When the water is boiling, drop a few fig leaves in and blanch for about 1 minute; remove with a spider or strainer and immediately plunge into the ice water bath to retain the green color. Repeat with the remaining leaves. Drain the leaves on a towel. (The blanched leaves can be wrapped in plastic wrap and stored in the refrigerator for a few hours before using.)

To make the fig butter: Preheat the oven to 400° F. On a baking sheet, toss the figs with the oil and roast for 20 minutes, until completely softened. (Reduce the oven temperature to 350° F for toasting the pecans in the next step.) Let the figs cool, then puree in a blender or a food processor until smooth. In a stand mixer fitted with the paddle attachment, combine the softened butter and half of the fig puree. On low speed, mix until combined and smooth, then add the remaining fig puree and mix on low to incorporate. Season with salt to taste. Transfer to a container, cover, and refrigerate. (The fig butter can be made up to 3 days in advance; leftovers are delicious on almost anything, especially toast in the morning.)

To toast the pecans: Place on a baking sheet and bake in the 350° F oven for 5 minutes. Immediately toss the hot pecans with the butter, salt, and sugar using a spatula. Return to the oven and bake for 5 minutes longer, until fragrant. Let cool, then transfer to a bowl or an airtight container and store at room temperature until needed, up to a few days. (Toasted pecans like these are great in a salad as well.)

To make the branzino: Season each portion of branzino with salt and pepper and top with 1 tablespoon of the fig butter. Carefully wrap each portion of fish by placing a blanched fig leaf on the counter, top with a fillet, and fold the leaf around the fish like an envelope. You may need to use another leaf on top to cover; if so, tuck the ends underneath. The fish should be enclosed completely to retain the moisture, but it does not need to be tightly wrapped.

Set up a saucepan with a bamboo steamer and fill the pan halfway with water. Cut 4 slices from the lemon. Add the lemon slices, garlic, rosemary, thyme, and bay leaf to the water in the pan. Place the wrapped fish in the bamboo steamer, cover, and steam for 5 to 7 minutes. To test for doneness simply peek into a packet to see that the fish is no longer translucent and is firm to touch. (If you do not have a steamer you can wrap your fish in the leaves, then in parchment, and finish with aluminum foil. Bake in a 400° F oven for 8 to 10 minutes.)

Serve each packet of fish immediately, placing the leaf directly on the plate and trying to reserve the natural juices as well as the fig butter. Partially unwrap the leaf and top with a squeeze of lemon and some toasted pecans as a garnish. ∗

Poached Shrimp, Melon, and Chile Soup

Serves 4

Melon water is something we make as readily as we do Tomato Water (page 213). We always have scraps of melon around the kitchen (byproducts of dicing and balling melons for other dishes), and it is a refreshing base for cold summer soups like this one. I like to use heirloom varieties of melons (see page 206), but cantaloupe or honeydew work fine here as well. If you have a food saver gadget that pulls air out of a bag to vacuum-seal your food, use it to compress the melon pieces. This concentrates the flavors and compresses the fruit to create dense and slightly translucent pieces that are perfect for a salad or soup—the melon pieces look almost like little gems. If you do not have a food saver, it's fine to just use small cubes or a couple of different sizes of balls. Use the best shrimp you can find—preferably local or regional, depending on where you live. We rely on freshly caught Georgia white shrimp brought up from Savannah for all of our shrimp recipes.

4 cups Court Bouillon (page 245)

1 pound shrimp (16 to 20 count, medium size),
peeled, deveined, and cleaned

1 cantaloupe

1 honeydew melon

1 watermelon

Kosher salt

Dry white wine or Champagne vinegar to taste

5 figs (preferably the Celeste variety),
stems removed and sliced

¼ cup chiles, thinly sliced
(preferably a mixture of cayenne and Padrón)

1 tablespoon extra virgin olive oil, plus extra for drizzling

Fleur de sel

Micro chervil or cilantro and thinly sliced radishes for garnish

In a large pot, bring the court bouillon to a boil over high heat. Meanwhile, make an ice bath by combining 2 cups ice with 2 cups cold water in a large bowl. Add half of the shrimp to the boiling court bouillon and poach for 2 to 3 minutes, until no longer translucent and slightly pink. With a strainer, transfer to the ice bath to stop the cooking. Repeat with the remaining shrimp. Once the poached shrimp have cooled, drain well and pat dry with paper towels. Refrigerate, covered, until ready to serve. (This can be done a couple of hours ahead of time but the shrimp will be the most tender if poached just before serving.)

Peel and seed the 3 melons. Trim and carefully cut up enough melon to yield 1 cup of small cubes or balls from each. Toss the 3 cups of melon cubes or balls together and set aside.

To make the melon water: Measure out 4 cups melon trimmings and any extra cut melon and puree in a blender or food processor until smooth. Strain into a medium bowl through a chinois or fine-mesh strainer lined with cheesecloth, leaving any solids behind. You should have about 2 cups of melon water. Season with salt and taste to see if you need to add any wine or vinegar to add a little acidity. You are looking for a sweet liquid with a little saltiness in the end—the vinegar or wine offers another dimension but should not be readily detected on the palate. You can make the melon water as well as the melon cubes or balls up to 2 days in advance.

In a large bowl, toss the shrimp, melon cubes or balls, figs, and chiles with the oil and fleur de sel to taste. Arrange in 4 bowls. Pour a scant ½ cup of the melon water into each bowl. Drizzle with a little more oil and garnish with chervil, radishes, and fleur de sel. ★

Chicken Roulades with Fig Stuffing

Serves 4

A roulade is a wonderful way to dress up a chicken. We use a heritage Red Ranger hen, but any high-quality, free-range bird is a good choice—especially if it comes from your local poultry farmer. Unless you are skilled at breaking down a whole chicken, you will want to ask your butcher to prepare the birds for you: The breasts should be removed from the bone cage with the skin intact. Remember to keep the food processor and blade cold and clean prior to making the fig stuffing, for safety and easy handling.

You can keep the assembled, uncooked roulades in the refrigerator for up to three days, or you can prepare and cook them completely before refrigerating, tightly wrapped, for up to a week. If you do cook the roulades in advance, reheat them just before serving alongside the Summer Vegetable Succotash (page 246).

½ pound figs (about 8), stems removed and halved

1 tablespoon olive oil

Kosher salt

2 (3¼-pound) whole chickens, breasts boned with skin intact; thighs, legs, and wings skinned and boned (see note above)

2 chicken livers

Pinch of ground cloves

Pinch of ground juniper

Pinch of ground allspice

Pinch of Insta Cure #2 (see "Curing Salt," page 16)

⅛ teaspoon ground white pepper

2 egg whites

¼ cup heavy cream

1 tablespoon Clarified Butter (page 246)

Place the bowl and metal blade of a food processor in the refrigerator for an hour to chill. Preheat the oven to 400° F.

Place the figs in a lightly oiled roasting pan. Brush the cut sides with the oil and season with salt. Roast for 15 minutes, just enough to soften the fruit. Let cool. Set aside 4 fig halves for garnish (if you like); finely chop the remainder.

In the chilled bowl of the food processor, place the skinned and boned leg, thigh, and wing meat from the chickens (you should have about ³/₄ pound). Add the livers, cloves, juniper, allspice, Insta Cure, 2 teaspoons kosher salt, and the white pepper. Process and slowly add the egg whites and cream. Pass the stuffing through a fine-mesh strainer into a bowl and gently fold in the chopped figs. Cover and refrigerate while you prepare the breasts.

Use a meat mallet to pound out each breast, skin side down, to form a 6 by 4-inch rectangle; season with salt and pepper. Place each breast on a large piece of plastic wrap, keeping the skin side down. Form a 2 by 6-inch log of stuffing at the bottom of the breast. Roll the breast around the stuffing, keeping the skin stretched over the entire outside. The skin should be loose enough to pull around the roulade nicely. Use the plastic wrap to form the roulade by wrapping it tightly and twisting the ends in opposite directions while rolling the roulade between your hands and your work surface. Seal tightly in several layers

of plastic wrap. Repeat to make 4 roulades. (At this point the roulades can be refrigerated for up to 3 days.)

To cook the roulades, create a warm water bath: You are looking for a water temperature of 160° F; a meat thermometer is the best way to judge this. A slow cooker set on the lowest temperature filled with warm water will work nicely for this, or a pot of water on the lowest setting of your stove—it should not come to a simmer or a boil if possible. Place the roulades (still wrapped in plastic) in the water bath and cook for 90 minutes, or until the roulades reach an internal temperature of 155° F (you will need to unwrap to check the temperature).

Transfer the roulades to a work surface, remove from the plastic wrap, and dry completely. The roulade may be refrigerated for a couple of days if sealed tightly. To serve, heat the clarified butter in a large skillet. Add the roulades and sear, rolling frequently, until the skin is uniformly golden brown. If you have made the roulades in advance and they were refrigerated, then you may need to place the browned roulades in an oven to heat through; baking at 400° F for 8 minutes should do it.

Slice the roulades straight through into round discs and plate individually, garnishing each plate with 1 of the roasted fig halves, if you like. ★

Yogurt Parfait with Fig Gelée and Peanut Brittle

Serves 4

At Bacchanalia we often serve a version of this treat as a small pre-dessert, a seasonal bite to excite our guests' palates before the dessert arrives. Though this recipe has several components, it is not at all difficult—don't be intimidated by the gelatin! If you want to cut out one step, you can substitute store-bought fig preserves or fig syrup for the fig gelée. The entire recipe can be made ahead, then assembled and served while the clafoutis is in the oven. The peanut brittle is a delicious snack on its own, or as a post-dinner nibble with a cup of coffee.

For the Parfait

1 ½ sheets gelatin,
or 1 ¼ teaspoons powdered gelatin

½ cup heavy cream

¼ cup granulated sugar

Pinch of kosher salt

1 cup whole-milk yogurt

½ teaspoon freshly squeezed lemon juice

For the Fig Gelée

10 figs (preferably the Kadota variety), stems removed and halved

1 cup granulated sugar

1 cinnamon stick

1 sheet gelatin, or ¾ teaspoon powdered gelatin

For the Peanut Brittle

1 cup raw peanuts, toasted

1 ½ cups granulated sugar

⅓ cup light corn syrup

1 teaspoon kosher salt

½ teaspoon pure vanilla extract

¼ cup (½ stick) butter

To make the parfait: Soak the gelatin sheets in 1 cup cold water until soft and supple, about 5 minutes. Squeeze out the water and set aside. Hand whip ¼ cup of the heavy cream into soft peaks and set aside. In a small saucepan over low heat, combine the remaining ¼ cup heavy cream, the sugar, and salt and warm through. Remove from the heat and add the softened gelatin sheet or the powdered gelatin, stirring until it dissolves. Let cool for 10 minutes, then add the yogurt. Fold this mixture into the bowl of whipped cream and add the lemon juice. Divide among four 4-ounce ramekins, glasses, or plastic cups and refrigerate until set, about 6 hours.

To make the fig gelée: Line a 6-inch round or square shallow flat-bottomed container (a cake pan would work nicely) with plastic wrap; set aside. In a 1-quart saucepan, combine the figs, sugar, cinnamon stick, and 2 cups water. Bring to a simmer over low heat and simmer for 10 minutes.

Meanwhile, soak the gelatin sheet in 1 cup cold water until it is soft and supple, about 5 minutes. Squeeze out the water and set the soft gelatin sheet aside. Strain the fig mixture through a fine-mesh strainer into a bowl. Return 1 cup of the fig poaching liquid to the saucepan. Reserve the remaining liquid for serving the parfaits and discard the fig pieces. Add the softened gelatin sheet or the powdered gelatin to the saucepan, stirring to dissolve the gelatin in the warm liquid. Pour into the lined container. Refrigerate, uncovered, until set, at least 2 hours.

Pull up the plastic wrap to remove the gelée from the container and dice into small cubes. (The gelée can be stored in the refrigerator for several weeks in a covered container. It is also delicious with cheese.)

To make the peanut brittle: Line a baking sheet with parchment paper and spray with nonstick cooking spray. In a 2-quart saucepan fitted with a candy thermometer, combine the sugar, corn syrup, salt, and 1 cup water. Place over medium heat and stir until dissolved. Raise the heat to high and cook the mixture until it reaches the hard-crack stage, or 300° F on the candy thermometer. Remove from the heat, add the vanilla and butter, and swirl to incorporate. Working quickly, add the toasted nuts, stir to coat, and slide out onto the prepared baking sheet. Let cool completely, about 1 hour.

Break the brittle apart either with your hands or a mallet and place the pieces in the bowl of a food processor fitted with the steel blade. Pulse until it is the texture of coarse meal. (Stored in an airtight container, the brittle will keep for several weeks and is an excellent topping for ice cream or yogurt.)

To assemble the parfaits: If you set the parfait in ramekins or glasses, they are quite easy to unmold: Take directly from the refrigerator, run a knife around the sides, and invert into individual serving bowls. If you have used plastic cups, you can make a small incision in the bottom of a cup and invert into a bowl—the parfait will slide right out. Put a spoonful of the fig poaching liquid in the bottom of each bowl and add the gelée cubes and a dusting of the peanut brittle powder. We garnished with a tiny fig leaf but a single leaf of mint would be nice as well. ★

Fig Clafoutis

Serves 4

The clafoutis is a traditional French peasant dessert typically made with cherries. It reminds me of a thick pancake—and really, what could be more delicious than that? But instead of cherries, for this menu we like to use small, thin-skinned, sweet Celeste figs. A little crème fraîche on the side is a nice counterpoint to the sweetness. As with any clafoutis, this recipe can be made in a large baking dish or in individual ramekins. We prefer ramekins or miniature cast-iron au gratin dishes, as the clafoutis remains inflated longer and looks more inviting. They should be served hot, directly from the oven. (Fortunately, the Yogurt Parfaits on the previous page give your guests something to enjoy while the clafoutis bakes.)

For the Batter

1 ½ cups granulated sugar plus 1 tablespoon for dusting ramekins

8 large eggs

2 cups whole milk

2 tablespoons heavy cream

1 ½ cups all-purpose flour

1 teaspoon pure vanilla extract

½ teaspoon kosher salt

For the Golden Fig Puree

6 large figs, preferably SLU golden variety, cut in half lengthwise

1 teaspoon granulated sugar

Pinch of salt

For the Clafoutis

1 teaspoon butter, at room temperature, for buttering ramekins

12 Celeste figs, stems removed and quartered

Confectioners' sugar, for garnish

Crème fraîche, for garnish (optional)

To make the batter: In a large deep bowl, combine the granulated sugar and eggs with an immersion blender held at an angle to incorporate air, until the mixture is thoroughly combined and very light in color. (Alternatively, you can do this in a blender.) Slowly add the milk and cream and continue to blend until well mixed. Add the flour, vanilla extract, and salt and continue to blend for 1 minute, until thoroughly combined. Allow to rest at room temperature for at least 1 hour. (The batter can be made up to 1 day in advance and covered and refrigerated. Remove from the refrigerator 1 hour prior to baking to come to room temperature.)

To make the golden fig puree: Preheat the oven to 350° F. Toss the figs with the sugar and salt. Spread the figs out on a baking sheet and roast in the oven for 15 minutes, until very soft. When the figs are cool enough to handle, scoop out the flesh and press it through a fine-mesh strainer. Set aside.

To bake the clafoutis: Preheat the oven to 425° F. Grease four 6-ounce ramekins or cast-iron pans with the butter and dust with the granulated sugar, tapping out the excess. Place 12 pieces of fig in each dish and add just enough batter to come halfway up the side. Place the filled ramekins on a baking sheet and bake, rotating the baking sheet after 8 minutes, for 10 to 12 minutes, until golden brown and the center is puffed. Serve immediately, dusted with confectioners' sugar and with a dollop of crème fraîche, if desired, and golden fig puree on the side. ★

Bread and Base Recipes

Brioche
Makes 32 miniature rolls

Brioche dough is fairly quick to make and very versatile; it can be transformed into a savory loaf or sweet cinnamon knots for breakfast. We often use it for little sandwiches, as it is rich and buttery. In this and all our bread recipes, we list dry ingredients by weight instead of by volume. We believe it's essential to use a scale for this kind of baking. This will ensure accuracy as the density of flour and other dry ingredients can vary significantly depending on the weather of the day, the humidity of your climate, the brand of ingredients used, and how the ingredients have been milled and stored.

11 large eggs
2 1/2 ounces fresh yeast or 1.25 ounces dried yeast
2 pounds 6 ounces all-purpose flour
6 ounces granulated sugar
1 tablespoon kosher salt
1 pound (4 sticks) unsalted butter, at room temperature

Combine the eggs and yeast in the bowl of a stand mixer fitted with the dough hook. Stir on low speed to combine for 1 minute. Add the flour, sugar, and salt and continue to mix on low speed. When the dough starts to come together, add 1 stick of the soft butter. Increase the speed to medium and continue slowly adding the butter 1 stick at a time, until all of it is added and the dough is soft but not tacky. Cover the mixer bowl with plastic wrap and allow the dough to sit for 1 hour. Refrigerate for at least 8 hours or up to 24 hours.

Remove the dough from the refrigerator 30 minutes before shaping. Using a scale, divide the dough into 1 1/2-ounce pieces, forming 32 balls.

Line a 12 x 18-inch baking sheet with parchment paper.

You should not need to add extra flour to work this dough, just a clean flat surface; we find a wooden board works best. Shape each piece of dough into a 2 x 1-inch rectangle that is about 1 1/2 inches thick. With one long side near you, fold the top edge down toward the center, then bring the bottom edge up over the top edge to form a cylinder. Gently roll the dough with your hands, pressing down on the seam using both hands and roll and stretch until the cylinder is about 3 inches long, 1 inch wide, and 1 inch thick. Place the roll on the prepared baking sheet and continue shaping the remainder of the dough portions. Arrange the rolls to make 3 rows of 8 down the length of the pan with little space between the rolls. By the time the rolls have finished proofing, they will be touching—this is what you want. Cover the pan with plastic wrap and allow to sit in a warm area for approximately 1 hour, until the rolls double in size.

Preheat the oven to 350° F. Remove the plastic wrap and bake the rolls until golden brown, about 15 minutes. A toothpick inserted in the center of a roll should come out clean. Allow to cool on the pan. After completely cooled, you may wrap the rolls tightly in plastic wrap and store at room temperature for up to 2 days, or freeze for up to 2 months.

Baguettes
Makes 6 baguettes

There is nothing more comforting than a warm baguette—the texture is especially wonderful when fresh. This is a simple dough that requires little hands-on time, and the dough is easy to shape. It is preferable to bake the baguettes on a stone, but they will bake fine on a baking sheet.

6 cups spring water, at room temperature
.8 ounce fresh yeast or .4 ounce dried yeast
4 1/2 pounds all-purpose flour
1.6 ounces sea salt
1 tablespoon olive oil

In the bowl of a stand mixer fitted with the dough hook, combine the water and yeast; stir together and let stand for 5 minutes. Add the flour and sea salt and mix on low speed until a slightly sticky dough forms.

Turn the dough onto a lightly floured work surface and knead by hand for 5 minutes, until the dough is smooth and elastic. You may need to dust your hands with a small amount of flour to keep the dough from sticking. Once the dough is smooth and elastic, place in a large, clean bowl coated with the oil. Cover the bowl with a kitchen towel and allow the dough to rest for 1 1/2 hours at room temperature (about 68° F), until doubled in size.

Line a baking sheet with a kitchen towel. Divide the dough into 6 equal portions of rectangular shape. Take one portion of dough and fold the two ends in toward the center as if you are folding a letter. Then roll into a log. On a lightly floured cutting board or countertop, roll the log into a long cylinder by gently rolling with both hands: Begin rolling in the center, then move outward with your palms flat against the dough until it is about 16 inches long. Place the log seam side down on the prepared baking sheet. Repeat with the remaining 5 pieces of dough until all the baguettes have been shaped.

Cover the baking sheet with another kitchen towel and allow the baguettes to rise for 30 minutes, until doubled in size.

Preheat the oven to 425° F. A baking stone is best for baking the baguettes, but if you do not have one, an upside down baking sheet would work as well. Place the baking stone or baking sheet in the oven and let it heat for 30 minutes.

Fill a small ovenproof pan with 1 cup of ice and place on the bottom rack of the oven right before you put in the dough—the steam created will make the baguettes brown and crusty. With a sharp paring knife or single-edged razor blade, slash 7 diagonal 1/2-inch-deep slashes down the length of each baguette. Carefully slide each baguette onto the hot baking stone or upside down baking sheet. Bake the baguettes for 20 to 30 minutes, until golden brown. To test to see if a baguette is done, rap the bottom with your finger; if it sounds hollow, it's done. Cool and store at room temperature. We do not store in plastic, as that causes the crust to lose its crispness. The baguettes can also be frozen, tightly wrapped in plastic, for up to 2 months. To recrisp the crust, spritz the baguettes lightly with water and reheat in a 350° F oven for 5 to 10 minutes.

Dark Bread

Makes 4 small loaves

This is a dense, hearty bread that toasts well and makes a great ham sandwich.

2 ounces fresh yeast or 1 ounce dried yeast
1 ½ cups molasses
1 cup dark beer
8 ounces old-fashioned rolled oats
1 pound bread flour
1 pound medium or light rye flour
¼ cup ground caraway seeds (ground in a spice or coffee grinder)
1 tablespoon dark cocoa powder
5 teaspoons salt
14 tablespoons (1 ¾ sticks) butter, softened
Olive oil for greasing

Combine the yeast, molasses, beer, and 1 cup water in the bowl of a stand mixer fitted with the dough hook. Stir and let stand for 5 minutes. Add the oats, bread and rye flours, caraway, cocoa, and salt. Mix on low speed until the dough starts to come together. Add the butter in 4 intervals, letting it incorporate in between each addition. Turn the speed up to medium and mix for 3 minutes. The dough should be smooth and pull away from the side of the bowl.

Turn the dough out onto a lightly floured surface and knead by hand for 4 minutes. The dough should be soft and tacky, but not sticky. Place the dough in large bowl coated with 1 teaspoon oil and cover with plastic wrap; allow to rest for 2 hours at room temperature (68° F).

Lightly grease four 6 x 2 ½-inch loaf pans. Punch the dough down and divide into 4 equal portions using a bench scraper. Shape each into a small log approximately 6 inches long, place in a prepared loaf pan, and cover with plastic. Allow to rise for 2 hours at room temperature (68° F), until the logs have doubled in size.

Preheat the oven to 425° F.

Place a small ovenproof pan filled with 1 cup of ice on the bottom rack of the oven right before baking the loaves. Place the loaves in the oven and bake for 10 minutes. Reduce the oven temperature to 350° F and continue to bake for 20 minutes, until a toothpick or wooden skewer inserted in the center of a loaf comes out clean. Allow to cool on a cooling rack for at least 1 hour before slicing. We sometimes will freeze our cooled bread in order to slice thinly. The bread will keep in the freezer, tightly wrapped in plastic, for up to 2 months.

White Bread

Makes 4 small loaves

This recipe is for a very versatile bread dough that we use in a variety of ways. Depending on what shape, size, and mold you choose, the dough can become a simple Pullman loaf for sandwiches, dinner rolls, or even sticky buns.

3.5 ounces whole milk
1 large egg
1.8 ounces fresh yeast or .9 ounce dried yeast
2.5 ounces butter, softened
2 pounds 3 ounces all-purpose flour
3.5 ounces sugar
1 tablespoon kosher salt
1 tablespoon olive oil

In the bowl of a stand mixer fitted with the dough hook, combine the milk, egg, yeast, and 2 ¼ cups water and stir by hand to combine. Let sit for 5 minutes. Add the soft butter and mix briefly on low speed. Add the flour, sugar, and salt and continue to mix on low speed, working the dough for 3 to 4 minutes, until the dough starts to come together. Increase the speed to medium for 5 minutes to work the gluten. The dough should be soft, not sticky.

Transfer the dough to a large bowl coated with the oil. Cover with plastic wrap and allow to rest at room temperature (68° F) for 1 ½ to 2 hours, until doubled in size.

Preheat the oven to 350° F. Lightly spray four 6 x 2 ½-inch loaf pans with nonstick spray.

Turn the dough out onto a lightly floured surface and punch down. Divide into 4 equal pieces using a bench scraper or small knife. Shape each into a small log approximately 6 inches long, place in a prepared loaf pan, and cover with plastic. Let sit in a warm area for about 30 minutes, until doubled in size.

Carefully remove the plastic wrap. Bake the breads for 15 to 20 minutes, until golden brown and a toothpick or wooden skewer inserted in the center comes out clean. Allow to cool before slicing or storing. Wrapped tightly in plastic, the loaves will keep for up to 2 days at room temperature. The loaves can also be frozen for up to 2 months.

Hoagie Rolls

Makes 16 rolls

After the first rise, turn the dough out onto a lightly floured surface and divide into sixteen 3-ounce pieces using a bench scraper or small knife; we like to weigh each piece on a kitchen scale for equal portions. Cover the pieces with a dry kitchen towel to prevent moisture loss while shaping each piece.

From one piece of dough, shape a 4 x 2-inch rectangle that is about 1 ½ inches thick. Form a cylinder with your hands on a lightly floured surface: With one long side near you, fold the top edge down toward the center, then bring the bottom edge up over the top edge to form a cylinder. Gently roll between your hands and the work surface by pressing down on the seam using both hands to roll and stretch until it is about 6 inches long, 1 ½ inches wide, and 1 ½ inches thick. Place the shaped dough on two parchment-lined baking sheets as you go—8 pieces to a pan (2 rows of 4). Cover the baking sheets with plastic wrap and allow to sit in a warm area for 30 to 45 minutes, until doubled in size.

Preheat the oven to 350° F or to 325° F if your oven has a convection fan. Remove the plastic wrap and bake for 15 minutes, until golden brown. To test for doneness, insert a toothpick into the center; it should come out clean. Allow to cool before slicing or storing. Wrapped tightly in plastic, the rolls will keep at room temperature for up to 2 days. They may also be frozen for up to 2 months.

Buttermilk Biscuits
Makes 12 biscuits

This is a simple, classic recipe. The quality of the buttermilk is what really makes these biscuits special. If you can find old-fashioned buttermilk, it will make a world of difference in your kitchen. Most store-bought buttermilk is labeled "cultured." This means it is made by adding enzymes or lactic acid to milk or cream, which then ferments to create a tart and thick buttermilk. "Old-fashioned buttermilk," on the other hand, is the liquid that remains after churning cream into butter. It is slightly less tart than commercial buttermilk and is often studded with rich little flecks of butter. Ask for it at your local farmers' market. We get ours from Cruze Farm in Knoxville, Tennessee, and use it for baking, dipping, and sipping. I highly recommend trying it for this recipe. Of course, if you can't find old-fashioned buttermilk, this recipe still makes a great biscuit with supermarket buttermilk.

4 cups all-purpose flour, sifted
4 teaspoons baking powder
1 teaspoon baking soda
2 ¹/₄ teaspoons kosher salt
¹/₂ cup (1 stick) cold butter, cut into small cubes, plus 1 tablespoon for topping
2 cups cold buttermilk

Preheat the oven to 500° F. Line a baking sheet with parchment paper.

In a large bowl, combine the flour, baking powder, baking soda, and salt. Add the ¹/₂ cup cubed butter. Using your hands, incorporate the butter into the flour mixture until the butter pieces are roughly the size of peas. Make a well in the middle of the butter-flour mixture and pour in the buttermilk. Gently stir the mixture until it comes together and you can form a ball with a pinch of the dough between your fingertips. Be careful not to overwork the dough or your biscuits will be tough.

On a well-floured surface, roll out the dough to a 1-inch thickness. Cut out rounds using a 2 ¹/₂-inch round cutter and transfer to the prepared baking sheet, leaving ¹/₂ inch between biscuits. Bake for 10 minutes, or until lightly golden brown.

While the biscuits bake, melt the remaining 1 tablespoon butter. Remove the biscuits from the oven, immediately brush with the butter, and serve.

Fresh Pasta Dough
Makes 4 (6-ounce) discs

10 large egg yolks
1 large whole egg
1 tablespoon olive oil
1 tablespoon milk
Pinch of kosher salt
2 to 3 cups pasta flour (finely milled flour, also known as "00" flour)

Combine the egg yolks, whole egg, oil, milk, and salt in the bowl of a food processor fitted with the metal blade. Pulse while adding the flour for 30 to 40 seconds. Add a total of 2 cups of the flour and check the dough: It should be soft and coming together around the blade of the food processor. If the dough is too sticky, add more flour.

Turn the dough out onto a lightly floured surface and bring together with your hands. Add a little more flour in small increments if the dough is too sticky. Knead by hand until the dough is supple and smooth, 2 to 3 minutes or until it just comes together. Cut the dough into four 6-ounce discs, wrap each piece in plastic wrap, and let it rest in the refrigerator for at least 30 minutes or up to 1 hour. You may refrigerate it for up to 6 hours, but if you do so, you must let the dough sit at room temperature for at least 30 minutes before rolling or working it; otherwise it will be too brittle.

★ **To roll out and cut the dough:** Roll or press the dough into a rectangle about ¹/₂ inch thick. Working with one disc at a time, roll the dough through the pasta roller, starting with the thickest setting. Continue putting the dough through the roller, folding it into thirds between each first few settings, and then just straight through down to the thinnest setting. You should be able to see your hand through the dough. Hand-cut the pasta into 1-inch-wide strips for long pasta, or cut into 3-inch rounds for filled pasta. The cut pasta will keep fresh for a day, in resealable plastic bags, in the refrigerator or frozen for a couple of weeks.

Chicken Stock
Makes 2 quarts

This recipe will produce a stock that can be used for anything from cooking legumes to poaching a fish. It is light, aromatic, and, if done properly, clear. It is light enough to use in a fish soup and can be reduced and/or fortified (with roasted chicken carcasses). It is simple but does take some due diligence in skimming and straining to get the purest result possible. For Turkey Stock, you can substitute for the chicken 2 turkey carcasses, cut into quarters, or 4 turkey legs.

2 whole chickens (3 to 4 pounds each), rinsed and quartered
Kosher salt
2 ribs celery, cut into 2-inch pieces
2 carrots, cut into 2-inch pieces
1 Spanish onion, quartered
1 whole head of garlic, cut in half
1 bunch fresh thyme
Stems from 1 bunch fresh parsley (leaves reserved for another use)
2 fresh bay leaves
1 teaspoon whole black peppercorns

Place the chickens in a large (8-quart) stockpot and add cold water (3 to 4 quarts) to cover. Season the water with salt. Bring to a simmer over medium to low heat, skimming frequently to remove impurities. Once it comes to a simmer, reduce the heat to low and continue to skim any foam that rises to the top. Add the celery, carrots, onion, garlic, thyme, parsley stems, bay leaves, and peppercorns. Simmer slowly for 3 hours, until the chicken is falling off the bones.

Transfer the chickens to a carving board and let cool slightly. Discard the skin and bones and reserve the meat for soup or salads (it also makes great dog food). Ladle the stock through a fine-mesh strainer lined with cheesecloth to strain into a large bowl. Place the bowl over ice to cool the stock, or transfer to smaller containers and chill in the refrigerator overnight. Skim the fat from the cooled stock. The stock can be refrigerated for up to 3 days or frozen in pint containers for up to 2 months. Before using, transfer to a medium saucepan and bring to a simmer over medium to high heat.

Lamb Stock
Makes 2 quarts

This same recipe can be used to create a fowl, pork, or veal stock by substituting the bones and scraps from any of those animals. It is a brown stock, as we roast the bones and vegetables to create caramelization that enriches and also colors the broth.

5 to 6 pounds lamb bones (leg, ribs, neck)
1 pound lamb scraps (as lean as possible; this can be the sinew from the leg or shoulder)
3 onions, peeled and quartered
2 leeks, cut in half, upper green portions discarded
2 ribs celery, cut into 2-inch lengths
2 medium carrots, cut into 2-inch lengths
2 heads of garlic, cut in half
2 cups red wine
4 sprigs fresh thyme
4 sprigs fresh parsley stems (leaves reserved for another use)
3 sprigs fresh rosemary
1 tablespoon kosher salt, plus more to taste
1 tablespoon whole black peppercorns

Preheat the oven to 450° F.

In a large flameproof roasting pan, evenly distribute the bones and scraps and roast for 30 minutes, until all the bones are browned. You may want to stir or shake the pan halfway through the roasting to make sure all the bones are roasting evenly. Add the onions, leeks, celery, carrots, and garlic and continue to roast for at least another 20 minutes, until browned and caramelized.

Transfer the bones and vegetables to a 12-quart stockpot and pour off any fat from the roasting pan. Place the roasting pan over medium heat on the stovetop. Deglaze the pan by adding the wine and scraping with a wooden spoon to remove any bits on the bottom of the pan. Cook over medium heat, stirring occasionally, for at least 10 minutes. Scrape what is left into the stockpot.

Add 4 quarts cold water to the stockpot, more if needed to cover the bones and vegetables. Over low to medium heat, bring to a simmer,

skimming any foam or fat that floats to the top. Reduce the heat to low, add the thyme, parsley stems, rosemary, salt, and peppercorns, and continue to simmer, skimming occasionally, for 2 hours. Ladle into a fine-mesh strainer lined with cheesecloth to strain into a large bowl. Place the bowl over ice to cool the stock, or transfer to small containers and chill in the refrigerator overnight. Season to taste with salt. The stock can be refrigerated for up to 3 days or frozen in pint containers for up to 2 months. Before using, transfer to a medium saucepan and bring to a simmer over medium to high heat.

Broccoli Stock
Makes 5 quarts

4 pounds broccoli stems, trimmings, and leaves
2 ribs celery, cut into 2-inch pieces
2 carrots, cut into 2-inch pieces
1 Spanish onion, quartered
1 whole head of garlic, cut in half
4 sprigs fresh thyme
Stems from 1 bunch fresh parsley (leaves reserved for another use)
1 bay leaf
Kosher salt

Place the broccoli in an 8-quart stockpot and add 6 quarts cold water. Bring to a simmer over medium to low heat. Reduce the heat and add the celery, carrots, onion, garlic, thyme, parsley stems, and bay leaf. Simmer for 1 hour.

Ladle into a fine-mesh strainer lined with cheesecloth to strain into a large bowl. Place the bowl over ice to cool the stock or transfer to smaller containers to chill in the refrigerator overnight. Season to taste with salt. The stock can be refrigerated for up to 3 days or frozen in pint containers for up to 2 months. Before using, transfer to a medium saucepan and bring to a simmer over medium to high heat.

Court Bouillon
Makes 5 cups

This aromatic broth is typically used to poach seafood or shellfish.

1 leek, trimmed of dark green tops and roots, cut in half, and rinsed well
1 large carrot, cut into 2-inch pieces
1 onion, quartered
1 cup white wine
12 whole black peppercorns
1 fresh bay leaf
1 sprig fresh thyme
1 sprig fresh parsley or a handful of parsley stems
1 small handful celery leaves
1 tablespoon kosher salt
1 lemon, cut into quarters

Combine the leek, carrot, onion, and 6 cups water in a 4-quart stockpot and bring to a boil. Reduce to a simmer and add the wine, peppercorns, bay leaf, thyme, parsley, celery leaves, and salt. Squeeze the lemon into the bouillon and drop in the quarters as well. Simmer for 15 minutes. Let cool slightly, then ladle into a fine-mesh strainer lined with cheesecloth to strain into a large bowl. Place the bowl over ice to cool the bouillon or transfer to smaller containers to chill in the refrigerator overnight. The stock can be refrigerated for up to 3 days or frozen in pint containers for up to 2 months. Before using, transfer to a medium saucepan and bring to a simmer over medium to high heat.

Homemade Mayonnaise
Makes 4 cups

2 large eggs
4 large egg yolks
1 tablespoon Dijon mustard
Juice of 1 lemon
4 cups canola oil
Kosher salt

In the bowl of a food processor fitted with the metal blade, combine the whole eggs, yolks, mustard, and lemon juice. While the processor is running, slowly add the oil through the feed tube until the desired consistency is reached: It should be a glossy, creamy white color and thick enough to form peaks. Transfer to a bowl and season with salt to taste. Covered, this will keep in the refrigerator up to 1 week.

Clarified Butter
Makes approximately 1 cup
Clarified butter is created when milk fat is rendered from butter by separating the milk solids and water from the butter fat. It is an excellent cooking medium, as it is flavorful and has a much higher burning point than butter.

1 pound (4 sticks) butter

Heat the butter in a 1-quart saucepan over low heat, without stirring, until completely melted. The butter will leave three distinct layers: solids floating on the top, the clear and yellow clarified butter in the middle, and a milky-watery liquid on the bottom. Skim off and discard the solids on top. Pour the yellow clear liquid (the clarified butter) through a fine-mesh strainer (to remove any errant solids that have lingered on the top) into a container. Discard the milky water left in the pan. Clarified butter will keep, covered, in the refrigerator for several weeks or in the freezer for many months.

Summer Vegetable Succotash
Serves 4 to 6

Kosher salt
1 cup fresh butter beans or baby lima beans
1 cup fresh pink-eyed, lady, or black-eyed peas
1 pound small cherry tomatoes
2 tablespoons Clarified Butter (previous recipe)
3 shallots, finely diced (about ⅛ cup)
1 cup fresh corn kernels
⅛ cup chicken stock (page 244)
1 teaspoon fresh thyme leaves
2 tablespoons cold butter
Freshly ground pepper

Place 2 quarts water in a 4-quart saucepan, add 1 tablespoon salt, and bring to a boil. Meanwhile, prepare an ice bath of 2 cups of ice and 2 cups of cold water in a 2-quart bowl; set aside.

To blanch the beans and peas, drop them separately into boiling water for 2 to 3 minutes and remove with a strainer or spider and plunge into the ice bath (leave them in the strainer in the ice bath so you can reuse the ice bath for the next batch). To peel the tomatoes, cut a small x-shaped slit in the end opposite the stem and drop them into boiling water for 30 seconds. Remove and plunge into the ice bath for a second. Gently remove the skin by using a sharp paring knife and peeling it back from the bottom of the tomato using the slits in the bottom as a starting point. Cut the tomatoes in half.

Heat the clarified butter in a large sauté pan over low heat, add the shallots, and sweat until translucent, about 5 minutes. Add the corn, butter beans, and pink-eyed peas and cook until the corn is tender, about 2 minutes. Add the stock, tomatoes, and thyme. Simmer over low heat for 5 minutes to form a shiny glaze. Turn off the heat, add the butter, and swirl to incorporate. Season with salt and pepper. Remove from the heat and serve.

Granola
Makes 1 cup

2 tablespoons butter
⅛ teaspoon pure vanilla extract
1 cup rolled oats
2 tablespoons granulated sugar
1 tablespoon light brown sugar
Pinch of kosher salt

Preheat the oven to 325° F. Line a baking sheet with parchment paper and coat with nonstick spray.

Melt the butter in a saucepan over low heat and add the vanilla. In a mixing bowl, combine the oats, sugars, and salt. Pour the melted butter over the top. Toss in the bowl to coat the ingredients.

Evenly spread the oat mixture on the prepared pan. Bake until golden brown, 10 to 15 minutes, stirring once halfway through. Once cool, break apart with your hands. Store in an airtight container at room temperature for several weeks.

Conversion Chart

All conversions are approximate.

Liquid Conversions

U.S.	Metric
1 tsp	5 ml
1 tbs	15 ml
2 tbs	30 ml
3 tbs	45 ml
¼ cup	60 ml
⅓ cup	75 ml
⅓ cup + 1 tbs	90 ml
⅓ cup + 2 tbs	100 ml
½ cup	120 ml
⅔ cup	150 ml
¾ cup	180 ml
¾ cup + 2 tbs	200 ml
1 cup	240 ml
1 cup + 2 tbs	275 ml
1 ¼ cups	300 ml
1 ⅓ cups	325 ml
1 ½ cups	350 ml
1 ⅔ cups	375 ml
1 ¾ cups	400 ml
1 ¾ cups + 2 tbs	450 ml
2 cups (1 pint)	475 ml
2 ½ cups	600 ml
3 cups	720 ml
4 cups (1 quart)	945 ml
	(1,000 ml is 1 liter)

Weight Conversions

U.S./U.K.	Metric
½ oz	14 g
1 oz	28 g
1 ½ oz	43 g
2 oz	57 g
2 ½ oz	71 g
3 oz	85 g
3 ½ oz	100 g
4 oz	113 g
5 oz	142 g
6 oz	170 g
7 oz	200 g
8 oz	227 g
9 oz	255 g
10 oz	284 g
11 oz	312 g
12 oz	340 g
13 oz	368 g
14 oz	400 g
15 oz	425 g
1 lb	454 g

Oven Temperatures

°F	Gas Mark	°C
250	½	120
275	1	140
300	2	150
325	3	165
350	4	180
375	5	190
400	6	200
425	7	220
450	8	230
475	9	240
500	10	260
550	Broil	290

Acknowledgments

I would like to dedicate this book to the people in my life past and present—specifically but not limited to—my maternal grandparents, Mae B. and W.H. Stiles, for the land that we sow; my paternal grandparents, Anne B. and Dr. Joseph C. Quatrano, for the generous food lessons that they taught me; my parents, Gulielma Stiles and J. Charles Quatrano, for supporting this path I took, both financially and emotionally; my husband and partner, Clifford R. Harrison, for his land and food stewardship; and my sister, Frances, for her impeccable customer relations at Bacchanalia over the past twenty years. I would also like to extend special thanks to the following: the executive chef of Bacchanalia and Quinones, David (Andy) A. Carson, for his enthusiasm for this project that is only matched by his talent and amazing eye for the art of food on a plate; all of the chefs and staff who took part in the cooking and styling of *Summerland*, with whom I have the great fortune to work daily and who make all that we do lovely, delicious, and enjoyable; the friends I have made along the way who are so indulgent, loyal, and kind; Liz and Henry Lorber for time spent on every shoot, making the days flow seamlessly; Kenn Rogers for all his his visual contributions; Sara Camp Arnold for arranging my scattered thoughts into the written words; my editor, Christopher Steighner, at Rizzoli for taming my acerbic humor in a kindly and patient manner; Jennifer S. Muller for her graceful layout and sweet artwork; and Brian Woodcock for his studied eye and stunning photography and for making the year we spent together feel like play not work. Lastly I would like to express a special debt of gratitude to our four-legged family who unconditionally love and support us each and every day.

Top row from left: Rutabaga, Petey, Otis and Anne,
Middle row from left: Clifford with W.H. Stiles "dub" and Sailor, Atticus, Jackson
Bottom row from left: Simon, Huckleberry, Rupert

First published in the United States of America in 2013
by Rizzoli International Publications, Inc.
300 Park Avenue South
New York, NY 10010
www.rizzoliusa.com

© 2013 Anne Quatrano
Photographs © 2013 Brian Woodcock
Design and Illustrations by Jennifer S. Muller

2013 2014 2015 2016 / 10 9 8 7 6 5 4 3 2 1

Distributed in the U.S. trade by Random House, New York

Printed in China

ISBN-13: 978-0-8478-4131-8

Library of Congress Control Number: 2013938942

Index